Women, Politics and Constitutional Change

POLITICS AND SOCIETY IN WALES SERIES
Series editor: Ralph Fevre

The Politics and Society in Wales Series examines issues of politics and government, and particularly the effects of devolution on policy-making and implementation, and the way in which Wales is governed as the National Assembly gains in maturity. It will also increase our knowledge and understanding of Welsh society and analyse the most important aspects of social and economic change in Wales. Where necessary, studies in the series will incorporate strong comparative elements which will allow a more fully informed appraisal of the condition of Wales.

Women, Politics and Constitutional Change

THE FIRST YEARS OF THE NATIONAL ASSEMBLY FOR WALES

By

PAUL CHANEY
FIONA MACKAY
LAURA McALLISTER

*Published on behalf of
The Social Sciences Committee
of the Board of Celtic Studies*

UNIVERSITY OF WALES PRESS
CARDIFF
2007

British Library Cataloguing-in-Publication Data.
A catalogue record for this book is available from the British Library.

ISBN 978–0–7083–1895–9

Printed in Great Britain by Antony Rowe Ltd, Chippenham, Wiltshire

In memory of Val Feld, member of the first National Assembly for Wales and former director of the Equal Opportunities Commission in Wales. A tireless campaigner for gender equality and social justice for all, she is sorely missed in Wales and beyond.

Er cof am Val Feld, aelod o Gynulliad Cenedlaethol Cymru cyntaf a chyn-gyfarwyddwraig y Comisiwn Cyfle Cyfartal yng Nghymru. Ymgyrchydd di-flino dros gyfartaledd i fenywod a chyfiawnder cymdeithasol i bawb, gwelir ei heisiau yng Nghymru a thu hwnt.

Contents

Foreword

Lisa Francis, Welsh Conservative AM for Mid and West Wales, 2003–7

Those who know me as a female politician opposed to all-women shortlists may very well be surprised to find me contributing to the foreword of a book which is clearly going to have quite a lot to say on the subject! Whilst I accept that, post-1997, the doubling of women MPs in the House of Commons had made the place more representative as a whole, I would still argue that what is more important than anything is the calibre of the person doing the representing – not what, or who, they are. Local associations want to be able to choose their own candidates – they want the person who is right for the job as they see it, not someone who is imposed on them by Central Office.

However, it would seem that Anne Widdecombe's words were prophetic when she said: 'When people look and see a lot of women Labour MPs and not very many Conservative women MPs, they will think this is something which needs to be redressed and this perhaps will be in the back of their minds at selection meetings.' And yes, it would be churlish indeed of me to fail to recognize and acknowledge the effect that shortlisting and ultimately a fifty-fifty gender split has had on politics within the National Assembly for Wales. The TV reality of seeing more women taking part in everyday politics has certainly encouraged more women-candidate recruits within the Conservative Party, both in Wales and over the border.

I continue to believe in a meritocracy, in spite of the welcome changes that have occurred in politics over the last eight years. In fact, I am far too insecure to do otherwise! I would hate for anyone ever to turn around and tell me that I was only ever selected or elected just because I'm a woman. Therefore, it is vital that existing women politicians extend the ladder to those who wish to follow by ensuring that candidates have better training and opportunities. In addition, we owe it to our own efforts and self-respect to ensure that all selection panels within the Welsh Conservatives are gender-balanced, to improve the representation of women in our party.

Jane Hutt, Welsh Labour AM for the Vale of Glamorgan
It is hard to imagine what contemporary Welsh politics would be like if the moves to seek fair representation of women in the National Assembly had not been successful. The commitment by the incoming 1997 Labour government to hold a referendum on devolution provided a once-in-a-generation opportunity to transform the political landscape by addressing the abysmal under-representation of women in Welsh political life.

Our aspirations for equal numbers of women in the Assembly have now been met. All parties have played their part, with the undoubted stimulus of Labour's 'twinning' mechanism, resulting in women making up the majority of Labour AMs. A major breakthrough has been a Welsh Assembly Government in which over the past eight years women ministers have held nearly every portfolio at different times.

As a campaigner for women's rights since the 1970s, I realize that the opportunities laid at our feet have been manifold and daunting. We now have our rightful places at the table, but this counts for nothing if we have not made a difference to the way we 'do politics' in Wales, to address inequalities that impinge principally on women's lives in relation to their status in the family, community and workplace.

This book provides a much welcome contribution to assessing the impact of devolution on the lives of women in Wales. I believe this should be judged, in large part, by our effectiveness in the delivery of public services. Improving health and tackling health inequalities are key. Investing in early years, in education and childcare are important for young women and women returners; enhancing the opportunities for women in community regeneration, as well as giving priority to strategies to tackle domestic violence and the pay gap, are important for all women. These are all government policies backed by the Assembly, with women AMs at the forefront of scrutiny.

In these early years of devolution, we are pioneers. We are beholden to prove the beneficial impact of devolution but, in doing this, we must inspire women in every walk of Welsh life to speak up and get involved, knowing the door is opening for them. We must continue to break down the barriers impeding the progress of women in political life. They must be able to relate to us as people whom they could replace, to take the journey forward. Our big challenge now is to act to bring black and minority ethnic women into the process – out of the wings and on to the stage. Only then will we have made use of this once-in-a-lifetime opportunity.

Helen Mary Jones, Plaid Cymru AM for Llanelli
It is a real privilege to contribute to the Foreword of this valuable insight into the role of women in politics in Wales today. Has gender balance in the Assembly made a difference? This book will help us judge. I believe it has – to some extent.

Issues like social care, children's rights and equality have received more attention from government and opposition than they would have done in a male-dominated institution. The tone of debate has been more constructive and consensual, particularly at committee. Some ministers have proved willing to work with the opposition and with outside organizations. But there are risks ahead. As the Assembly is transformed into a proper parliament, which I believe it will be, we have to ensure that the move to a clearer split between government and opposition does not lead to perpetual knee-jerk confrontation. This will be more of a challenge because the media on the whole find cooperative politics 'boring'.

The current gender-balance in membership did not happen by accident. It was achieved largely by the two biggest political parties making conscious decisions to right historic wrongs. Can that be sustained? Within my own party, complacency is a bigger threat than backlash. As members see women speaking for the party on the national stage, the underlying barriers to women's participation may become invisible and remain unaddressed. Those barriers must be dismantled if lasting equality is to be achieved. Helping a few women over them is not enough. The first years of the Assembly demonstrate that it is not enough to have women present on the political stage. It is women who identify with other women and feel a duty towards them – feminist women – who make the difference. We need to weave gender equality not just into the fabric of our national democracy, but into every aspect of our national life. We have made a start, but we still have a great deal to do.

Kirsty Williams, Welsh Liberal Democrat AM for Brecon and Radnorshire
Whilst Wales's new democratic institution has marked a different era in women's political participation, the aftershocks from this political earthquake remain unfelt in large parts of the country. An equal split of male and female AMs has been one of the proudest achievements of the National Assembly for Wales. The adoption of 'family-friendly' hours has also been a step forward, although whether they are very friendly to AMs who live outside Cardiff is another matter. At a stroke, with its creation, the Assembly achieved a numerical equality never seen either in Westminster or in town halls across Wales. But the danger is that we get carried away with our 'success'. The Assembly's less confrontational style contributes to its lack of status, although the new powers may well change that. Moreover, the strength of opposition to all-women shortlists – in all parties – shows that while battles have been won, the fight for equality still rages.

Wales's political make-up has changed – this much is true. But the political face underneath the eyeliner and lip-gloss is still overwhelmingly white, male and middle-aged; and it is propped up by a wider civic society which still does much of its business in golf clubs or at the mart. The Assembly made a spectacular start to changing a particularly backward political culture. There are now more women MPs, too. But the work needs to continue. For all the talk of progress, we have yet to see a woman First Minister, neither have we seen a woman elected to lead an Assembly group or Welsh party. So don't get fooled by the numbers. While significant progress has been made, better does not automatically mean good. Young women in political life still face being patronized, ogled and worse. But political life is merely a reflection of the values of the society it represents. Only when this prejudice is no more part of society, will politics be a truly equal forum.

Mary Lloyd Jones, Artist
I am delighted that the authors want to use my image *Dal dy Dir* for the cover of the book *Women, Politics and Constitutional Change*. I am totally in sympathy with the themes of the book and very happy to be associated with this publication.

Acknowledgements

The authors wish to thank all those who gave generously of their time during our research and provided invaluable material for this book though interviews, correspondence and informal conversations, and also by affording unique access to original documents and records. There are too many to mention, but specific thanks go to Leighton Andrews AM, Professor Deirdre Beddoe, Penni Bestic, Professor Nickie Charles, Rhian Connick, Angharad Davies, Dr Charlotte Aull Davies, Janet Davies AM, Dr Julia Edwards, Siân Edwards, Sue Essex AM, Jill Evans MEP, Lisa Francis AM, Hywel Francis MP, Mair Francis, Edwina Hart AM, Jane Hutt AM, Mari James, Helen Mary Jones AM, Mary Lloyd Jones, Gloria Lumley, Julie Morgan MP, Diana Stirbu, Joyce Watson, Kirsty Williams AM and Leanne Wood AM.

Our thanks go to Hâf Elgar, who provided valuable research assistance to the Gender and Constitutional Change project in the summer of 2001. We also acknowledge the support of the bodies that have funded the research projects on which parts of this book are based, including the Economic and Social Research Council, the University of Wales Board of Celtic Studies and the University of Liverpool Research Development Fund. We are also grateful to the Politics and Society in Wales series team, especially the editor, Professor Ralph Fevre, and the University of Wales Press for their support and assistance in the completion of this project.

As co-authors we have each played a role in planning, writing and editing *Women, Politics and Constitutional Change*, and have contributed our different ideas, data, feedback and analysis. As such, this book is very much the product of a collective endeavour. However, we should also like to acknowledge the key role played by Paul Chaney in driving this venture from inception to completion.

Lastly, we would wish to pay special tribute to our families, friends and colleagues for their patience, support and encouragement during the writing of this book.

Series Editor's Foreword

A decade ago the idea that a book about UK politics might one day feature the words 'women' and 'constitutional change' in the same title might have seemed wildly optimistic. If it was suggested that most of the empirical evidence for such a book would be drawn from Welsh politics, this would have confirmed the idea was being embellished for comic effect. But this book is not a satire, and nor is it a miserable litany of all the ways in which women are kept out of politics. It is a careful and authoritative analysis of how a major political transformation has been achieved.

The remarkable transformation that is described in this book could not have occurred without the constitutional change referred to in the title, but we would be very wrong to conclude that we owe this entirely to the UK Government's programme for constitutional reform. The book explains the way that women activists grasped the opportunity afforded by this programme to shape constitutional change. As Trevor Phillips, the first Chair of the Commission for Equality and Human Rights, has pointed out, Wales is leading the UK in many aspects of equality and diversity. Wales is in this position because of the influence women activists exerted over the manner in which devolution has taken place here. The two most obvious examples of their influence are the National Assembly's statutory equality duty and its standing committee on equality of opportunities. The origins and effects of both of these innovations are discussed at length in the book.

Nobody is as well placed as Paul Chaney, Fiona Mackay and Laura McAllister to tell this extraordinary tale. Paul has been responsible for a ten year stream of research on the attempts to create a new kind of politics in Wales. This work has been influential in informing both researchers and practitioners elsewhere about shaping the further reform of governance. Laura has been researching Welsh politics for even longer than Paul and has made her own contribution to reform, particularly through her work as a member of the Richard Commission on the Powers and Electoral Arrangements for the National Assembly for Wales that reported in March 2004. Fiona has written extensively on equal opportunities, political representation and political participation; she also provided research advice on equality mainstreaming to the Consultative Steering Group on the Scottish Parliament and the Scottish Executive.

The authors have put a great deal of effort into thinking about how we can really measure, and evaluate, the depth and extent of the transformation and they have meticulously gathered evidence before reaching conclusions. From their careful analysis of data – on anything from the style and content of deliberation in the Assembly to the role of NGOs in policy-formation – the authors conclude that much has been achieved already. Nevertheless, they clearly agree with the opinion of those women politicians who say in the foreword that there is still much to be done. For equality campaigners elsewhere, however, there is much to be learned from the transformation that has already been wrought. This book analyses the main steps – often with extracts from key documents – that were taken to get to this point.

Ralph Fevre
Cardiff
March 2007

Tables

Figures

Illustrations

1

Introduction

In a nondescript office block overlooking Cardiff Bay, an extraordinary moment of political history was played out this week. It passed without any great fuss or fanfare in the wider world, but, in the long history of women's struggle for proper political representation, it was ground-breaking, earth-shattering, almost incredible. Following last week's elections, the Welsh Assembly, created in 1999 following devolution, has become the first legislative body in the world to be made up of equal numbers of men and women. Did you catch that? In the 60-strong Welsh Assembly, there are 30 men and 30 women. Parity! And in Wales of all places, home of patriarchal old Labour, born out of the coal and steel industries, and steeped in male-dominated trade-union politics. Better than Sweden, which has long been a beacon for female political representation, whose parliament is 45.3 per cent female. Better than Blair's Babes. Better than anywhere.[1]

People may think Wales is leading the way for women because of the number of female AMs we have in the National Assembly but ... Wales is still not in the 21st century as far as its treatment of women in politics is concerned ... The mines have gone in Wales and times have changed – but attitudes to women have not. We are still in the Dark Ages.[2]

The paradox of women and contemporary politics in Wales is neatly summed up in these two seemingly contradictory assertions. On the one hand, Wales has seen a dramatic shift in the gender balance of political power, as evidenced by the equal numbers of women elected to the new devolved Assembly in the context of the promotion of new inclusive democratic values (see Chaney and Fevre, 2001a; Mackay, 2004a; Chaney, 2006a). This achievement, an apparent world first,[3] focused international attention – some hyperbolic – on Wales. On the other hand, equal representation in the National Assembly for Wales (NAW) was achieved in an historically unpromising climate with powerful continuing legacies of stereotypical attitudes that marginalize and exclude women from public and political life, and a largely unreconstructed overarching political culture entrenched within parties and existing political institutions. The seeming 'gender coup' that was delivered by devolution presents a set of puzzles about how such a breakthrough was achieved and what its significance is for women as political actors, civic activists and citizens.

The under-representation of women in political and public life – their chronic minority status – is a global feature of institutions (IPU, 2005).[4] It has become an issue of increasing political concern as governments, political parties and other global, regional, national and local bodies have come under pressure from the demands of women's movements, particularly feminist activists, for action, including quotas (Karam, 1998; Sawer, 2000, 2002). As such, 'the "under-repre-sentation of women" [has become] a slogan of great discursive power, resulting in policy initiatives at every level of the political system' (Sawer, 2002: 5). Apart from demonstrating 'fair play' or justice, the presence of women in substantial numbers brings with it a set of theoretical expectations relating to the enhanced quality of deliberation, democratic workings of institutions and social legitimacy. More controversially, there are expectations that female politicians will act as agents for the substantive representation of women: in other words, that they will not only 'stand for' women, but that they also will 'act for' and in the interests of women.[5]

As elsewhere, women have long been marginalized in Welsh politics, particu-larly in elected office (see Tables 1.1, 1.2 and 1.3). Historically levels of represen-tation have been yet lower than the dismal records of England and Scotland, themselves laggards in world tables.

Devolution changed all that. The first elections to the National Assembly for Wales in 1999 delivered a step-change, with 40 per cent women's political repre-sentation. Four years later women achieved their goal of equal representation in Wales, taking up 50 per cent of the seats at Cardiff Bay in 2003. In addition to achieving high visibility as elected members, women also hold prominent pos-itions of power in the National Assembly and the Welsh Assembly Government, as ministers and committee chairs. For most of the first Assembly, women were in a majority in the Cabinet and took around equal shares of subject and standing committee chair positions.

Women's presence as elected representatives is the most visible sign of change. In addition, aspirations to inclusive politics have led to new mechanisms and practices which have given voluntary organizations, including women's groups, unprecedented access to the policy-making process. Furthermore, the National Assembly for Wales (NAW) has also been subject to a statutory duty, set out in the Government of Wales Act 1998 and in NAW standing orders, to promote equality of opportunity in the exercise of all its functions and with regards to all people. The duty has underpinned a raft of reforms aimed at promoting equality, including gender equality. Together, these have resulted in a reprioritization of equality matters; since 1997, unprecedented time, political will and resources have been invested in promoting reform to 'mainstream' equality.

Women, Politics and Constitutional Change is first and foremost an investigation and account of how Wales reached this point and the consequences of these devel-opments. We examine the relative role played by political parties, women's movements and other factors, such as institutional design, on outcomes in terms of the 'descriptive representation' (or numerical presence of women), and the

Table 1.1 **Numbers of women candidates in Welsh constituencies (elected) in Westminster elections 1918–2005.**

Year	Welsh Labour[6]	Welsh Conservative	Liberal/ Welsh Liberal Democrat etc.	Plaid Cymru	Other	Total women candidates	Total women elected
1918	1	–	–	–	–	1	0
1922	1	2	–	–	–	3	0
1923	–	–	1	–	–	1	0
1924	–	1	–	–	–	1	0
1929	–	1	2 (1)	–	–	3	1
1931	1	1	1 (1)	–	–	3	1
1935	–	2	1 (1)	–	–	3	1
1945	1	–	1 (1)	1	–	3	1
1950	2 (2)	–	1 (1)	–	1	4	3
1951	3 (1)	–	1	–	–	4	1
1955	2 (1)	1	–	1	1	5	1
1959	3 (2)	1	–	–	1	5	2
1964	2 (2)	2	–	1	1	6	2
1966	2 (2)	–	1	–	1	4	2
1970	1	2	1	–	–	4	0
1974 Feb.	1	–	3	2	–	5	0
1974 Oct.	–	1	4	1	–	6	0
1979	–	1	2	1	3	7	0
1983	2	1	3	6	1	13	0
1987	3 (1)	–	5	9	2	19	1
1992	4 (1)	2	8	7	4	25	1
1997	5 (4)	4	10	7	11	39	4
2001	5 (4)	9	5	7	18	44	4
2005	9 (6)	10	11 (1)	4	22	56	7

Sources: Evans and Jones, 2000: 227 and *www.electoralcommission.gov.uk.*

creation of new mechanisms and channels to promote gender equality – as well as other dimensions of equality and social justice. Our aim is to examine the dynamics and impact of institutional restructuring processes on women's descriptive and substantive representation (see below for a discussion of these terms) in the new political space of the National Assembly, and to question how, and in what ways, politics has opened up to women and their diverse concerns. We seek to provide a rich chronological narrative, drawing upon a wide range of primary and secondary sources, to chart the run-up to devolution, the creation of new institutions, and the dynamics and developments of the first session of the Assembly in the period 1999–2003. It is an account that puts Welsh women in the picture.

Table 1.2 Number of women candidates in Welsh constituencies (elected) in European elections 1979–2003.

Date	Labour	Conservative	Liberal/ Liberal Democrat	Plaid Cymru	Other	Total women candiates	Total women elected
1979	1 (1)	2 (1)	1	–	–	4	2
1984	–	2 (1)	1	–	1	4	1
1989	–	1	–	1	1	3	0
1994	2 (2)	2	2	1	3	10	2
1999	3 (2)	0 (–)	1 (–)	2 (1)	8	14	3
2004	3 (2)	1 (0)	2 (0)	2 (1)	9	17	3

Note: Following boundary changes, the number of Welsh Euro-constituencies decreased from 5 in 1999 to 4 in 2004.
Sources: Elected women MEPs *www.qub.ac.uk/cawp/UKhtmls/UKMEP1.htm*; women candidates *www.europarl.org.uk/guide/candidates99/wales.html*; women candidates/MEPs 2004 *www.europarl. org.uk/guide/Gelectionsmain.html*.

Women, Politics and Constitutional Change is designed to engage with a variety of audiences, from the general reader to those with a specialist interest in women, politics and constitutional change. It is also designed to act as a teaching resource across a range of disciplines, including politics, gender studies, public policy and contemporary history. We include many tables and figures, which reproduce statistical analysis and extracts from key documents (many hitherto unpublished), such as the minutes of women's NGOs and devolution campaign documents, as well as illustrations of the ways in which gender equality has been addressed in a range of Assembly Government policy documents.

Our analysis of the impact of one of the most significant shifts in politics over recent decades is based on extensive empirical evidence, derived from documentary sources and from the views and experiences of participants. The book is the first *single* study that examines the impact of post-1997 gender 'settlement' in Wales, and the first book to date on the gender dimensions of devolution in the UK. Throughout, we chart parallel developments associated with devolution elsewhere in UK, particularly in Scotland, and by analysing empirical developments on gender and politics in a theoretically sophisticated way we intend this book to inform ongoing and future analysis of women, politics and constitutional change in the UK. In these respects, it breaks new ground.

DEFINITIONS AND COMPETING EXPLANATIONS

One of our key questions is to what extent did Welsh women activists – within the women's movement, broadly defined – and feminist ideas play a role in influencing the 'gendering' of constitutional change and the prioritizing of women's

Table 1.3 Women councillors and council leaders (2000 and 2004), Welsh unitary authorities.

| Unitary authority | 2005 situation (after 10 June 2004 elections) | | | | | 2000 situation (after 6 May 1999 elections) | | | | |
| | Number of councillors | | | | Number of women council leaders | Number of councillors | | | | Number of women council leaders |
	Female	Male	Total	% women		Female	Male	Total	% women	
Blaenau Gwent	4	38	42	10	0	4	38	42	10	0
Bridgend	16	38	54	30	1	14	40	54	26	1
Caerphilly	17	56	73	23	0	17	56	73	23	0
Cardiff	28	47	75	37	0	23	52	75	31	1
Carmarthen	12	62	74	16	1	9	65	74	12	0
Ceredigion	4	38	42	10	0	4	38	42	10	0
Conwy	15	44	59	25	0	15	44	59	25	0
Denbigh	10	37	47	21	1	9	38	47	19	0
Flint	13	57	70	19	0	10	60	70	14	0
Gwynedd	17	58	75	23	0	12	71	83	14	0
Ynys Môn	2	38	40	5	0	3	37	40	8	0
Merthyr	1	32	33	3	0	5	28	33	15	0
Monmouth	10	33	43	23	0	8	34	42	19	0
Neath Port Talbot	13	51	64	20	0	12	52	64	19	0
Newport	9	41	50	18	0	6	41	47	13	0
Pembrokeshire	11	49	60	18	0	8	52	60	13	1
Powys	20	52	72	28	1	18	36	54	33	0
Rhondda Cynon Tâf	18	57	75	24	0	23	52	75	31	1
Swansea	21	51	72	29	0	17	55	72	24	0
Torfaen	15	29	44	34	0	15	29	44	34	0
Vale of Glamorgan	14	33	47	30	0	9	38	47	19	0
Wrexham	6	46	52	12	0	9	43	52	17	0
TOTAL	276	987	1263	22	4	250	999	1249	20	4

Source: D. Balsom (ed.), *Wales Yearbook* (Cardiff: HTV, 2000, 2005).

representation in Wales, and to what extent were these developments the consequences of an interplay of other factors? We first define women's movements,
before turning to set out two possible frameworks for understanding the
dynamics of change.

Women's movements are notoriously difficult to define; the patterns of
women's activism do not fit neatly into models of social movements, especially
those that focus upon particular organizational forms (Briskin, 1999). Banaszak
et al. (2003: 2) define women's movements as 'those movements whose definition,
content, leadership, development, or issues are specific to women and their
gender identity'. We also include autonomous community-based organizations
as well as women's sections inside mixed organizations, institutional feminism,
in the form of gender experts and academics, service-oriented groups and identifiable feminists working with others for change (Ferree and Martin, 1995;
Briskin, 1999). Ferree and Martin (1995) note that patterns of activism are not static
and that there is 'two-way traffic' between community-based organizations and
other more institutionalized forms.

One of the factors that helps to explain the changing forms and trajectories of
women's movements in western industrialized democracies (such as Canada, the
US, Australia and countries of the European Union, including the UK), is the
impact of state interactions with women's movements. The main trend that can
be discerned has been of increasingly institutionalized interactions with state
bodies and complex alliances with state and quasi state institutions (for example,
political parties) and other civil society actors. The advantages of the institutionalization of women's movements is insider status and the potential to
influence and shape policy; the disadvantages experienced include fragmentation, loss of strategic focus, de-radicalization and co-option.

SYSTEM-LEVEL AND STRATEGIC EXPLANATIONS

Two main approaches are used to understand the comparative trends in women's
representation: system-level and strategic explanations. System-level approaches
focus upon systematic factors, particularly the electoral system. A number of
comparative studies have demonstrated that the type of electoral system is a key
variable for explaining different country performances: women candidates are
likely to fare better under proportional-representation (PR) systems than under
first-past-the-post (FPTP) majoritarian systems (Lakeman, 1982; Rule and
Zimmerman, 1994; Norris, 2004). There are a number of reasons put forward,
which relate to the different logics of candidate selection that operate under
the two systems (a 'balanced slate' versus 'winner takes all'), and to the different
sorts of incentives and costs involved in parties promoting women candidates
(Caul, 1999, 2001; Matland, 2002). The main barrier, at least in western liberal

democracies, is not a prejudiced electorate but the party 'gatekeepers' who control the earlier nomination stage. Put simply, in Westminster-style first-past-the-post voting systems, party selectors are likely to opt for the 'standard' or 'ideal' candidate – who appeals to the greatest number of voters – rather than for a candidate who is perceived as more 'risky'. Comparatively speaking, women have fewer resources (time, money, power, contacts, networks and status) than men. Women (and minority ethnic hopefuls) must overcome the cumulative disadvantages of social and economic inequality and cultural stereotyping to reach the pool of eligibles in the first place. Once there, they may appear less convincing, 'riskier' candidates than their male, white, middle-class counterparts. The experiences, qualifications and attributes of women as non-standard candidates are often undervalued and underappraised. In the context of intense competition for a single nomination, they are also less likely to have the backing of powerful party factions. Conversely, in more proportional voting systems, where slates of candidates are run for multi-member districts, party selectors have an incentive to present a list that 'looks' more like the electorate. An all-male or all-white list might look 'odd' and send out the wrong signals. In this context, there are incentives to nominate women (Matland and Studlar, 1996).

Perhaps more importantly, demands for gender party quotas are more easily met within PR systems, and a process of 'contagion' is also more likely to occur than under FPTP. Contagion relates to the process whereby the adoption of gender policies, such as candidate quotas, by one political party may lead to action by other parties, who also adopt measures, formal or informal, in order to improve their performance (see, for example, Matland and Studlar, 1996). Thus, the dynamics of party competition can be mobilized to support demands to increase the number of women in politics.

However, few researchers suggest that voting systems provide the whole answer. Strategic agency approaches focus on agent-centred accounts of change, examining the actions of political parties, the dynamics of party competition and the role as pressure groups of organized feminists, both inside parties and in wider women's movements, in explaining increased levels of female political representation (Lovenduski and Norris, 1993; Wängnerud, 2000; Beckwith, 2003; Lovenduski, 2005).

As noted earlier, breakthroughs in women's representation also relate to successful campaigns for parties to implement gender quotas (Lovenduski and Norris, 1993; Caul, 1999, 2001; Beckwith, 2003). Gender quotas are among a range of measures that parties can implement to correct against institutional bias in recruitment and selection processes, for example, by setting party rules for minimum proportions of female and male candidates on shortlists, drawing up all-women shortlists for certain contests, or alternating female and male names on party lists.[7] At their strongest, they are designed as 'equality guarantees', ensuring gains in the number of women candidates who become elected members (Lovenduski, 2005). The experience in Wales confirms findings from other studies that stress: the importance of feminist interventions in political parties; the relative receptivity of political parties as 'carrying agents' for women's demands for reforms, including quotas; and the ability of feminists to frame their claims within prevailing discourses (Banaszak et al., 2003). Contexts are significant, and the Welsh case-study provides more evidence of the way in which processes of institutional restructuring and constitutional reform provide 'windows' or 'moments' of opportunity for political agents to press for improvements in women's political representation, although positive outcomes are not inevitable (see Britton, 2002; Brown et al., 2002; Banaszak et al., 2003; Beckwith, 2003; Dobrowolsky and Hart, 2003a, 2003b; Mackay et al., 2003).

POLITICAL OPPORTUNITY STRUCTURES

A common approach taken in the study of the interaction of social movements with states is one which focuses on *political opportunity structures* (Tarrow, 1994) or *interaction contexts* (Banaszak et al., 2003). These comprise the frameworks that may act to inhibit or enable organized groups to effect change. Political factors relate to *political culture.* This includes: the basic values and prevailing norms which set the parameters for political debate and behaviour (Banaszak et al., 2003: 17); institutional and political *configurations of power* (for example, patterns of party competition, the relative strength of trade unions, the composition of the government of the day); and the patterning of power relations amongst societal interest groups (Kriesi, 1995, cited by Banaszak et al., 2003: 18). Struggles over the meaning of key terms, such as equality and democracy, also present discursive opportunities and dangers for would-be reformers (Snow and Benford, 1992; Beckwith, 2000).

The relative effectiveness of social movements in taking advantage of prevailing political opportunities is conditioned by a number of further factors. These relate to issues of strategy and timing, and to the sum of resources that a social movement, such as a women's movement, commands (Banaszak et al., 2003), together with its *mobilizing structures,* which are broadly defined as coordinating mechanisms, practices and procedures that enable strategic collective working and coalitions (McAdam et al., 1996). In other words, social movements need not only resources, vision and luck, but also the ability to act in concert.

Political change and state reconfigurations are identified in the literature on women's movements as providing important political opportunities for organized women to make claims for improved political representation, political voice and input into policy processes. In our case, devolution has provided the key context. Timing and the framing of demands within prevailing debates are important factors in explaining the relative success or failure of reform attempts. The breakthrough of the 'electoral project' by party women and women's movement activists in Britain was made possible by the coincidence of two reform trajectories in the 1980s and 1990s: the Labour Party's internal debates at the United Kingdom (UK) level, and the broader pressures of devolution in, first, Scotland and, later, Wales. According to Mackay (2006: 173):

> these reform trajectories are set within three wider contexts: reaction to the radical programmes of neo-liberal restructuring undertaken by successive Conservative governments over this period; the gathering pace and activism of global campaigns to tackle the chronic minority status of women in political and public life; and elite debates in advanced welfare democracies about the so-called crisis of democracy and the disengagement of citizens as evidenced by the falling electoral turn-out and rising levels of mistrust and cynicism in politicians, parties and political processes.

Together, these contexts provided a structure of opportunities, political, institutional and discursive, for organized women in Wales, as well as Scotland and, to a lesser extent, Northern Ireland, to press for improvements to political representation and participation.

There are considerable difficulties in 'demonstrating the independent effect of collective action on social change' (MacAdam, McCarthy and Zald, 1988; Briskin, 1999: 24). For example, it is difficult to prove a direct causal link between women's activism and concrete outcomes, or to demonstrate that it was that action – above all other factors – that made the difference. However, we can make judgements about potential effects by looking for evidence of change in terms of political outcomes, policy outcomes, mobilization outcomes and cultural or discursive outcomes. In the case of women's mobilizing in Wales success can be judged by the extent to which there have been post-devolution gains in women's descriptive and substantive representation; the extent to which women and ideas of gender equality can be found within institutional blueprints like Assembly rules or policy frameworks; and, finally, the extent to which 'politics as usual' has been challenged and political culture altered. We address these issues throughout the book and consider the extent and significance of outcomes in chapter 10, Conclusions.

WOMEN AND CONSTITUTIONAL ACTIVISM

Political opportunities are created by reform processes – such as devolution – and the chance to be in at the start of a new institution. Comparative research from countries as diverse as Canada, South Africa and the UK shows that a number of factors contribute to the successful promotion of women's representation and women's policy interests more broadly: first, the operation of a 'dual strategy', whereby women mobilize within parties and state institutions as 'insiders', as well as bringing pressure to bear from outwith through autonomous women's organizations (Lovenduski and Norris, 1993; Wängnerud, 2000). This can take the form of affiliated and autonomous women working separately but in parallel, or through instances of groups of women having 'dual' or 'multiple militancy': in other words, where gender concerns are promoted by the same women through their multiple memberships of different organizations, both autonomous and mixed, and through the interaction of their different political identities (Beckwith, 2000, 2003). 'Dual goals' feature in a number of successful mobilizations, whereby women demand improved descriptive representation, through increased numbers of female elected representatives, and enhanced substantive representation, through the institutionalization of women's 'voices' and the creation of women's policy machinery (Brown et al., 2002; Britton, 2002). Other contributory factors include: the strength of the women's movement or movements; the ability to form time-limited coalitions (Britton, 2002); the existence of sympathetic and powerful allies or 'carrying agents', principally political parties, that can promote women's demands; and the framing of women's demands within discourses and arguments that have mainstream legitimacy or congruence with party or state agendas (Lovenduski, 1999, 2005; Dobrowolsky and Hart, 2003a, 2003b; Banaszak et al., 2003a, 2003b; Mackay et al., 2003).

The Welsh case provides further evidence that a period of rapid institutional change, such as devolution, creates opportunities for substantial progress to be made with respect to the political representation of women, and for prospects for the regendering of politics to make space for women, women's issues and women's perspectives. In turn, organized women, in women's movement organizations and as elite actors, and feminist ideas – about democracy, representation and equality – played a significant role in the shaping of new institutions.

Defining 'women's issues' and 'women's perspectives' is a tricky business, given our understandings of the heterogeneity of women and the complexities of identities. For the purposes of simplicity, we follow Trimble and Arscott by defining women's issues as those 'where policy consequences are likely to have a more immediate and direct impact on significantly larger numbers of women than on men' (2003: 185). These issues or concerns may have biological factors (for example, reproductive rights, provision of breast cancer treatment, maternity services and so on) or social factors (for example, policies relating to the gendered division of labour, such as work-life balance and childcare provisions), or some combination of the two (Lovenduski, 1997). Lovenduski and Norris (2003: 88) suggest women's issues refer to 'all political issues where women and men may disagree ... women's shared interests are those policies that increase their autonomy ... [Thus] recognition of women's issues is a process of politicisation ... [where] the inequalities of power between the sexes are acknowledged'. We define women's perspectives as 'women's range of views as well as their approaches to all policy issues, not just those with an immediate and direct impact on women' (Trimble and Arscott, 2003: 185).

We evaluate the extent to which post-devolution politics has become 'women-friendly' – or 'feminised' (Lovenduski, 2005) – by looking at the following dimensions:

Descriptive representation, by which we mean the political representation of women in the new elected bodies in terms of their physical presence. To what extent do the new institutions resemble wider Welsh society with regard to gender balance?

Substantive representation, by which we mean the extent to which women's issues, concerns and perspectives have become integrated into political debate, policy agenda and programmes. Evidence for this may be charted through: first, female politicians 'acting for' women in terms of raising and articulating issues; second, in terms of the political agenda of the Assembly Government and the Assembly as a whole displaying the emergence or reprioritization of women's issues and equality issues, and of matters of concern to women; third, the institutionalization of women's concerns and gender equality through commitment to 'mainstream' gender in policy-making; and fourth, the engagement of women in public policy-making through inclusive mechanisms, such as consultative fora and mainstreaming strategies.

THE POLITICAL REPRESENTATION OF WOMEN: CONCEPTUAL ISSUES

Our first set of questions relates to the dynamics and developments in the run-up to the creation of the new political institutions. The entry of substantial proportions of women into the National Assembly for Wales provokes another set of questions, relating to the impact of the presence of women on politics and the substantive representation of women. As the issue of women's representation gained legitimacy and momentum in the 1980s and 1990s, so, too, did the expectations that increasing the numbers of female politicians would automatically lead to 'better' representation for women. Political parties and institutional advocates, such as the UN, often assume there is a simple relationship between descriptive and substantive representation. The 'magic' number of 30 per cent is often cited by such bodies as the tipping point, after which women will be able to 'transform' politics (Dahlerup, 1988).

Originating from research into US organizations (Kanter, 1977), 'critical mass' (or proportions) models assert that there are qualitative differences in the capacity for substantive representation, dependent upon the proportion of women present in a political institution. It is predicted that once women move from a small to a large minority – or achieve a 'critical mass' – there will be significant changes in institutional culture and policy outcomes. Whilst present as 'tokens' or as 'small minorities', their behaviour will be constrained and distorted by majority norms and structures.

Simple models of critical mass – which assume that there is an automatic relationship between numbers or proportions and impact – have been undermined empirically and theoretically. Such models also fail to build upon all of Kanter's original insights, which highlighted the crucial role of feminist champions *whatever* the proportion of women present in an institution, and also pointed out that the increased presence of women may result *both* in the increased potential for transformatory coalitions *and* in the potential for fragmentation of the identity 'woman', as the diversity of individual women becomes more apparent (Childs and Krook, 2005). Comparative research is building up a picture of the contingent and complex character of substantive representation in established political institutions, such as the UK House of Commons (Childs, 2001, 2002, 2004a, 2004b; Cowley and Childs, 2003; Lovenduski and Norris, 2003; Childs and Withey, 2004), the Congress and State legislatures in the US (for example, Duerst-Lahti and Kelly, 1995; Thomas, 1996; Thomas and Wilcox, 1998; Reingold, 2000; Dodson, 2001; Swers, 2002; Carroll, 2003), Canadian Federal and Provincial legislatures (Tremblay and Andrew, 1998; Tremblay and Trimble, 2003; Trimble and Arscott, 2003), the Nordic parliaments (Skard and Haavio-Mannila, 1986; Skeije, 1991; Karvonen and Selle, 1995; Wängnerud, 2000), to name but a few, as well as in new institutions, such as the South African Parliament (Albertyn, 2003), the Scottish Parliament (Mackay et al., 2003) and the Northern Ireland Legislative Assembly (Cowell-Meyers, 2001, 2003).

There are apparent (although modest) differences in the attitudes, motivations and policy priorities of female and male parliamentarians, but these are mediated – and sometimes trumped – by political party. Women consistently report that they behave and experience political institutions in different ways, although these differences are difficult to quantify. There is evidence to suggest that women politicians tend to recognize the connections between themselves and other women who either aspire to office, want greater access to their government, or want to see policy changes. They are also more likely to consult a wider and more diverse range of opinion when considering policy options than are men (Kathlene, 1998). Contact with women's organizations is an important dimension of substantive representation and signals that parliamentarians recognize women as a social category. Substantive outcomes are most obvious in the Nordic countries, where high levels of female representation over a sustained period have had a discernible impact on the shaping of welfare state policy, particularly around care politics. Even there, cautious notes are sounded about the difficulty in isolating gender from other factors, the need not to overplay the extent of gender differences in parliamentary behaviour, and, conversely, the need not to underplay the important of other factors, such as party (Skeije, 1991; Karvonen and Selle, 1995; Wängnerud, 2000). In a recent review Mackay (2004b: 108) noted:

it is clear that empirical studies undermine any simple assumptions that numbers alone provide adequate explanations. Whatever is going on, it is too complex and messy to be captured by simplistic notions of critical mass. Few scholars now expect numbers alone to guarantee substantive outcomes. Instead there is growing consensus that substantive representation is 'probablistic' rather than 'deterministic' and that numbers are mediated by political party and other institutional factors and environments.

(See also Childs and Krook, 2005.)

Lovenduski and Norris reinforce the need to be sensitive to the institutional context and conditions of change; 'to understand what happens when the numbers of women rise, it is necessary to understand under what conditions change can be expected to occur and how institutional effects will distort or delay this process' (2003: 89). Childs's study of the 1997 new cohort of women MPs in the House of Commons has explored and elaborated some of the problems facing critical-mass models in specific institutional and political contexts. Party identity and the institutional constraints of strong party parliamentary systems impact upon women MPs' capacity or inclination to 'act for' women (Childs, 2001, 2004a, 2004b; see also Beckwith, 2002). International studies suggest that the overall proportion of female elected members may be less significant than the positional influence of sub-groups of women. In this context, it is argued that the proportion of women backbenchers belonging to the executive party or parties (Grey, 2002) or the proportion of women holding ministerial office (Karam, 1997/2002) is of primary importance in predicting substantive outcomes. On the basis of their comparative study, Studlar and McAllister (2002) argue that, beyond numbers, women need to be representatives of parties that are sympathetic to women's substantive policy goals and require the strategic capacity to frame demands and exercise influence within their party groups. A number of scholars have observed that the increase in descriptive representation 'has not necessarily been associated with shifts in policy discourse, let alone increased expenditure' (Sawer, 2002: 10). We concur with this scepticism that 'critical mass' will inevitably lead to the substantive representation of women. Instead, we adopt the 'politics of presence' framework, as developed by Anne Phillips (1995), which theorizes the link between the presence of women and any substantive representation of women (and their concerns) as complicated and contingent. Whilst it is plausible that women representatives may act for women, there are no guarantees: shifting identities, differences amongst women, partisan loyalties and institutional factors are all seen to play a part in shaping and constraining their inclination and capacity to 'act for women'. However, the presence of women is important: it is important on the grounds of justice done – and seen to be done – and to reinforce the legitimacy of political institutions, especially in the eyes of women. It is crucial that women – in their diversity – are present in politics in order to contest, deliberate and inform the 'politics of ideas', particularly issues that have not yet become part of established political agendas (Phillips, 1995). There is no assumption that all women will think the same way, or that women will necessarily be feminist. However, a substantial presence is needed in order that a diversity of women's perspectives can be inserted into political debate, improving deliberation and enhancing vertical and horizontal representation (Mansbridge, 1999; Young, 2000).

NOTES OF OPTIMISM AND CAUTION

Notes of both optimism and caution can be sounded in the case of Wales. As the following chapters will demonstrate, progress has been made with the feminizing of politics through the descriptive and substantive representation of women. However, as the paradox raised in the opening quotations of this book highlights, there are also unpromising legacies with which to contend. With the notable exception of one or two local councils and bodies such as Chwarae Teg, there is little track record or expertise in gender equality – and equalities more generally – as an area for public policy, organizational strategy or political concern. This is the case at the all-Wales level (see chapter 8) and within local government. For example, research on the development of equal opportunities policies in Wales and Scotland in the mid 1990s concluded that equalities development in Welsh local government has been slower and less systematic or advanced than in their counterparts in Scotland (Breitenbach et al., 1999). It is also the case that there were far fewer local government women's committees in Wales than in England and Scotland, and, too, fewer key spaces and platforms for the articulation and promotion of women's issues and gender equality demands than elsewhere in Britain in the 1980s and 1990s (Edwards, 1995). Cultural gender stereotypes may have loosened somewhat (Beddoe, 2000), but they are still remarkably persistent in everyday life and in the public domain. For example, recent research concluded that such stereotypes continued to pose a serious barrier to women seeking promotion to senior management in Wales (Charles and Davies, 2000). The high visibility of women in the National Assembly for Wales stands in stark contrast, then, to their continuing low profile in other branches of politics and positions of public and economic decision-making. A recent report by the Equal Opportunities Commission Wales and the Wales Women's National Coalition (2004) revealed that women hold fewer than one in five of the top jobs in public life. According to the report, there are no female chairs of police authorities, chief Crown prosecutors, university vice-chancellors or party leaders in Wales. Only 9 per cent of local authority chief executives and 14 per cent of council leaders are women.[8] Meanwhile, there have been significant improvements in the proportion of women MPs representing Welsh constituencies (20 per cent elected in 2005), albeit from a low base;[9] and modest gains at local government level, where women councillors now make up 22 per cent of local councillors (Equal Opportunities Commission Wales, 2004).

Taking these factors into account, we predict that developments will not be even and linear; rather, they will be characterized by modest gains, checked by faltering momentum, drift and setbacks. The extent to which gains at the level of the Assembly are sustainable has been a crucial question for our study, and will drive future research in this field.

WOMEN AND POLITICS

We do not claim to offer here a comprehensive account of all aspects relevant to women and contemporary politics in Wales. For example, we do not consider in detail the experiences or representative trends for women at other levels of conventional electoral politics, in local councils, at the Westminster Parliament or the European Parliament. Neither do we examine at length the myriad forms of women's experience and activism that can be characterized as the politics of everyday life, of community activism, and of the articulation and expression of cultural identities in Wales and elsewhere.[10] This was a conscious choice, whilst recognizing that further work will be crucial to augmenting our study.

Ground-breaking work has been undertaken by feminist historians and social scientists to map aspects of women's lives, experiences, identities and politics in Wales. Four pioneering works stand out: two edited collections, *Our Mothers' Land* (John, 1991) and *Our Sisters' Land* (Aaron, Rees, Betts and Vincentelli, 1994), and two monographs, *Out of the Shadows* (Beddoe, 2000) and *Women and Work* (Rees, 1999a). John and her collaborators (1991) document chapters in Welsh history from 1830 to 1939, stopping at the outbreak of the Second World War. Beddoe (2000 and earlier writings) covers the span of the twentieth century, bringing the story up to elected devolution. Both Beddoe and Rees (1999a) chart the impact on women's lives, roles and work of wider trends of socio-economic change. The lives of women and men in Wales have been affected by the dramatic economic restructuring in the last quarter of the twentieth century, heralding the collapse of Wales's traditional industries of coal, steel and agriculture and the growth in service-sector industries; this has gone hand in hand with social reforms and changing family forms, and with the introduction of equality legislation changes that have challenged traditional gender stereotypes and gender hierarchies. Rees assesses the impact of the equality legislation of the mid 1970s and provides a detailed review of key trends in educational attainment, employment patterns, balancing work and family lives, and attitudes to both gender equality and equal opportunities, in relation to ethnicity, disability, the Welsh language and urban/rural divisions (see also Rees, 1994, 1999b).

According to Beddoe (1986 and 2000), social change for women has been slower and more contested in Wales than elsewhere in the UK, and the cultural, social and political representation of women has been limited and constrained. This can be summed up in stereotype of the Welsh Mam: the self-sacrificing, stoic, domestic icon, defined by home and family (Beddoe, 1986). The 1988 film *Mam* – made by the women's film cooperative Red Flannel Films – marked a cultural challenge to these limiting stereotypes and 'was a landmark in demolishing the myth of the Welsh Mam and substituting a range of other images more accurately reflecting the diversity and complexities of women's lives in modern Wales' (Rees, 1999a: 6).

The publication of *Our Sisters' Land* a decade later had a similar powerful impact. The volume combined leading-edge academic research across a range of issues, including: changing family forms (Betts, 1994); the refuge movement and domestic violence (Charles, 1994); women and labour-market participation (Rees, 1994); women in agriculture (Ashton, 1994); gender and colonization (Aaron, 1994); women, nationalism and feminism (Davies); as well as personal voices and activist accounts. These included Angharad Tomos's account (1994) of her own and other women's roles and activism in the campaigning group for Welsh-language rights, Cymdeithas yr Iaith Gymraeg, and the testimonies of women who had struggled to reconcile and express multiple and complex identities, for example Roni Crwydren's account of finding a place as a Welsh-speaking lesbian feminist, with no word for lesbian in her Welsh dictionary (1994), and artist Mary Lloyd Jones's reflections on achieving creative success despite being 'the wrong sex, living in the wrong place at the wrong time' (1994: 275).

The University of Wales Press has provided an important publishing outlet for works that, by the double marginalization of their subject (Welsh women), might otherwise have been hard to find a home. Similarly, the Equal Opportunities Commission in Wales has also played a pivotal role in commissioning and publishing research on women across a range of areas; examples include women and the pay gap (Blackaby et al., 2001), women in management (Blackaby, 1999), and gender and the Welsh language (Jones and Morris, 1997). The organization also provides annual statistical summaries of the position of women and men in Wales. These works, and the wider writings of contributors to this volume and others, have created a body of work that reclaims, documents and analyses women's history, and takes forward the project of redefining and reflecting contemporary women's lives, in all their diversity.

Women, Politics and Constitutional Change seeks to build upon this groundwork and to act as a springboard for other research. Much remains to be studied, and we see this volume as part of an ongoing process to record, map and analyse in order to build up a holistic picture of women as political and social actors in Wales. We return to this theme in the Conclusions.

MAKING COMPARISONS

Our concern is to develop the specifics of the Welsh case within a broader theoretical and empirical context. Whilst there is not the space in this volume to develop a systematic comparative analysis, we draw upon contemporary research in Scotland and Northern Ireland and endeavour to locate our story within the wider international context.[11] Whilst our study is temporally and geographically specific, we suggest that our findings have wider relevance to theoretical and practical debates about women and politics, and to the development of an equality agenda in the UK and elsewhere.

EVIDENCE AND METHODS

The book is based on interview material and documentary analysis gathered as part of a number of overlapping projects, which were undertaken by the authors and colleagues between 1999 and 2003. These included:

1. The 'Gender and Constitutional Change' project which was part of the Economic and Social Research Council's 'Devolution and Constitutional Programme' (project reference L2192520233).[12] This comparative study charted and analysed the participation of women activists in campaigns for devolution in Wales, Scotland and Northern Ireland, and evaluated the impact they have made and continue to make as the process of constitutional change evolves and develops. Second, it analysed the impact of constitutional change and the new devolved institutions on women, their political roles and identities, and gender relations. The approach was largely qualitative, drawing upon documentary materials and in-depth interviews with 150 key actors involved in the process of constitutional change. A total of 50 interviews were carried out in Wales with politicians, civil servants, party activists, academics, trade unionists, advocates from equality agencies and representatives from women's organizations. Interviewees were all identifiable actors in the process.
2. A University of Wales Board of Celtic Studies project entitled 'The Effectiveness of Inclusive Governance: A Study of the Participation and Representation of Minority Groups in the First Two Years of the National Assembly'.[13] This study commenced prior to the first elections to the National Assembly and charted the legislature's development during its first two years. Participant observation, document analysis and over 100 semi-structured interviews with candidates, Assembly Members and a range of policy actors were used to examine the extent to which the new Assembly was able to meet the aspiration of 'inclusive governance', as articulated during the 1990s devolution campaign.

3.   The study 'Social Capital and the Participation of Marginalized Groups in
      Government 2001–04'. This was an Economic and Social Research Council-
      funded project (reference R000239410).[14] By focusing on the first term of the
      National Assembly, this research built on the aforementioned Board of
      Celtic Studies-funded project, and was a sociological study of experiments
      in giving marginalized groups a say in government. It concentrated on the
      types of social capital that link government, organizations and individuals,
      and on the influence on government of the participation of marginalized
      groups and the effectiveness of the new institutions. This project used a
      mixture of qualitative and quantitative research methods, including over 150
      interviews with a broad range of political and policy actors, in order to test
      the fundamental tenets of social capital theory.
4.   A study of women candidates in the 1999 elections: this research, funded by
      the University of Liverpool Research Development Fund, on women candi-
      dates in the four main parties for the 1999 Assembly election, was carried out
      as part of a wider programme of research undertaken on devolution.[15]

We have also utilized data from the Wales Life and Times Study 2003, conducted
by Dr Richard Wyn Jones, University of Wales Aberystwyth; Professor Anthony
Heath of the Department of Sociology, University of Oxford, and the National
Centre for Social Research (NatCen) (Economic and Social Research Council
L219 25 2042).

CHAPTER BY CHAPTER

In chapter 2 we focus upon the women's movements and their role in the 1990s
devolution campaign in Wales. We set the form and trajectory of developments
within a comparative context, drawing upon developments in Scotland and
Northern Ireland. We argue that issues of gender equality – and the strategies of
women activists – have played a significant role in the different processes of institutional change in Wales, Northern Ireland and Scotland. Constitutional reform
processes opened up opportunities for women to mobilize around the issues of
political representation in its broadest sense. Being involved, albeit in different
ways, in the design of new electoral systems and new institutions has meant that
women activists have played a part in improving descriptive and substantive
representation.

   Chapter 3 builds upon the themes outlined in chapter 2. It focuses on the period
from the eve of the 1997 devolution referendum to just prior to the first National
Assembly elections in May 1999. Attention is focused on how elements of the
women's movement, led by key 'strategic women', continued to lobby for
gender equality. Our purpose is to evaluate the manner and extent to which
women shaped the institutional 'blueprint' of the new Assembly, thereby, in turn,

determining the future capacity of national government in Wales to address the long-standing patterns of discrimination, exclusion and alienation from national politics experienced by successive generations of women. By institutional blueprint we mean the formal rules, structures and mechanisms of the post-devolution Assembly. In particular, we focus upon the development of a statutory equality duty, a means by which equality considerations were institutionalized. The desire was to create political institutions that were more responsive to women's concerns and more likely to tackle structural discrimination, and in which women could play a full role. We argue that the response of the UK government – as well as establishment figures and 'gatekeepers' in Wales – to the calls for gender equality provided a litmus test for the promise of a 'new' and 'inclusive' post-devolution phase of politics. The institutional developments outlined in this chapter indicate the extent to which the political climate for gender equality had shifted significantly from the earlier exclusive and discriminatory practices of administrative devolution.

International evidence suggests that political parties are crucial carrying agents for women's demands for a greater voice and place in conventional politics. In chapter 4 we examine the historic and changing role of women in political parties in Wales, focusing primarily upon the major party, Welsh Labour, and its closest electoral rival, Plaid Cymru: The Party of Wales. As elsewhere in the UK and other western liberal democracies, feminists from the second-wave women's movement entered political parties (in particular Labour and Plaid Cymru) in the 1980s and, together with other supportive party women, began to make claims to improve women's position inside party structures, through women's sections, forums or committees, and in electoral politics. The central focus of the chapter is the struggle by women and their supporters inside political parties to press through demands for positive action to ensure substantial progress was delivered, and the response of existing party hierarchies and power structures to reformers' demands. We examine intra- and inter-party dynamics, especially in relation to candidate selection.

In chapter 5, we move from an examination of women politicians and leaders, and of organized women in political parties and women's organizations, to explore female political behaviour at mass level in relation to the National Assembly. Specifically, attention is focused on: voting patterns, party identification, interest in politics, attitudes towards political parties, constitutional preferences and opinions on public policy issues. It is clear that issues of gender equality have become a feature of electoral competition in Wales. We explore available evidence in order to assess whether post-devolution electoral politics is characterized by gender differences in political behaviour, and whether voting patterns are shaped by gendered responses to political factors, such as party ideology and party leadership style, as well as intersecting identities based on language, age, class and nationalist orientation.

Chapter 6 examines the gender dynamics of the National Assembly. Specific attention is focused on the link between the descriptive and substantive representation of women in political debate. In so doing, this chapter provides initial evidence of the extent to which women Assembly Members were able to set and shape the political agenda, effect a qualitative change in parliamentary discourse and meet general expectations that women would 'make a difference' to national politics in the wake of elected devolution. We explore whether women AMs are more likely than men to engage in debate on gender-equality issues, and the role of ministerial interventions and the actions of individual women 'equality champions' in advancing the substantive representation of women. Attention is also focused on the extent to which gendered, cross-party cooperation, or a putative 'sisterhood', may be seen to operate in Assembly discourse. We also examine various qualitative aspects of plenary debate. These include: the 'direction' of speakers' interventions (in other words, whether they are for, against or neutral in respect of gender equality); the breadth of policy areas covered by women AMs' interventions to promote gender equality; and whether women speakers draw upon their own direct, gendered life-experience to inform debate.

The pro-devolution rhetoric emphasized the need for a new 'participatory democracy'. In chapter 7 we explore the links between the Assembly and women in civil (and civic) society. Specifically, we examine: the mechanisms through which women have engaged in policy-making; the development of the principal women's policy network; and the types of policy issues that characterize the engagement of women's NGOs with the Assembly. Using the results of earlier research, including interviews with members and managers of women's NGOs, this chapter sets out an assessment of the effectiveness of, and challenges associated with, women's political participation during the first years of devolved government. It begins with a succinct summary of the arguments for inclusive and participatory democracy that featured at the time of the devolution campaign. These effectively provide a benchmark for the subsequent analysis that evaluates developments, including the reconfiguration of women's organizations, as part of the ongoing development of a nascent women's lobby. The evidence presented in this chapter suggests that women's growing participation in the policy process has lent greater democratic legitimacy to national decision-making. However, it is also clear that further challenges remain before the earlier hopes for a 'participatory democracy' are fully realized.

Equality mainstreaming, including gender equality, is a key mechanism by which the substantive representation of women was to be achieved. For us it acts as one proxy measure of the substantive representation of women. Thus, in chapter 8, we present an analysis of the application of mainstreaming, an ambitious and transformative approach to public policy that was adopted by the Assembly Government in July 1999. We assess the progress made to date in developing the institutional prerequisites necessary for mainstreaming gender – and other dimensions of – equality. Attention is also focused on selected examples of policy and law. These have been chosen because they provide early evidence of measures to promote gender equality following devolution. They include reform of the public appointments process and of education policy, as well as numerous examples of Welsh legislation passed by the Assembly. The concluding sections of this chapter assess the impact of these new developments by reference to evaluation reports published during the Assembly's first years, and a comparative analysis of parallel measures undertaken by the Scottish Executive. In particular, this chapter examines whether, in respect of mainstreaming, there is evidence of 'decoupling', or the situation whereby the devolved government is managing a disjunction between its political vision for equalities, the formal rules and practices of the bureaucracy, and actual policy outcomes.

This book is intended to provide an empirically rich narrative account of the 'devolution moment'. Throughout, we give space to the voices of women protagonists, drawing upon our extensive interviews with female activists from a wide range of backgrounds. In order to deepen our understanding of the major effect that constitutional change has had on the role of women and politics, chapter 9 adopts a singular approach. It differs from the preceding analysis by presenting the first-hand accounts of women candidates and Assembly Members (a comparative dimension is also provided by selective reference to the experience of male politicians). This material was gathered during a series of approximately 200 research interviews undertaken between 1998 and 2005. In respect of women and politics, these recollections provide clear evidence of the extent of the changes associated with constitutional reform and the hard-won nature of the advances made to date. By allowing women's voices to be heard in this way, the accounts presented in this chapter provide unique insights, impossible to gain through a traditional narrative approach and academic analysis. In terms of the structure of this volume, this chapter is also designed to summarize for the reader the progress, challenges and achievements in a journey that has, thus far, taken a little over a decade. Our purpose, then, is to gain an understanding of what it was like to participate in the events analysed in earlier chapters – and thus be better placed to re-address this book's key themes in chapter 10, the concluding chapter.

2

Women's Movements, 'Strategic Women' and Feminist Ideas: En-gendering the 1990s Devolution Campaign?

> It was one of those 'tingle-down-the-back-of-your-neck' type of 'I was there' moments! And it was terribly empowering! ... As women, it was one of those 'can do' moments, empowering moments when you knew you couldn't go backwards.[1]

Women around the world have mobilized during periods of constitutional change to make demands for inclusion in the process of constitution making and to stake claims for equality, representation and rights. Their activism is underpinned by a knowledge that, 'without their own efforts to frame the rules of membership, access and the exercise of power, their concerns may go unrepresented, under-represented and/or misrepresented' (Dobrowolsky and Hart, 2003a: 2). In this chapter we discuss the extent to which, and in what ways, women's movements and key 'strategic women' shaped constitutional politics in Wales by engaging with the campaign for increased levels of self-government. To what extent can we distinguish feminist ideas about gender equality and claims for descriptive and substantive representation within wider debates about the future of Welsh politics?

The Labour government that came to power in 1997 promised and delivered extensive constitutional reforms (Hazell, 2000; Ridley and McAllister, 2000; Bogdanor, 2001). These reform processes were the culmination of lengthy campaigns, which went back to before the failed devolution campaigns of the 1970s. However, unlike previous phases of home rule campaigns, this time around there were concerted efforts by women determined to influence 'constitutional politics' and to open up politics to women and women's ideas. Modern constitutional politics in the UK has been characterized by marked increases in the numbers of women in political institutions and the post-1997 diversity of electoral systems, institutional arrangements and parliamentary spaces. These developments make the UK 'a rich laboratory – and an important international case study – for examining the role played by systems, parties, actors and ideas in shaping the descriptive and the substantive representation of women' (Mackay, 2004b: 113).

NORTHERN IRELAND AND SCOTLAND: COMPARATIVE CONTEXTS

The origins and dynamics of women's involvement differed across jurisdiction; however, both Northern Ireland and Scotland saw the mobilization of women's movements – in the case of Northern Ireland, across significant community divisions – in response to the political and institutional opportunities created by processes of constitutional and institutional reform.

In Northern Ireland the concern to end violent conflict was the primary motivating factor for the most powerful players, and it was only at the latter stages of the peace process that women from the grassroots community sector were able to intervene effectively in debates and promote broader ideas of inclusion into political dialogue. The constitutional moment was provided by plans for the creation of an elected Forum and multi-party talks to negotiate a constitutional settlement, a process that culminated in the 1998 Belfast – or 'Good Friday' – Agreement.[2]

Female activists, drawn from women's centres, community groups, networks, such as NI Women's European Platform and the National Women's Council of Ireland, and academia, worked to create a cross-community women's party in a matter of just six weeks in order to fight the elections in 1996 and secure a place for women's voices at the table (Fearon, 1999). The Northern Ireland Women's Coalition (NIWC) was not the inevitable next step in the movement to promote women into Northern Ireland's political arena, but was spurred on by the combination of political opportunity afforded by the elections and the indifference and intransigence of the mainstream political parties to the demands of women in the grassroots sector (Brown et al., 2002: 78). At the subsequent elections NIWC was ranked the ninth most popular party out of twenty-four, which gave it two elected Forum members and a team at the multi-party talks.

Although the legacy of violence and community divisions limited the space available for the NIWC to put gender on the agenda, the party and its support structures in the grassroots movement did succeed in getting some of its concerns reflected in the final Agreement (Roulston, 1999; Brown et al., 2002). The Agreement contains a list of rights to which the (pro-Agreement) political parties reaffirmed their commitment. These include 'the right of women to full and equal political participation' (NIHRC, 2004: 12). In addition, the provisional Bill of Rights for Northern Ireland[3] addresses the rights of women as a 'systematically disadvantaged group' (Harvey, 2003: 138; NIHRC, 2004). Furthermore, such processes have resulted in the development of a pioneering new equality and human rights framework. Integral to this is the comprehensive 'Section 75', mainstreaming equality duty and associated institutions (McCrudden, 1996, 2004; Donaghy, 2003, 2004; Hinds, 2003). According to Fearon (1999: 163), these aspects of constitutional reform have 'lift[ed] the veil on politics, to make it a less difficult enterprise to engage with. It [politics] has been revealed as an accessible, even attractive entity. And this is how the Agreement will have perhaps the greatest import for women.' However, it is not clear whether the political stalemate and suspension of the Assembly until 2007 will necessitate a re-evaluation of this assessment.

The Women's Coalition and the wider mobilization of women sought to influence the parties to field more women candidates, but with only modest results. Women comprised only 17 per cent of candidates contesting the 1998 election and 14 per cent of members elected to the first Northern Ireland Legislative Assembly. However, this represented a step-change to the patterns of gross under-representation at the old Stormont, the Westminster Parliament and the European Parliament.[4]

In Scotland, conditions were more favourable than those in Northern Ireland in terms of political contexts, the stances of political parties as carrying agents (see Introduction), and the process and form of the devolution process. Scotland perhaps also provides a more pertinent comparator for Wales. The women's movement in Scotland – broadly defined – mobilized in the 1980s and 1990s to campaign for '50:50' gender parity in representation and the creation of more 'women-friendly' politics. The mobilization comprised women from different backgrounds and organizations, including grassroots autonomous women's groups, trade unions, traditional women's organizations, feminist academics, gender-equality experts and political parties. Over a period of more than ten years, they successfully intervened, with the support of key male allies, to make specific claims about women's representation and to gender wider civil society campaigns to redress the so-called 'democratic deficit' and promote the case for greater democratic participation and 'new politics'. Using the political, institutional opportunities presented by the reform process, and the discursive framing opportunities created by new politics debates, they worked to build a public and political consensus around the key aims of improving representation of women in political office (descriptive representation) and institutionalizing gender concerns in a new Scottish Parliament, through policy machinery and channels for consultation and participation (a form of substantive representation) (Brown, 1998; Brown et al., 2002; Mackay et al., 2003).

The women's movement in Scotland had dense inter-linkages: groups had long traditions of working together in coordinated action and co-working at an all-Scotland and local level in the context of administrative devolution around multiple issues, including women's poverty, violence against women, gender-sensitive public services and women's representation (Breitenbach, 1990, 1996), and the mobilizing opportunities of the European Union and United Nations.[5] The flourishing of municipal feminism in Scotland in the 1980s and 1990s through local government women's committees (Edwards, 1995; Breitenbach and Mackay, 2001) provided further opportunities for networking and joint campaigning, of which the Zero Tolerance Campaign is an exemplar (Mackay, 2001b; Cosgrove,

2001). The women's movement became more distinctively Scottish in the 1980s, in the context of the resurgence of devolution campaigns after the failed referendum of 1979 and growing Scottish opposition to neo-liberal welfare state reform, which was seen to impact disproportionately upon women (Breitenbach, 1989; Brown, 1991; Brown, 1998).

Activists in the women's movement in Scotland can also be characterized as displaying dual or multiple militancy (see Introduction). In other words, many women were active in autonomous women's organizations and women's sections within political parties and trade unions, as well as in the mainstream of political and civic organizations, including the range of devolution campaign groups. As a result, they were able to exert leverage, maintain momentum, broker deals and build coalitions.

In addition, the movement was operating in the context of a strong, politically focused civil or civic society. Civil or civic society is a concept that is historically contested and vaguely defined, but which has gained wider currency post-devolution. It typically refers to all of the various institutions and organizations through which citizens organize collectively in the space between private life and the state. The Centre for Civil Society at the London School of Economics provides a useful working definition:

> Civil society refers to the arena of uncoerced collective action around shared interests, purposes and values. In theory, its institutional forms are distinct from those of the state, family and market, though in practice, the boundaries between state, civil society, family and market are often complex, blurred and negotiated. Civil society commonly embraces a diversity of spaces, actors and institutional forms, varying in their degree of formality, autonomy and power. Civil societies are often populated by organisations such as registered charities, development non-governmental organisations, community groups, women's organisations, faith-based organisations, professional associations, trades unions, self-help groups, social movements, business associations, coalitions and advocacy groups.[6]

Institutional expression of a relatively strong civil society in Scotland can be seen in the creation and work of the Scottish Constitutional Convention, an unofficial body established by key groups in civil society together with some political parties, which debated and considered potential blueprints for a Scottish parliament during the 1980s and 1990s. Many of the recommendations of the SCC were adopted by the incoming Labour government in 1997 in its White Paper *Scotland's Parliament* (for details see Brown, 1998). From an early stage, women members of the SCC and their activist networks ensured that gender equality was debated and taken into consideration at each stage of the design process. Whilst an early recommendation for a statutory mechanism (SCC, 1992) was diluted to a commitment to the principle of equal representation, the SCC debates put pressure on the political parties. The two main political partners in the SCC, Labour and the Liberal Democrats, signed an electoral agreement as part of the final SCC publication, committing themselves to fielding equal numbers of male and female candidates in the first elections to a parliament elected under the additional Member system (SCC, 1995). In the 1997 White Paper, the government added its weight by stating its concern for diversity and equal opportunities in candidate-selection procedures.

Whilst the introduction of a more proportional system removed a systematic barrier to women's representation (see Introduction), the focus was on party action to deliver results. As a result of intensive campaigning by women's organizations, under the umbrella of the Scottish Women's Coordination Group (SWCG), and women activists inside political parties on '50:50', three of the four main political parties made commitments to take steps to improve gender balance. This was done through: improvements in selection and recruitment procedures; 'soft' positive action measures, such as balanced shortlists; and quota-type measures, such as the 'twinning' of constituencies or the alternation of male and female candidates on regional lists. In the final event, the Labour Party was alone in introducing official quota measures, in the form of 'twinning', when proposals for positive action failed to find sufficient support from the membership of the SNP and the Liberal Democrats. However, a 'contagion' effect could be discerned in the case of the SNP, who, faced with the prospect of unfavourable comparisons with their main electoral rival Labour, used unofficial positive action, in terms of encouraging the placement of women in favourable positions on their regional lists. In contrast to Northern Ireland, there were substantial gains made in descriptive representation in the first elections, with 37.2 per cent female Members of the Scottish Parliament in 1999, rising to 39.5 per cent in 2003 (Mackay, 2003).

In addition, the institutional 'blueprints' of the Parliament contained important statements and mechanisms for promoting the enhanced participation and influence of women in policy development and creating more accessible working practices and political cultures. Women working through the SCC, women's organizations and the Equal Opportunities Commission all played a role, as did women members of the Consultative Steering Group on the Scottish Parliament (CSG), the body established in 1998 to advise on standing orders and procedures. These gains included: the inclusion of equal opportunities as one of the four key principles of the Scottish Parliament, alongside power-sharing, accountability, and access and participation; the adoption of 'family-friendly' sitting hours in the Parliament and the observation of school holidays; the establishment of a visitors' crèche in the parliament building; and the creation of a parliamentary Equal Opportunities Committee and an Equality Unit in the Scottish Executive. Equal opportunity is a key principle of the Parliament and a stated priority of the government. Both are committed to 'mainstreaming' equality – including gender equality – across all their areas of work, including legislation and policy-making; the Parliament has the power to encourage equal opportunities and to impose duties on public bodies to ensure they have due regard to equality legislation;[7] and memoranda accompanying executive bills must include an equal opportunities impact statement.

Northern Ireland and Scotland present examples of grassroots mobilization, in the case of Scotland interconnecting with the mobilization of strategic elite women inside parties and other mainstream organizations. An early assessment of Wales in comparative focus reached the conclusion that, unlike Northern Ireland and Scotland, there had been little appreciable mobilization of the women's movement(s) in Wales. Instead, an elite cadre of 'strategic women' – 'leaders without a movement' – had capitalized upon the opportunities presented by devolution in a top-down process that mirrored the predominantly top-down nature of Welsh devolution as a whole (Mackay et al., 2002).

The remaining sections of this chapter examine the pattern and nature of women's movement mobilization within wider reform processes, and the role of 'strategic women'. Such 'strategic women' can be characterized by their shared feminist conviction, and by their membership of women's NGOs and other 'gender' organizations. They were individuals who used the political opportunities presented by devolution in order to develop the infrastructure of women's organizations in Wales. Importantly, these were women who were well connected in key social and political networks and able to exert political influence. Whilst confirming the generally top-down nature of women's constitutional activism in Wales, we argue that a more nuanced analysis of the process reveals a complex set of developments, in which women's movements reconfigured and played an increasingly important role, particularly in the latter stages. First, we turn to map briefly the origins and trajectories of women's movements in Wales in the 1970s, 1980s and 1990s.

MAPPING THE WOMEN'S MOVEMENT

In this section we briefly map key developments in the 1970s, 1980s and 1990s.[8]

Women's movements in the 1970s: protest, consciousness-raising, feminist institution-building, conferences and joint actions
Narratives of the women's movement in Wales are dominated by two events of the 1980s: Greenham and the 1984–5 Miners' Strike (see below). In many accounts, this is seen to mark the beginning of a distinctively Welsh feminism (Dubé, 1988: 10). There is less reportage of women's movement activism from the earlier period of the 1970s. For some, this is evidence that the women's movement started later than its counterparts in England, Scotland and Northern Ireland and was less radical. Rolph cites the Welsh historian Kenneth Morgan, whose smug assertion was that 'there is scant evidence that the more aggressive or

---

TIMELINE

1970s

1970   First Women's Liberation Movement (WLM) group in Wales (Cardiff Women's Action Group).

1972   WLM group set up in Swansea.

1974   First All-Wales Women's Liberation Conference.

Women's Rights Committee for Wales set up to monitor Sex Discrimination and Equal Pay Acts.

Cardiff Women's Aid formed.

1975   First women's refuge in Wales opened in Cardiff.

WRWC delegation presents first UK petition to European Parliament in Strasbourg.

1977   Welsh Women's Aid founded.

Swansea Women's Aid refuge opened.

Rhiannon, a bilingual feminist paper launched.

1978   Equal Opportunities Commission Wales office opened.

1979   Swansea Women's Centre opened.

Socialist-feminist conference in Swansea on 'The Welsh National Question and the Proposed Assembly'.

1980s

1981   Cardiff Women's Centre opened.

Women for Life on Earth peace march from Cardiff to Greenham Common. Start of Greenham Common protest and peace camps.

1982   'Embrace the Base' mass protest at Greenham Common

Wales Women's Euro Network.

March Against Women's Unemployment, organized by WRCW.

1984   Wales Assembly for Women set up to report on the UN Conference for Women.

Wales TUC Women's Advisory Committee formed.

1984–5   Women in south Wales mining communities mobilized around the miners' strike against pit closures. Establishment of women's support groups.

1985   DOVE Workshop set up to provide training and education for unemployed women and women returners. Established by women who had been active in the Swansea, Neath and Dulais Miners' Support Group.

South Glamorgan Women's Workshop set up to provide training and education for unemployed women and women returners.

South Glamorgan County Council Women's Committee established.

1985–6   Blaenau Ffestiniog Women's Support Group formed to support slate quarry workers' strike action.

1986   Honno women's press set up to publish English- and Welsh-language books by Welsh women writers.

1990s

1992   Chwarae Teg consortium set up by EOC Wales, the Welsh Development Agency and Business in the Community to support and promote women's participation in the workforce.

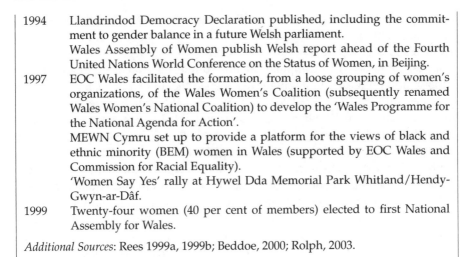

1994	Llandrindod Democracy Declaration published, including the commitment to gender balance in a future Welsh parliament.
	Wales Assembly of Women publish Welsh report ahead of the Fourth United Nations World Conference on the Status of Women, in Beijing.
1997	EOC Wales facilitated the formation, from a loose grouping of women's organizations, of the Wales Women's Coalition (subsequently renamed Wales Women's National Coalition) to develop the 'Wales Programme for the National Agenda for Action'.
	MEWN Cymru set up to provide a platform for the views of black and ethnic minority (BEM) women in Wales (supported by EOC Wales and Commission for Racial Equality).
	'Women Say Yes' rally at Hywel Dda Memorial Park Whitland/Hendy-Gwyn-ar-Dâf.
1999	Twenty-four women (40 per cent of members) elected to first National Assembly for Wales.

Additional Sources: Rees 1999a, 1999b; Beddoe, 2000; Rolph, 2003.

Figure 2.1 Women's movement: selected landmarks.

misanthropic forms of "Women's Lib" made much impact in a friendly country like Wales' (2003: 44, citing Morgan, 1981: 352). However, according to others (Beddoe, 2000; Rolph, 2003), feminism was 'alive and well' in the 1970s with a radical and active women's liberation movement, which set the groundwork and radicalized many of the key activists for developments in the 1980s. Many of the 'strategic women' involved in engendering devolution campaigns in the 1990s had their roots in 1970s Women's Liberation Movement (WLM) groups and their offshoots.

The 1970s can be characterized as a period when the women's movement in Wales followed similar patterns to its counterparts in England, Scotland and elsewhere. Women's groups sprang up, influenced by key American feminist texts (books and pamphlets) and in response to wider social trends. It is no surprise that these groups were primarily concentrated in urban south Wales; WLM groups comprised young educated women, many drawn from university circles (Beddoe, 2000; Rolph, 2003). The first group to be set up was the Cardiff Women's Action Group in 1970, followed in 1972 by groups in Swansea (see Figure 2.1). However, activism was not confined to major conurbations, and groups were set up elsewhere, including Aberystwyth, Abergavenny, Bangor, Carmarthen, Harlech, Lampeter, Newport, Pontypridd and the Rhondda valleys (Beddoe, 2000: 160; Rolph, 2003: fn. 1). Nor was feminism solely a middle-class phenomenon, with working-class women active in some groups, particularly in the Swansea area (Rolph, 2003: 47–8). Issues and activities followed similar lines to elsewhere, with consciousness-raising groups, study and education activities, and campaigning around reproductive health, maternity and abortion services, equal pay and equal opportunities, childcare and violence against women. The first Women's Aid group was set up in Cardiff 1974 as a feminist collective (see Charles, 1994, 2004) to campaign against domestic violence and to provide support and refuge. Its first refuge was opened the following year.

Protest rallies and national conferences were held, bringing ideas and values to a wider audience; Welsh women also attended WLM conferences and events in England and Scotland (Rolph, 2003). Activists also responded to the new equalities legislation of the 1970s, joining the newly formed Women's Rights Committee for Wales to work with older, liberal, equal rights feminists, in order to monitor the implementation of the Sex Discrimination and Equal Pay Acts.

From the early days, there was both collaboration and also tension with English feminism and feminist groups. As in Scotland (Breitenbach, Brown and Myers, 1998), activists in Wales complained that London-based organizations marginalized and misunderstood the Welsh context, in particular the significance of the Welsh language and nationalism. This led, for example, to the establishment of Merched y Wawr in response to the perceived Anglocentric culture of the Women's Institute (Jones, 1999: 148). One of the founding members of Women's Aid, interviewed in our study, reported that they had been determined not to be subsumed under England and therefore lobbied the Welsh Office for funding to set up a separate Welsh Women's Aid. There were also early attempts to bring together English- and Welsh-speaking women, with the publication of the bilingual paper *Rhiannon* (Beddoe, 2000: 163). There is also evidence of public debate amongst feminists on women and devolution in the run-up to the failed referendum of 1979 (see Figure 2.1). The legacy of this decade of activism can be traced in the next decade, according to Rolph:

> Cardiff Women's Action Group included women from local mining areas, and many of the women who became heavily involved in the women's peace movement in Wales had been involved in feminist groups and actions of the 1970s. By the time women became involved in the campaigns of the 1980s, there was a well-established, if small, feminist network with an already enviable record of visible achievements. (Rolph, 2003: 44)

1980s: Oppositional protest politics and mass mobilization, then fragmentation and deradicalization

'Feminism took a new direction in the 1980s' (Beddoe, 2000: 163) with the creation of a women's peace movement, Women for Life on Earth (WFLOE). Women had been involved in the Campaign for Nuclear Disarmament but the decision to site Cruise missiles in Britain at the Greenham Common airbase in Berkshire provoked Ann Pettit, from Llanpumsaint, and four friends to organize a peace march from Cardiff to Greenham in 1981. The marchers, about forty in total, set up a permanent peace-picket outside the base (Pettit, 1985), which turned into an international movement involving thousands of women. As Aaron remarks, 'throughout the eighties the peace camp served as a potent symbol for many Welsh women, English-speaking and Welsh-speaking alike, and became a way of life for some' (Aaron, 1994: 127). The protest galvanized women to further peace actions focused on other military installations in Wales, such as those at Caerwent US military base,[9] the Brawdy US base and ROF Llanishen in the period 1982–4 (White, 1984).

The second event that galvanized women as activists was the miners' strike against pit closures, from 1984 to 1985. The dispute sparked an unprecedented organization and mobilization of women, with far-reaching and long-lasting consequences. As in English and Scottish coalfields, women went beyond their traditional role of running soup kitchens and welfare, taking a more proactive and public role, including picketing, pithead occupations, organizing rallies, public speaking and fund-raising tours (Evans, Hudson and Smith, 1985). Women's support groups in local communities and their central body, the South Wales Women's Support Group (SWWSG), started to call for recognition of their contribution by the South Wales Area National Union of Mineworkers. However, as Beddoe notes, 'in many valleys the strike brought a new respect for women. In other places men felt threatened by this new demonstration of women's power' (2000: 165).

Some commentators see this heightened militancy as a sign that women had been influenced by feminist ideas and the 'role-model effect' of Greenham Common (Day, 2000: 114). Participants' comments certainly provide evidence of a radicalizing influence. One woman activist, interviewed in 1983, said, 'we're out on the streets and the picket lines. Before, I never fully understood the Greenham women. *Now* I realise how important it is for women to organize themselves.'[10] Another such activist underlined the enduring effects of the strike and said, 'there's no way I'm going to sit down in the house after this is over, after being so active. We've been so strong now that it would be pointless not to stay together.'[11] Another woman added, 'this strike has had extraordinary effects. Out of something that is terrible, something very good has grown. We know we have the strength to do a lot of things.'[12]

The impact of the miners' strike in terms of women's new self-confidence and autonomy was illustrated by their role in setting up the DOVE women's training workshop in Dulais Valley and the South Glamorgan Women's Workshop (Rees 1999b: 258), as well as entering higher education and running their own enterprises (Beddoe, 2000: 165–6). SWWSGs continued to exist and rallied to support other industrial actions, such as the Blaenau Ffestiniog quarry strike of 1985–6, but gradually dissipated, becoming loose associations rather than a united body (Adler, 1989).

These two events had a lasting impact on women's lives and connections. Networks from this time were frequently referred to by interviewees in our research. It is also clear that strategic women were able to call upon these connections to take forward their campaigning around devolution and gender equality in the 1990s.

As well as oppositional politics and mass mobilization, the decade saw a growing self-determination – and unprecedented visibility – through the growth of a distinctively Welsh women's voice through feminist publishing and film-making ventures (Rees, 1999a; Beddoe, 2000), and other expressions of cultural politics.

The latter half of the 1980s saw a fragmentation of the women's movement – if it could ever really be seen as a unified movement – with neither the critical events nor the coordinating mechanisms to provide momentum. There was also a flourishing of small-scale projects and grassroots organizations, many funded through European streams of funding for women's projects (Rees, 1999a). However, they had little strategic function and were primarily concerned with day-to-day work to improve the lives of women in their communities. The Wales Assembly of Women (WAW), an umbrella organization, provided some coordin-ation of Welsh perspectives to take to the UN Nairobi World Conference on Women in 1985, and thereafter represented Welsh women's organizations on the UK official consultative body, the Women's National Commission (WNC). It was seen by some of our interviewees as the only strategic-level feminist organization to have been active during 'the dark days' of the 1980s and 1990s in keeping Welsh issues on the agenda. However, WAW was not viewed as a representative body.

Meanwhile, feminists entered institutions such as political parties, trade unions, voluntary sector bodies and local government. The 1980s saw the creation of women's structures in the Wales Trades Union Congress (TUC) and the estab-lishment of South Glamorgan County Council's Women's Committee, whilst some women's sections of political parties were reinvigorated. Of particular note is the Plaid Cymru Women's Forum (see chapter 4), where key women's movement activists – and 'strategic women', such as Helen Mary Jones (a future AM), Jill Evans (a future MEP) and Janet Davies (a future AM) – were active; and a small number of Wales Labour Party branch-level women's sections. Riverside women's section in Cardiff was lively in the 1980s, with a group of women – who had been active in the women's movement – lobbying the party hard to adopt women-friendly childcare and housing policies, and campaigning for improve-ments in the representation of women in internal party positions and as candidates and elected representatives. The section included Jane Hutt, Sue Essex and Jane Davidson, who later became local councillors and subsequently AMs and Welsh Assembly Government (WAG) ministers.

1990s: 'Respectable feminism' and devolution

By the 1990s, Beddoe remarked that 'respectable organisations and pressure groups represented the public face of feminism in Wales' (2000: 167), taking the values and ideas of feminism into institutions. The Equal Opportunities Commission (EOC) became an active player and source of strategic leadership in Wales under the directorship of Val Feld. She began to build support infrastructure, consisting of organisations like Chwarae Teg,[13] founded in 1992 as a network to support women's enterprise and increase women's participation in the labour market, and MEWN Cymru, a network set up in 1993 to provide a platform for the views of black and minority ethnic women in Wales. The EOC used local-government reorganization and the 1995 UN Platform for Action as network-building/mobilizing opportunities, culminating in the creation in 1997 of a coalition of women's organizations, the Wales Women's National Coalition (see later discussion).

CHARACTERISTICS OF THE WOMEN'S MOVEMENT

Feminist activists, as elsewhere, comprised only a small minority of women in Wales but have had a wider, indirect influence on women's lives (Beddoe, 2000: 160), through concrete social, legal and policy gains and through the transmission of ideas. In some respects the trajectory of the movement has mirrored that of movements elsewhere, in that it has become fragmented, less visible, less protest-oriented and more 'respectable'. A division between reform and radical or revolutionary feminism is common in the study of comparative women's movements; however, in Wales we see women active in both reformist organizations, such as WRCW in the 1970s and Welsh Assembly of Women in the 1980s and 1990s, and in more radical groupings. Socialist feminists worked with radical feminists and liberal feminists. In other words, there was a strong pragmatic streak and a willingness to work across divisions around common goals, necessary tactics in a small country; so there were not the battles over ideology and identity that fractured the women's movement in the 1980s in England (Lovenduski and Randall, 1993). The women's movement was active, localized and internationalist in outlook and, for the most part, activists and workers were oriented to service delivery and community development. It had little engagement with Wales-level institutions and generally lacked strategic capacity (see later discussion).

Feminism and nationalism
The dimension of the women's movements in Wales that most distinguishes them from English counterparts is the interplay between feminism and nationalism (linguistic and political). There are differing views about the role that nationalism, and particularly Welsh-language activism, has played, in terms of working with or against feminism. On the one hand, Reeves (1988) argued that it had partly stifled the growth of feminism, pointing to the traditional attitudes of some

language campaigners. Similarly, Davies (1993) suggested that linguistic nation-alism diverted and 'absorbed the political energies of many women' who might have otherwise been active in women's movements in the 1970s. On the other hand, it is evident that the two movements over time have interacted and affected each other, resulting in a strong strand of feminism in the nationalist movement and a strong sense of Welshness in the women's movements.

Women have been active in the Welsh-language rights organization, Cymdeithas yr Iaith Gymraeg (CYIG)[14] since the 1960s, 'manifest[ing] their toughness, and capacity for direct action' (Aaron, 2001: 201–2) and increasingly taking leadership roles, to the point where, in 1988, Reeves commented that it 'had virtually been taken over by women' (1988: 217). One of its leading voices, Angharad Tomos (1994, 2001), has written about the feminist as well as cultural consciousness-raising consequences for many women of language activism and contact with the criminal justice system. The Welsh-language feminist poet and peace campaigner, Menna Elfyn, famously reported that 'I ... went to prison myself as a language activist, but came out a feminist' (1994: 282). Aaron argues that although feminism was still viewed as an alien Anglo-American import by many Welsh-identified communities, it has since the 1970s 'combined interest-ingly with a resurgence in confidence in Welshness to produce a new and strong female voice within both Welsh and English-language cultures of Wales' (1994: 183–4). In a similar vein, Rolph argues that 'the Welsh language and ideas of Welsh nationalism ... played a large part in shaping the nature of the WLM in Wales' (2003: 43–44).

THE WOMEN'S MOVEMENT AND DEVOLUTION

Devolution provided a potential mobilizing opportunity to the Welsh women's movement. However, although the movement was not in abeyance in terms of day-to-day activism, it lacked the strategic capacity, infrastructure and the resources to mobilize as either a unified force or a time-limited coalition. Few funds were available for networking, and most organizations were involved in 'practical feminism', delivering front-line services and support rather than taking part in strategic planning. Several of our interviewees characterized Welsh femi-nism as 'practical feminism', concerned with the politics of everyday life, with groups working in isolation to provide services or initiatives around giving women a stronger voice in their communities, or working 'together spontan-eously on campaigns but [without] strategic or organized links'.

Reeves suggested, in her review of the women's movement in Wales in the 1980s, that the shared legacy of campaigns would provide a trigger to coalesce the movement at critical moments: 'the Welsh women's network, connected strand by durable strand over the last twenty years of campaigning, giving us hope that it will always be there to bring women together in times of crisis' (Reeves, 1988: 222). There were multiple connections, but by the 1990s few opportunities or mechanisms for organizational mobilization and strategic work at a movement level. It was also the case that devolution had low salience in the context of scarce resources, and it did not constitute the critical trigger for mobilization.

Instead, the campaign to engender the devolution reform process comprised largely 'insider' strategies, of women working through institutions (see later discussion). However, connections formed in earlier phases of the women's movement were utilized by strategic women – gender equality experts, elected politicians and party officials, trade union officials, directors of women's NGOs, academics and policymakers – to find ways to work together to press their case for gender equality in the run-up to devolution. The shared legacies still serve to underpin a sense of sisterhood in the Assembly (see chapters 6 and 9). As one female AM subsequently explained:

> Many of the women who work in this institution on different sides of the political divide have a tradition of working together on other issues before we got here. Jane Hutt the Health Minister was the first ever national coordinator of Welsh Women's Aid, the body that campaigns to counter domestic violence. I was one of its first national chairs – now you don't bring that shared experience of twenty years working on women's issues together into an institution and then instantly drop it as soon as one of us is elected with a green rosette and one of us is elected with a red one. And I just use Jane and I as an example, there are lots and lots of examples of that. There are photographs of Sue Essex, the Environment Minister, standing at the fence at Greenham Common fifteen years ago with the Shadow Environment Minister Janet Davies. So those shared experiences, those *are* important.

WOMEN, GENDER EQUALITY AND THE WELSH DEVOLUTION CAMPAIGN(S) IN THE EARLY 1990S

In Wales, gender equality issues were mostly absent from the initial concerns of the pro-devolution campaign that emerged from the wreckage of the 1979 referendum, a movement that was boosted by the widely perceived injustice of the 1987 UK General Election result. As a popular graffito put it, 'Wales voted Labour, got Thatcher'. Launched in the same year, the Campaign for a Welsh Assembly (CWA) was 'the most significant coalition for democratic devolution, the nearest Wales ever came to having a cross-party Constitutional Convention' (Morgan and Mungham, 2000: 97–8). However, the CWA's 1988 *Strategy Paper One* made no reference to gender equality (CWA, 1988); instead, it restricted itself to arguments about the most effective structural arrangements for governing Wales within the UK.

Within the left-of-centre political parties at this time there were (mostly female) voices raised which sought to link the issues of gender equality and constitutional reform, arguing that any new Welsh parliament must ensure women had an equal role. In her paper presented to the 1990 Plaid Cymru summer school Michele Ryan stated:

> There are many women working hard at a local level. Indeed, in many cases women form the backbone of the local parties. Something is blocking their access into decision-making and positions of influence ... There are still male chauvinists in Plaid who think that women's issues should be left until we have achieved self-government – a position adopted by Lenin and the Bolsheviks and look at the position of women in Russia ... Unless we want to reproduce the same inequalities and discriminations that exist in the present nation-state, we have to work now to ensure that when we have the first government in Wales, half of those serving on it will be women. (1990: 14)

This process of lobbying to ensure gender equality was at the heart of the emerging devolution proposals that began to gather momentum in the first half of the 1990s, when women such as Siân Edwards and Val Feld started to exert a discernible influence in the CWA. In 1993, CWA further developed its plans for financial and legislative powers for a future Welsh Assembly. In March of the following year, the CWA, now renamed the Parliament for Wales Campaign (PWC), convened a 'Democracy Conference'. At this stage in the pro-devolution campaign, there was strong hostility to devolution from within the Welsh Labour Party (WLP) establishment. The academic commentators and devolution activists Morgan and Mungham (2000: 88) claimed:

> [M]atters came to a head [at the] Democracy Conference in Llandrindod Wells ... the WLP Executive spared no effort to prevent MPs and Party members from attending; in fact it even organised a rival conference on the same weekend in Newport, which proved an embarrassing failure. Nevertheless, such was the pressure that prominent pro-devolutionists in the party, like Rhodri Morgan and Wayne David, eventually withdrew from the Llandrindod conference. Only three Labour MPs defied the ban – Paul Flynn, Peter Hain and Jon Owen Jones – all of whom were summoned before the Executive and reprimanded for liaising with outside bodies and for defying the injunction to keep the devolution debate inside the Party.

The main purpose of the conference was to develop the 'Draft Democracy Declaration', the PWC's blueprint for a future parliament. Although, again, there were no references to equality issues in this document, according to one participant, three arguments for 'the involvement of women in a Welsh Parliament' subsequently featured in conference debates and workshops tasked with producing a final Declaration (Edwards, 1994: 146). These were:

1. Democracy is based upon the participation of all in political decision-making. Women constitute at least half of any population and it is axiomatic therefore that they should be represented proportionately.
2. Political participation requires the articulation and defence of the interests

of the group or groups that are represented. Women are more aware of their own needs and interests, and are therefore better able to press for them.
3. Involving women in a gender-balanced Welsh Parliament will improve the culture of the decision-making process itself.

Women's organizations did participate in the Llandrindod conference (Andrews, 1999: 58). Edwards (1994: 147) concludes that the final debate on women's future role in the Welsh legislature was: 'won by the words of [a male delegate] who said, 'I would like to say, very briefly, that I support this clause. I am totally in favour of positive discrimination; after all, it has served us men very well down the centuries.' As a result, the following article was approved and added to the Declaration at PWC's annual meeting in July 1994: 'a future Welsh Parliament will ensure, from the start, that there is a gender balance in its elected representatives, and will ensure that its procedures will enable women, men and minority groups to participate to the fullest extent' (PWC, 1994a: unpaginated). Coincidentally, the same month saw the publication of the Welsh Labour Party document *Shaping the Vision: A Consultation Paper on the Powers and Structure of the Welsh Assembly.* The aims of this document were partly influenced by events in Scotland – where, before the 1992 General Election, the Scottish Constitutional Convention had agreed on a proposed statutory obligation on political parties to put forward an equal number of female and male candidates in future devolved elections. The principle of '50:50' had first been proposed by the STUC Women's Committee in 1989 and subsequently had become the official policy of both the STUC and the Labour Party in Scotland (Brown, 1998/2001). In a similar vein, the WLP document stated: 'the Party has also committed itself to equal representation for men and women in the new Assembly' (WLP, 1994: 4).

Just four months after the WLP's *Shaping the Vision,* the PWC published its own report, *Empowering the People.* In it, the PWC said that it welcomed the WLP's proposals for securing equal representation of men and women as being 'likely to lead to a much improved political culture within Wales' (PWC, 1994a: 7). *Empowering the People* proceeded to ask:

Yet how is [equal representation] to be achieved in practice? It should be possible to reach consensus on the following six propositions:

1. The current level of representation of women in Wales is unacceptable.
2. We should not allow the under-representation of women at Westminster to be reproduced in a new Welsh Parliament.
3. A system of government which claims to be democratic cannot deny the right of both men and women to enjoy full participation in political decision-making.
4. Action needs to be taken to ensure the desired gender equity in a Welsh parliament.
5. The desire for gender balance is not threatening or unusual, but a reflection of broader changes in the roles of men and women in society and in the labour force, and is in line with trends in other European countries.

6. We should seek agreement on a proposal which does not alienate the broad constituency in support of gender balance, and which attempts to meet the needs of all legitimate interests involved. (PWC, 1994a: 22)

In 1994, the prevailing view of many feminists within PWC was against a laissez-faire or voluntary approach; instead, it was held that the equal representation of women and men should be built into the institutional blueprint of the future Assembly as a statutory requirement. Thus, in a PWC document, reference is made to the scenario 'if parties themselves were *required* to select an equal number of men and women as candidates' (PWC, 1994a: 22, original emphasis). Advocates were clear on the need to seize the initiative on this issue. *Empowering the People* states:

> Even given the advance that has occurred in the thinking in Wales regarding women's rights, such arrangements [positive action in a future Assembly electoral system] would be bound to have a dynamic and innovative effect on Welsh politics. It could be that they [positive action statutory clauses] would be subject to review after two, or perhaps three elections. There could also be a 'sunset clause' in relation to the legislation establishing the electoral arrangements for the new Parliament. Nevertheless, any suggestion of waiting until we see how bad the situation is before we act is a recipe for inertia. If we are to achieve change, the time to do it is at the start before political and personal interests have become entrenched. Establishing a Parliament for Wales provides a unique and exciting opportunity to improve dramatically the representation of women in Welsh life. *To be successful,* as the [PWC Llandrindod] Declaration states, *that opportunity must be seized from the start.* (PWC, 1994a: 23, original emphasis).

In terms of wider public and political debate amongst opinion-formers, there would appear to have been little airing in influential periodicals, such as *Barn* and *Planet – The Welsh Internationalist,* of the issue of women's political under-representation in the context of devolution, until Deacon's article in *Planet* in 1996. In it, he noted that the gender deficit in terms of women's representation had been overshadowed by other obvious deficits in democratic politics in Wales, but that the WLP, Plaid Cymru and the Liberal Democrats had each committed themselves to equal representation in a new parliament (Deacon, 1996: 126–8). The secondary literature on the run-up to devolution similarly has little to say on women, equality and representation.

INCLUSIVE POLITICS?

In May 1996, the WLP's *Preparing for a New Wales* reported on a major setback to plans for gender balance, in the following terms:

> there has been an assumption within the Party that equality for women, in terms of representation in the Assembly, could be fulfilled by each two-member constituency returning a man and a woman. However, following the recent employment tribunal

judgement on all-women shortlists, the [GB] National Executive Committee has established a Working Party to investigate its implications for the Party's selection procedures. (WLP, 1996: 3)

At a British level, sustained activism by feminists in the Labour Party (including women activists from the Welsh and Scottish parties) had resulted in agreement that the quota-type mechanism, all-women shortlists (AWS), would be used to select candidates in half of the party's inheritor seats (where a Labour MP had retired or stood down) and in the party's target seats (key marginals, currently held by other parties, which Labour assessed were winnable) in the run-up to the 1997 General Election (Lovenduski, 2005). This controversial measure was only partially implemented before the process was halted in 1996, after a successful legal challenge was brought at an industrial tribunal in Leeds by two male would-be candidates. The tribunal judgement – itself controversial – 'changed the political landscape by ruling that the role of a parliamentary candidate could be considered as employment for the purposes of the Sex Discrimination Act' (Russell, 2000; Lovenduski, 2005: 120).

The ruling created legal uncertainty about what measures were lawful in promoting women's political representation, not only at a Westminster level, but also for the new institutions in Wales and Scotland, if devolution went ahead. In Scotland, work had begun earlier than in Wales in terms of prioritizing electoral systems and party rules, as a result of the sustained work undertaken by the Scottish Constitutional Convention over this period and the role of women within it. Female members of this forum, and their activist networks, used lessons from other countries in Europe and elsewhere, first, to expose Scotland and the UK's poor international record, and, second, to press the SCC to assess the implications of different electoral systems for women's representation (Brown, 1998). Despite the legal uncertainty, Scottish activists worked to tailor party positive-action measures to the AMS system that was eventually proposed for Scotland and, subsequently, Wales. With respect to lobbying the political parties about their candidate-selection procedures, 'zipping' was advocated for parties whose strength lay in the regional list vote. 'Twinning'[15] was the quota-type measure designed for Labour, which was likely to win most of its seats through the FPTP constituency contests. The mechanism was devised by Labour women activists and academics in Scotland as a way around any possible legal challenge to positive action in the aftermath of the tribunal ruling. Party activists, bolstered by detailed analysis and the vocal groundswell of support from the broad-based '50:50' campaign, applied sustained pressure to get 'twinning' accepted, first by the Scottish Labour leadership and then endorsed by the GB leadership and the Women's Representation Taskforce, convened by the then chair of the NEC Women's Committee (Russell et al., 2003). In turn, twinning became the preferred option proposed by Welsh Labour Party women, including female MPs, who were supported by the GB NEC and by party modernizers in Wales.

However, female activists also continued to press for equal representation of women to be built into the institutional blueprint until – and during – the time, three years later, when the Government of Wales Bill passed through the UK Parliament. One such advocate was Julie Morgan MP, who asserted:

> One of the most important ways of ensuring equal opportunity for all people is to have members who represent the range of people in Wales. That means that women should be there [in the Assembly] in equal numbers ... The Bill leaves the means of getting equal representation to the political parties. I welcome the element of proportionality in the Bill [that is, the Additional Member System elected by proportional representation] ... Now that an 80-member Assembly, with one man and one woman for each seat, is no longer an option, it may be difficult to achieve equal representation. Is it possible to put something in the Bill to allow political parties to take positive action to ensure that women are present in equal numbers?[16]

We return to discuss these developments in more detail in chapter 4.

BLUEPRINTS FOR SUBSTANTIVE REPRESENTATION

Turning away from issues of descriptive representation, the WLP's 1996 devolution policy document *Preparing for a New Wales* also marked a significant step in women's future substantive representation in Welsh politics. The policy document exemplifies the way in which new political institutions offer new opportunities for gender equality. It stated:

> The Parliamentary Act which establishes the Welsh Assembly should include an Equal Opportunities clause which will require the Assembly to adopt procedures which are non-discriminatory, [and] to establish a system of monitoring the success of the Assembly in implementing enabling measures for the participation of women and minority groups ... the Assembly will be concerned with promoting and overseeing the development of equal opportunities generally in Wales by:
>
> i)   scrutinising policies and developing new strategies to achieve equality
> ii) setting up procedures to ensure equal opportunities in the selection for public bodies
> iii) ensuring that economic development strategies take account of the need to fully utilise women's skills and tackle low pay. (WLP, 1996: 6)

This brief review illustrates that, from the early 1990s, women and their allies in political parties[17] and in the CWA/PWC used the framing opportunities presented by debates on devolution to press the case of women's political representation. They were able to take advantage of prevailing ideas of 'inclusion' and new politics, which became hallmarks of the campaign as it gathered pace and support (Chaney, 2002). Evidence can be found in the gradual 'en-gendering' of policy statements and declarations. The inclusion of a commitment to gender balance in the final Llandrindod Declaration bore the hallmarks of internal lobbying by influential feminists. However, as we noted earlier, during this period there was no sustained mobilization of grassroots women's organizations. From interviews, it appears that women worked within parties, and behind the scenes, to influence their party's policies (see chapter 4).

THE 1997 REFERENDUM CAMPAIGN: WHERE WERE THE WOMEN?

In contrast to Scottish home rule campaigns, in some quarters at least, ambivalence characterized much of the devolution developments in Wales. Public debate was hesitant and low key, and political debate was largely kept internal to each political party. In particular, the Welsh Labour Party's reluctance to become involved in wider public debates – and its antipathy to Plaid Cymru – prevented the establishment of a constitutional convention based on the Scottish model and limited the potential for a mobilization of the public and of civil society.

Up to mid 1996, the three principal drivers of the Welsh pro-devolution campaign were the pro-devolution wing of the WLP, Plaid Cymru and the PWC. At this stage in the devolution campaign, developments in Scotland – where the Constitutional Convention had steadily built cross-party support for devolution – posed a dilemma for the Welsh Labour Party executive; Morgan and Mungham (2000: 87) explain:

> Should it [the WLP executive] lend its weight to a cross-party movement as in Scotland or should it go it alone? There was never a shadow of doubt as to what the WLP Executive would do. It would go it alone because this seemed like the least-cost option on two counts: first, it meant that the WLP did not have to share control with other organisations; and second, going it alone seemed the surest way to preserve Party unity in Wales because centralist-minded Labour MPs would never entertain joint action with nationalists.

Morgan and Mungham (2000: 88) concluded that: 'there is no mystery as to why a cross-party Constitutional convention did not emerge in Wales as it did in Scotland and the answer is twofold: the "exclusivist" politics of the WLP and the weakness of Welsh civil society'. Thus, there was little opportunity for effective engagement with the issue until the announcement that a public referendum would be held by any incoming UK Labour government to endorse its plans for constitutional change (McAllister, 1998).

The announcement of 27 June 1996 that referendums would decide whether Welsh and Scottish legislatures would be established, if Labour won the election, necessitated a change of attitude to cross-party and 'non-party'[18] working in Wales. It was only at this stage that the cross-party group 'Yes for Wales' (YFW) was formed at the end of 1996. It was led at the outset by Peter Hain MP and included academics, broadcasters and trade unionists. The cross-party 'Yes for Wales' campaign was formally launched at a series of events during January and

February 1997. However, the campaign proper did not start until after the general election in May 1997, and thus had only a few months to try to engage public debate and interest, and to promote arguments of new 'inclusive' politics.

This also marked a step-change in terms of the visibility of women and the issue of women's representation. Women were prominent from the start in the campaign, from the inclusion of a woman, Lesley Smith, as a speaker at the launch event setting out her aspirations for the Assembly, to the informal convention that public platforms should have a gender balance of personalities and that women should feature in the campaign's public image (Andrews, 1999: 114, 70–1). As Mari James, one of the key figures in the 'Yes for Wales' campaign, recalled in a recent interview:

> [Gender balance] was definitely a characteristic of the campaign and we made sure we had rules for all our public events, all our press conferences, all that, we had a gender balance, either gender-balanced platforms or more women than men [...] because sometimes we couldn't deliver as many men [...] maybe two or three times we had press conferences that were entirely women and we hadn't decided to have them entirely women, it was just that I was chairing and Val [Feld] was kind of on duty that day doing stuff [...] but the journalists always said 'Now this is emphasising your theme, isn't it? That Wales will change?' So even when that wasn't the only point we were making, it was something that was being perceived as what we were doing [...] That is not what Wales's political campaigns usually look like, they don't look like they are women-led, so it did look different and yes, it was absolutely spot on.

Importantly, 'Yes for Wales' developed a number of affiliated campaign groups including 'Women Say Yes' (WSY).[19] The latter grouping was launched in June 1997 (Figure 2.2). It involved strategic women who were also leading members of the overall campaign, such as Val Feld, who served as treasurer of YFW. The connection between devolution and the promotion of women's substantive representation (see Introduction) was made explicit in campaign materials. One of its publicity leaflets, entitled 'Women of Wales – Have your Say!', urged women to vote for the creation of an assembly in the forthcoming referendum. It argued that the new body would be better able to tackle women's low pay, improve childcare provision, and act on women's health issues (such as the higher incidence of heart disease and breast cancer in Wales) (see Figure 2.3). As a campaigning alliance, WSY comprised a diverse range of groups, from those representing women employed in agriculture to the Minority Ethnic Women's Network (MEWN) Cymru. Organizers within 'Women Say Yes' were concerned that support for constitutional reform might be undermined if it were seen as a party-political campaign group. In response, as an activist recalls, 'one of our mantras was that "devolution is too important to be left to the politicians" – which brought in people who hadn't been involved in mainstream political parties'.

IT'S WOMEN'S TURN TO SAY 'YES' FOR WALES

A women's campaign for a 'Yes' vote is launched in Cardiff today at the Temple of Peace. Women prominent in the community and across the political spectrum in Wales have come together to argue the case for a Welsh Assembly. They are also urging Secretary of State Ron Davies to make known his proposals for ensuring equal opportunities in the Assembly's activities and the way that Members are selected.

Women Say Yes plans to hold a rally in Cardiff in July to encourage women across Wales to take part in debate about the Assembly and to be working for a 'Yes' vote. Mari James, Vice-Chair of Yes For Wales said: 'The Assembly offers the opportunity for a new kind of politics – one in which women's contribution can be heard and valued.'

They believe there are particular reasons why the Assembly will be important to women:

- Bringing under democratic control services that matter to women such as housing, health, and further education
- Ensuring the development across Wales of other key services such as childcare, social services and education
- Bringing decision-making closer to home so that women with family responsibilities can participate
- Helping partnerships to develop to tackle poverty and low pay, and to build prosperity

Women Say Yes want to ensure that women's voices are heard at an early stage. In their letter to the Secretary of State they point to the historical under-representation of women in all levels of political life. Even after the last election there are only four women MPs out of 40 and only 20% of women amongst 1200 local authority councillors in Wales.

Women establishing the group come from a range of backgrounds. All are involved in a personal capacity. They include: Pat Phillips, Jenny Randerson, Stella Matthews, Cherry Short, Julie Morgan MP, Eluned Morgan MEP, Edwina Hart, Val Feld, Ruth Parry, Jane Hutt, Christina Casseldine, Jill Evans MEP, Helen Mary Jones.

Figure 2.2 The text of a press release on the launch of 'Women Say Yes', 23 June 1997.[21]

The group's aims were stated in the following terms:

We believe that the Assembly offers a real opportunity for a new kind of politics. Women in Wales have been seriously under-represented in political life for generations ... We want an Assembly where women's contributions can be heard and valued ... we want to ensure that equal opportunities are built-in from the start – it will not work if it is an add-on later.[20]

Through an extensive series of meetings and publicity activities, 'Women Say Yes' succeeded in raising the profile of gender equality within the context of the overall 'Wales Says Yes' devolution campaign. A key role was played by 'strategic

---

WOMEN OF WALES HAVE YOUR SAY!

- The average weekly wage for women in Wales is £250. In Britain as a whole it is £283
- In Wales there are far less childcare places than in the rest of Britain
- More young people in Wales leave school with no qualifications than in England
- Women in Wales are more likely to have breast cancer and heart disease compared to women in England

We are getting a bad deal! Our families, our health and our jobs are suffering thanks to unwanted, unelected quangos! And we've had no choice and no voice until now.

On September 18th we can change things. The Welsh Assembly will be able to speak up for Wales in Britain and in Europe. It will mean our voices are heard and we can set our own priorities on the services that matter most to women.

'Yes' to bringing more women into politics and getting women's voices heard.

A new organisation brings the chance to build in equality right from the start. Working together we can find solutions to the problems we face. The Assembly can use the ability of all of our citizens.

Figure 2.3 The text of a 'Women Say Yes For Wales' campaign leaflet c.1997.[22]

women'. As one recalled, 'we were all part of a women's network weren't we? That network had existed for a long time. I mean some of the women in that network were women that were active in the 50s and the 60s pushing the feminist agenda.' Another participant confirmed the importance of 'strategic women', adding:

> It wasn't so much that a women's *movement* was attached to the 'Yes' ['For Wales'] campaign but there were individual women who had perceived themselves as having been in the Women's Movement who were attached to the 'Yes' campaign. There were women who had been on the Greenham Common march who came and joined us in Whitland [see below] and others who got involved. The real involvement in those campaigns brought people back. It [devolution] was the same sort of urgent single-issue campaign [as the Greenham march] that would effect women's involvement.

Foremost amongst the 'strategic women' was Val Feld. Speaking of 'Women Say Yes for Wales' a sister activist recalls: 'it was very much Val's responsibility'. She continued, 'One of her brainchilds [sic] was leaflets. She was keen to get out to the [women's] networks, which was quite something. Her idea was that you receive a leaflet personally rather than just read about it in the paper.' This observation is supported by Andrews's account of the referendum campaign (Andrews, 1999: 138):

Val Feld remembers, 'we produced all these leaflets in the different languages and they just went, I mean thousands of them'. Val was delighted – and stunned – by the response from ethnic minority groups. She attended a big festival in Swansea for Indian and Pakistani independence and set up a *Yes For Wales* stall. She found that there was a real desire to support the [pro-devolution] campaign, [Feld added] 'they understood exactly what this was about because they knew about colonialism'.

The most significant public rally organized by Feld and others in 'Women Say Yes' was billed as 'a gathering of women from across Wales to support the campaign for equality for women through a Welsh Assembly'. It took place in late summer, on Saturday 30 August 1997, just over two weeks before the devolution referendum. The rally was attended by several hundred women. The location was Hendy-Gwyn-ar-Dâf – or Whitland – in west Wales (see photographs reproduced in this volume). When asked about this event, one organizer remarked: 'that meeting, the rally in Whitland? – I still meet people who were there and say that it changed their attitude to politics'. Another described 'an enormous feeling of optimism and hope – and a tremendous feeling that we were actually about to change things'. According to the manager of a women's NGO, who was present at the event, this confidence was based on the belief that constitutional reform would mean that:

> There would be somewhere that we would count on, in a way that hadn't happened in Westminster – that women would actually have a say in a way that they haven't had before in Wales. That was a sort of feeling really that you were carving your own destiny and you actually had the power to do that, which probably had been lacking in formal politics before. I think that the devolution movement bought in women to be active in that sort of way and that was very, very important.

The rally was held in Whitland because of the town's connection with Hywel Dda, the codifier of medieval Welsh law. In specific circumstances, this afforded women legal rights equal to those of men – including the right to inherit property through the female as well as the male line (Jenkins and Owen, 1980). The symbolism of the location consciously tapped into feminist nationalist discourses. In debates about whether nationalism or feminism should be prioritized, feminist nationalists in Wales have pointed to the Laws of Hywel Dda, which gave women more rights than the English laws that replaced them, as evidence that the status of women in Wales deteriorated after the arrival of the external oppressor. The delivery of home rule would serve as a precursor to the development of fairer systems and greater gender equality (Davies, 1994: 253).

Accordingly, the WSY event organizers stated in their publicity material that Hywel Dda's town was 'the place where Welsh women were first granted rights'. The publicity sheet for the rally went on to say that the Acts of 'union' with England had effectively 'swept away' these rights. Campaigners in 'Women Say Yes' resolved to 'plan for a women's campaign to ensure that equality is at the heart of the Assembly's activities'.[23] The Whitland publicity leaflet ended by

saying: 'join us to ensure that women's voices are heard in the new Wales'.[24]
According to one woman organizer:

> We made a big fuss about setting up a crèche in the middle of Whitland. We were split
> between wanting lots of women there and [having] well-known faces. We didn't have
> to worry about the well-known faces because the people who were worried about it
> were [prominent WLP women politicians] ... The meeting was a walk through
> Whitland and then speeches at the end of it. But, because it was 'come with your chil-
> dren and do whatever you want' – but also – come *as women* – it was one of those 'can
> do' moments, empowering moments when you knew you couldn't go backwards.

Even participants who were initially sceptical were converted. As one younger
activist recounted:

> [I wondered] how much difference would a group of women with pushchairs and
> babies in slings and T-shirts planting a tree make ... [would it] make the female elect-
> orate of Wales suddenly change their opinion about devolution? ... but there was a
> great feeling at the end that everything was going to change.

Overall, such 'Women Say Yes' events were designed to presage a new politics
following devolution. In the words of one activist:

> One of the things the women were very determined about when we were running the
> Campaign was that it would be a microcosm of how the new Wales would be run.
> So we always had a gender balance on our platforms ... that kind of thing was to say
> 'this is what Yes For Wales, and the new assembly politics looks like'. In Whitland
> everyone had seen that and recognized that and said: 'yes! this is what is happening
> now. This is the way forward'.

Another activist recalls the co-working and solidarity of the period:

> We were very positive. A lot of us were already active with women's issues anyway,
> Val [Feld] with equal opportunities, DOVE workshop, there were women from the
> Labour Party that were very active in women's issues, so we all had that sort of fem-
> inist view of how we were going to carry this agenda forward, and there was a
> gathering momentum that there was going to be a change of government ... and there
> were a group of us [WLP activists] that got together to look at how we could push
> the whole thing about childcare and how important it was to have the provision of
> childcare, on the Labour Party agenda, and so there was a group of us that worked
> very closely with that and it was pioneered and carried forward by Jane Hutt as part
> of Chwarae Teg. So that all linked in you see. It was all those sorts of movements really
> that were *coming together* to push that forward.

DEBATES WITHIN THE WOMEN'S MOVEMENT ON DEVOLUTION

In the 1980s and 1990s in Scotland, there were vigorous debates inside the
women's movement on devolution and the shape that reformed politics might
assume. Discussions took place through conferences and rallies, reports, newsletters, pamphlets, articles and manifestos, such as the *Woman's Claim of Right in*

Scotland (1989), and submissions by women's groups to the Scottish Constitutional Convention. The paper trail in Wales is fainter, providing less evidence of sustained debate or a settled view of the women's movement in Wales. Yet early public statements can be found, such as a 1983 interview with Susan Lamb, a Welsh woman protester at Greenham Common (subsequently imprisoned for her protest activities at the base), who linked such activism with the growing pressure for constitutional reform. She stated:

> I believe in devolution. I voted for it [in 1979] ... how can someone in Westminster who's never visited, for instance, the Rhondda valleys, understand the particular problems of this area? I would like to see devolution for Wales because it would mean that problems of Wales will have at least been dealt with by people within Wales.[25]

According to our interviewees, debates were going on inside women's organizations, even traditional women's organizations, over this period and there was 'a sense that it would be better for women if some of these decisions were being made in Wales ... women's organizations felt their capacity to influence the national assembly would be much bigger than their capacity to influence the appropriate government departments'. There appear to be a number of reasons underpinning this supportive attitude. First, that 'anything was better' than the status quo, which marginalized women and their concerns; second, the attraction of more localized decision-making; and, third, what was seen as a discursive opportunity to en-gender traditional Welsh values of social justice to include women. As one activist explained:

> In a devolved Wales you would have an opportunity [...] to get decision-making based on [Welsh] political culture which would be about a more redistributive agenda, about more social justice and in the context of the women's movement a better chance to make the case for gender equality. [It would not be] ... a foregone conclusion but a better chance to make that case.

However, these discussions were low profile and did not translate into broad-based mobilization. Explanations for this varied amongst interviewees, but were thought to relate to issues of resources and infrastructure, the relative salience of the issue and, finally, because, according to some at least, nobody thought it was going to happen.

> We were women involved in women's organizations in Wales through the 80s and 90s, we were surviving, you were keeping a refuge open, you were finding funding for women's training programmes, you were desperately trying to sort out how you were going to provide child care for this or that event if you wanted women to go [...] Devolution wasn't a priority.

We take up some of these themes in the concluding section of this chapter. However, we note that in contrast to Scotland there were relatively few public spaces or forums in which devolution and the costs and benefits to be derived for women could be discussed. Most discussions were low key and internal to organizations and political parties.

In addition to discussions within the women's movement, activists in Cymdeithas yr Iaith Gymraeg also focused on influencing the latest devolution proposals (cf. Cymdeithas yr Iaith Gymraeg, 1998). As ever, primary concern centred on the language, but Cymdeithas's concerns deserve attention here as part of the emerging equalities agenda.[26] Lobbying activities by Cymdeithas included written submissions to the National Assembly Advisory Group (NAAG, 1998: 60) and, in August 1998, publication of its 'Agenda for the National Assembly for Wales'. This lobbying document went beyond language rights and set out a broad range of equality demands for the new Assembly (Figure 2.4), as Cymdeithas subsequently did to the Richard Commission in 2002–4.

As a Society we believe that the Welsh language belongs to all in Wales . . . it is in our view essential that, from the very outset, the Assembly is established as a body able to act effectively to empower the Welsh language and promote the development of free, vigorous, Welsh communities. One of the priorities of the Assembly should be to ensure that there are adequate resources to develop the teaching of Welsh and in the medium of Welsh throughout the spectrum from nursery to adult education. The aim is that everyone has a fair and equal opportunity to participate in our Welsh heritage

Modern Ways of Working.
We reiterate our belief as a Society to the following principles and we shall be calling on the Assembly to base its day to day working on the following principles:

Participatory Democracy. The Assembly must work in a way that is anti-oppressive ensuring real equal opportunities for all to take part in the Assembly. This would mean that the Assembly has fair and reasonable working hours and adequate child-care facilities and provisions for the disabled. The Assembly should also establish a shadow youth Assembly.

A Representative Democracy. We expect the Assembly to represent and discriminate positively in favour of oppressed 'minorities'. The Assembly should represent all communities in Wales. In order to promote representative democracy, the Assembly must ensure ways of holding a real and continuing dialogue with pressure groups seeking to lobby Assembly Members and with the voluntary sector. The Assembly should ensure space and resources to assist pressure groups and representations of the voluntary sector in Wales.

We insist that the time has now come to the people of Wales to act for themselves in a responsible, relevant and truly Welsh government, a government which is ready and able to meet the challenge of building a new Wales where we can truly be 'All for Welsh', and truly say, 'Welsh for All'.

**Figure 2.4 Extracts from Cymdeithas yr Iaith Gymraeg's
'Agenda for the National Assembly for Wales' (c.1998).**

WOMEN'S MOVEMENTS AND THE DEVOLUTION CAMPAIGN: AN ANALYSIS

In terms of political opportunity structures, whilst it is clear that devolution opened up opportunities, the circumstances were less advantageous for women in Wales than for those in Scotland until relatively late in the day. Matters were complicated by the general indifference of many sections of civil society to the devolution project, the weak infrastructure of the women's movement and the insular nature of the Welsh Labour Party, which prevented the development of important spaces for civil society and cross-party debate and dialogue, like that offered by the Scottish Constitutional Convention.

However, against this rather unpromising backdrop, a small group of influential women activists – gender experts, 'femocrats', politicians and trade union officials – did manage to insert themselves and concerns about gender equality into political dialogue. In a process that mirrored the top-down character of the general reform project in Wales, these 'strategic women' staked a claim for women and promoted measures for their improved descriptive and substantive representation. Once devolution looked a possibility, these activists could link demands for a new gender settlement with the need to deliver a 'yes' vote, and with the importance of women as a target group of sceptics and the undecided.

In terms of framing processes, although traditional gender stereotypes presented a continuing barrier for women, there were a number of discursive opportunities. For example, debates around devolution provided a chance to link traditional social justice concerns with gender equality. The strategic women were able to take advantage of prevailing ideas of 'inclusion' and new politics, which became hallmarks of the campaign as it gathered pace and support. According to some commentators, such as Osmond, explicit connections were made between campaigns for gender equality and struggles around the Welsh language, debates that had a wider cultural acceptance. Osmond was a key male ally and supporter of gender balance and women's contribution to new politics. He promoted the issue inside the PWC, as well as through his publications (1995, 1996/7), and as Director of the Institute of Welsh Affairs.

The reason why there was not an earlier, more organic, mobilization of women's movements in Wales has its roots in the form and unfolding of the wider reform campaigns. It can also be explained by the fragmentation and division within the women's movement in Wales and the lack of a unifying infrastructure. Women's networks were characterized by relatively weak and underdeveloped mobilizing structures, ill suited to operating at a coordinated, all-Wales locus of political action.

These underdeveloped mobilizing structures in turn reflected the general weakness of specifically 'Welsh' civil society as a whole during the period of administrative devolution (Paterson and Wyn Jones, 1999). Here, the absence of a vibrant Welsh policy process centring on the Welsh Office denied women's (and other) non-governmental organizations a clear focus for coordinated action. In such circumstances, the difficulties of achieving a 'bottom-up' movement of grassroots activism necessitated the adoption of a predominantly 'top-down' approach by 'strategic women activists' in order to ensure that gender-equality claims were advanced effectively during the 1990s devolution campaign.

However, this was accompanied by a purposive programme to build the infrastructure and capacity of the women's movement by the key strategic gender-equality body in Wales, the Equal Opportunities Commission, under the directorship of the most pivotally placed of the strategic women, Val Feld. She had the vision and determination to create new networks and strategic mechanisms that would enable women's organizations – and other equality groupings – to be in a position to influence and reap the benefits of devolution and other sorts of political and institutional opportunities. As noted, this work had began in the early 1990s with the creation of the strategic network Chwarae Teg to influence economic development policy; the creation of MEWN Cymru in order to create infrastructure to enable the development of a strategic voice for minority ethnic women; the fostering of a local government equality officers' network around the time of local government reorganization in the mid 1990s; and, most crucially for devolution, the support given to growing the 'cross-network' of women's organizations that was to become the Wales Women's Coalition in 1997 (and subsequently the Wales Women's National Coalition, WWNC). This infrastructure-building work was done in defiance of an equivocal, if not hostile, EOC management at British level, which was opposed to activities that might be construed as the EOC in Wales engaging with the devolution process, an activity seen by some as too 'political' for public servants in an arm's-length government-sponsored body.

In its early days, the women's network was developed by a number of individuals, including Helen Mary Jones, Plaid Cymru activist and newly appointed as a senior manager with EOC Wales. She recalls:

> Spen[ding] a lot of time talking to key figures of each organization in turn about why it was in the interests of each of the groups of women to have this coalition of women's organizations working together – and it gelled! and again, it was coming at a time when there seemed to be a climate of political change ... We then, of course, found that with devolution coming we had something to focus around much more clearly in terms of now there was going to be a democratic body [the Assembly] and we needed to have a proper forum for women's organizations to relate [to it] ... and by the time of devolution statute we'd managed to establish the Coalition as a legitimate voice for women's organizations in Wales.

The significance of this network-building was such that there was an organized and credible women's coalition in place in time to back the strategic women's demands in the intensive period of institutional design in 1997–8 (see chapter 3).

These developments point to the importance of timing and of changes over time. The first period of 1989–96/7 was fairly low key, with relatively few instances of women's mobilization or en-gendering of debates. Without the high stakes of constitutional change in the Northern Ireland context or the momentum of popular support for reform in Scotland, most grassroots organizations in Wales were too busy with the 'politics of everyday life' to focus energies and scarce resources on a campaign for a new political institution whose prospects looked far from certain.

However, there was strategic work being undertaken behind the scenes in parties (see chapter 4) and elsewhere. Meanwhile, as noted above, this was also a period of capacity-building, in other words building the mobilizing structures necessary for acting in concert as a women's lobby.

The year 1996 marked a step-change. As a Labour victory at Westminster became more likely, so, too, did the promise of delivering devolution. As a result, the pace of campaigning intensified. It became a political necessity to be 'inclusive', and the perceived problem with women's support for devolution provided key opportunities and frames. Overall, during the period between 1996 and 1998, the political context in which feminist and equality claims were being advanced in the devolution campaign shifted. It was gradually becoming easier to advance such demands, because such an agenda fitted well into the developing concept of 'inclusiveness' that became the buzzword of the gathering Welsh devolution campaign. Initially, in the face of opposition from Welsh Labour's 'old guard', this term had been code for introducing proportional representation into the electoral system of the Assembly. By this time, however, its meaning had broadened to signal a general concern with equality of opportunity and pluralism. Thus, the term served several key purposes: it encouraged cross-party working; it garnered support for devolution from hitherto marginalized social groups; and, crucially, it signalled a clear break from the exclusive and discriminatory politics of the past (Chaney and Fevre, 2001a, 2001b, 2001c). This developing context provided prevailing political opportunities for 'strategic women activists' and other members of the women's movement in Wales to lobby hard for a 'new' politics, one where women had an equal role to men. Thus, on its launch day in June 1997, 'Women Say Yes': 'urge[d] the Secretary of State to make known his proposals for ensuring that equal opportunities are part of the Assembly's activities and the way Assembly Members are selected'.[27]

The short but intensive window of opportunity from 1996 to 1998 presented in 'quick-time' the opportunities that the SCC had afforded women activists over a decade in Scotland. The referendum campaign and WSY events provide the clearest evidence of a degree of grassroots mobilization. However, we would argue that it was not a straightforward case of women's movement mobilization, but one of a more diffuse influence and a more disjointed process. Strategic women with women's movement credentials, many with personal networks rooted in earlier phases of the women's movement mobilization, adopted a mainly insider and elite strategy, but also worked to remobilize and re-energize the women's sector.

The story of women's movements, strategic women and devolution does not end here. Subsequent chapters focus in detail on parties and the role of strategic women in internal party debates and lobbying (chapter 4) around measures for delivering greater gender parity in descriptive representation. In the following chapter we examine the official response to the demands of strategic women to 'build equality' in with the bricks of the new institution, how women continued to press for equality, and the extent to which their actions shaped the institutional blueprint of the new Welsh legislature.

3

Gender and Politics: A Blueprint for Change

We have been able to integrate equality into the foundations on ... which the Assembly is built and ... in the way in which it is working and I do believe very strongly that we must all take credit for this. We have all of us in a number of different ways, different areas, and different activities, pushed very hard over the recent years to try to achieve some real change in Wales.[1]

The period from the eve of the 1997 devolution referendum to just before the first National Assembly elections in May 1999 provided a short and intensive period of opportunity for women activists to press their claims for a new 'gender settlement'. We focus here on the efforts of key 'strategic women', backed by women's movement organizations to lobby for gender equality. Their goal was to shape the 'institutional blueprint', or structures and procedures of the new Assembly: to build features of gender equality 'in with the bricks'. This marked a new phase of activism, a shift from influencing *proposals* for constitutional reform, hitherto debated within political parties and, to a lesser extent, devolution campaign groups, to efforts to influence the shaping of official government policy. The first priority was to make sure that the gender-equality measures advocated by the left-of-centre parties and the 'Yes For Wales' campaign were now included in the devolution White Paper to be put before Parliament and the people of Wales. Following the endorsement by the majority of voters of the creation of an assembly in the 18 September 1997 referendum, the challenge was to ensure gender equality was enshrined in the devolution statute and accompanying internal Assembly procedural law (in other words Standing Orders and associated procedures).

In this chapter we focus primarily on lobbying and developments around substantive representation: specifically, the institutionalization of women's voice, needs and interests through mechanisms and statutory duties. In the following chapter we return to the struggle within political parties for gender parity in candidate selection to the new Assembly (descriptive representation).

INSTITUTIONALIZING EQUALITY

In June 1997, the Secretary of State for Wales, Ron Davies, responded to the demand by 'Women Say Yes' that he 'make known his proposals for ensuring that equal opportunities are part of the Assembly's activities'[2] by agreeing to discuss such matters with representatives of the Wales Women's Coalition (subsequently renamed Wales Women's National Coalition, WWNC)[3] and the Equal Opportunities Commission Wales. This encounter took place on Friday 5 September 1997. Managers from three Coalition member organizations (National Federation of Women's Institutes Wales, Minority Ethnic Women's Network (MEWN) Cymru and Wales Assembly of Women) were joined by the director and commissioner of the Equal Opportunities Commission Wales. Under the sub-heading 'Getting the mechanisms right', the minutes of the meeting note that those present 'stressed the opportunity presented by a possible Welsh Assembly to mainstream equality'. At the meeting, Val Feld and the EOC Commissioner for Wales, Teresa Rees, drew the Secretary of State's attention to a draft equality clause that could be included in a future Government of Wales Bill. This idea had previously been advanced at the Welsh Labour Party Conference of 10–11 May 1996.[4] It required that the future Assembly promote equality in the exercise of its functions and the conduct of its business. The minutes record, 'RD [Ron Davies] responded positively to the importance of integrating equality and stated that VF [Val Feld] should discuss these matters further with civil servants.'[5]

Helen Mary Jones (at that time the deputy director of EOC Wales) recalls this process of 'securing' the equality duty:

> The key figure was Val [Feld], she was absolutely key. She was key in terms of getting everybody involved and there was a lot of 'juggling around'. There were lots of informal lunches and a lot of egos to be flattered. Then there was the work with the Coalition that I did predominately with Val's guidance, which was working with women's organizations to get them all signed up to the actual clause. We were very clear that nobody was that interested in how the Assembly was going to conduct itself; it was going to be about what the Assembly did ... But; *we* wanted something that was going to change what the Assembly did *as well as how it conducted itself* ... So we looked for a clause, we looked for something simple, we did get advice from people in the EOC – really at a lower level – in terms of wording of the clause. We took it to Ron [Davies] and the senior civil servants in two ways. One was a series of meetings with the Wales Women's National Coalition and then there was a series of meetings with representatives from all the equality bodies and we presented the clause: we made the case.[6]

Val Feld recalled:

> I remember the day that I suggested to Ron Davies that it might be intelligent to put a requirement for equality into the legislation that was being passed. He said to me that if I could persuade his civil servants that it was practical, he would do it. Many people put in their time and took a leap of faith to give the Assembly this unique

responsibility ... In the years ahead, it will enable us to judge the Assembly's progress in tackling the entrenched problems of inequality across a range of sectors in Wales.[7]

The influence of earlier lobbying can be seen in the tenor of the devolution White Paper (Welsh Office, 1997). It asserted the need for gender equality amongst elected representatives and in the policy process; in other words, the importance of improving the descriptive and substantive representation of women. It stated:

> The Government is committed to establishing a new, more inclusive and participative democracy in Britain ... in particular, the Government attaches great importance to equal opportunities for all – including women, members of the ethnic minorities and disabled people. It believes that greater participation by women is essential to the health of our democracy ... The Government also urges all political parties offering candidates for election to the Assembly to have this in mind in their internal candidate selection processes. (1997: 24, para. 3.7)

With respect to policy, the White Paper continued: 'the Assembly will let the Welsh people express their own priorities ... it will ... take decisions which can reflect the needs and circumstances of Wales, and most importantly the views of the people' (ibid., 5, 9, para. 1.23).

On 18 September 1997, a majority (albeit slender) of voters supported the government's White Paper proposals, and within less than two months the Government of Wales Bill was having its first reading in Parliament. The Bill contained the following equality clauses:

> Section 48. The Assembly of Wales shall make appropriate arrangements with a view to securing that its business is conducted with due regard to the principle that there should be equality of opportunity for all people.

> Section 120. (1) The Assembly shall make appropriate arrangements with a view to securing that its functions are exercised with due regard to the principle that there should be equality of opportunity for all people.

> (2) After each financial year of the Assembly, the Assembly shall publish a report containing:

> (a) a statement of the arrangements made in pursuance of subsection (1) which had effect during the financial year, and
> (b) an assessment of how effective those arrangements were in promoting equality of opportunities.

In terms of developing a fuller analysis of the way in which gender equality mechanisms were included in the institutional blueprint of the Assembly, a further crucial process merits attention here. It is one that reveals the salience of the new social movements' literature (see chapter 1) to an understanding of the engendering of devolution. Thus, the nascent mobilizing structures of the women's movement in Wales were able to use the political opportunity structures presented, not only by UK developments, but also by international, governmental

National Agenda for Action calls for:	What do we want to see	Progress to date	To achieve equality in Wales	Progress to date
Simplified accessible laws and procedures for the prevention and redress of discrimination. Equal treatment for women in all areas of nationality, citizenship and immigration.	Creation of a duty upon public bodies 'to work towards the elimination of discrimination on grounds of sex or marriage and to promote equality of opportunity between men and women generally.	Proposals drafted.	To ensure that any elected all-Wales body has responsibility for ensuring that an appropriate 'equality agenda' is developed to provide supporting legislation for women.	Responsibility in Government of Wales Bill.
			Legislation by any elected Wales-level body for improved statutory rights for carers and volunteers, where women largely predominate.	Probably not possible, unless secondary legislation.
Additional measures to improve women's participation in decision-making.	NGOs to campaign to remove barriers to women's participation in decision-making.	Some progress.	Action to address disproportionate under-representation of women in central and local government.	Some progress – Labour Party twinning and Project 99. Plaid Cymru target 50% on Assembly. Lib Dems 50% on shortlists.
			To ensure that any elected Wales-level body established in the future works in an inclusive, family-friendly way from the outset.	Yes – NAAG proposals include clear requirements.
			To ensure that any elected Wales-level body established in the future is structured to ensure equal opportunities in its representation from the outset.	Yes – progress in NAAG proposals, legislation and selection of candidates.

			We also need:	
Specific actions by government to implement the Global Platform nationally.	With immediate effect.	Very limited progress – responsibility unclear.	The Welsh Office and all Welsh organizations to disaggregate statistics by gender, ethnicity, language and disability.	In discussion and in Assembly proposals.
Evaluation of all proposed new legislation and, periodically, existing legislation for its impact on equality between the sexes.	Government machinery to be strengthened with adequate resources.	?	The Welsh Office and local government to establish mechanisms to evaluate the input of policy decisions on men and women and under-represented groups.	In discussion and in NAAG proposals.
Publication of all official statistics by gender, and, where possible, ethnicity, age and disability, in order to measure progress and to identify areas for future action.	Government to carry out audit of official statistics ... and improve the range and quality of disaggregated statistics.	Some progress – EOC local government framework and guidelines for National Assembly launched. EC structural funds project.		
	Pilot projects on mainstreaming across a range of policy, employment and service delivery areas.	Progress in Wales only.	To disseminate examples of cost-benefits of equal opportunities practice.	?
	Official documents, including legislation to include gender-neutral language.	NAAG response recommendation.	To promote the use of gender-neutral language in Welsh.	Some progress – NAAG proposals.
			The establishment of an Equal Opportunities Committee in any elected Wales-level body that may be established in the future.	Some progress – NAAG proposals.

Figure 3.1 Selected extracts from the National Agenda for Action Programme for Wales: evaluation of progress so far (c.July 1998).[8]

developments in the promotion of gender equality. Specifically, this strand in shaping the institutional blueprint of the Assembly links constitutional reform in Wales with the 1995 Fourth United Nations World Conference on Women, held in Beijing. This meeting agreed a Global Platform for Action on promoting gender equality. In response, national governments were required to draw up their own National Agenda for Action. Linked to the UK's National Agenda, in 1997, women's NGOs in Wales (as the Wales Women's Coalition), together with the EOC, began to develop the 'Wales Programme for the National Agenda for Action'. Devolution coincided with this process, and many of the action points in the Wales Programme were adapted to focus on, and influence, the blueprint of the future Assembly (see Figure 3.1).

One of the action points related specifically to the Assembly's equality clauses. Here, there was guarded satisfaction with the progress made thus far. The records of the Wales Women's National Coalition's meeting of November 1997 refer to the successful outcome of their earlier meeting with the Secretary of State. The minutes record that:

> The Coalition member organisations were very pleased to see the Equality Clauses in the National Assembly Bill. It was agreed that it will now be important for the Coalition to maintain pressure on the Welsh Office and the political parties to ensure that these Equality Clauses are put into full operation when the National Assembly is established.[9]

Consistent with this aim, women parliamentarians acted as both advocates and defenders of the equality clause during the Welsh devolution Bill's passage through the UK parliament. During one House of Commons debate, and in the face of some opposition to the Bill, Julie Morgan MP asserted:

> I am pleased that two clauses ... refer to equal opportunities ... starting afresh, with a new body, we should be able to make certain that those principles lie at the heart of the Assembly. One of the most important ways of ensuring equal opportunity for all people is to have members who represent the range of people in Wales. That means that women should be there in equal numbers ... Ensuring that the Assembly's business is conducted in a way that is conducive to equal opportunities, both for members and for the public, means that the needs of men and women – with children and dependants – should be taken into account.[10]

The National Assembly's main equality duty is an example of a 'fourth generation' equality law (Fredman, 2000). These are so-called because they move away from the earlier legal and policy approaches to equality that were based on anti-discrimination, equal treatment and positive action. The Assembly's duty is unique amongst the devolution statutes (Chaney and Fevre, 2002a; Chaney, 2004a), for it requires government to take a proactive stance and promote equality for *all* persons and in respect of *all* Welsh Assembly Government functions. According to law academics, this equality duty is a development of 'potentially greater significance' than the human rights clauses in the Government of Wales

Act. In their view, 'the people of Wales [we]re the first in the UK to be given a series of positive rights to exercise, and if necessary, to enforce through the courts in Wales' (Clements and Thomas, 1999: 10).

THE NATIONAL ASSEMBLY ADVISORY GROUP

In December 1997, three months after the devolution referendum, and in order to develop the legal framework for the new Assembly, the then Secretary of State, Ron Davies, established the National Assembly Advisory Group (NAAG). Its remit was to provide guidance to the Standing Orders Commission, to advise the Secretary of State, and 'to produce recommendations on which consensus has been established and which contribute to the establishment of an Assembly' (National Assembly Advisory Group, 1998: 4). The Group's final recommendations of August 1998 were agreed to by the Secretary of State 'almost in their entirety' (Bryant, 1998: 1). Subsequently, following work by the Standing Orders Commission, the agreed recommendations were enshrined in the Assembly's internal law, or standing orders (NAW, 1999a).

The whole NAAG process was closely controlled by the Secretary of State. The membership was drawn up in such a way that every item of the agenda of 'inclusiveness' could be checked off: political pluralism, gender, geography, pressure groups, business and trade unions. Thus, the Advisory Group's members were drawn from a wide range of fields, including the four main political parties, the 'Yes' and 'No' referendum campaigns, business, local government, trade unions, equal opportunities bodies and the voluntary sector. Davies concluded that this diverse membership 'augurs well for the inclusive form of Assembly we are looking to create' (Davies, 1998a). Whilst the involvement of such organizations and interest groups, including women's NGOs, drawn from both civil and civic society marked a positive step-change from the pre-existing mode of 'top-down' government administration under the Welsh Office, some observers were critical, and highlighted limitations in the process. For example, in his study of constitutional law and devolution, Rawlings (1998: 508) concluded:

> there was a contradiction at the heart of the process. The government has preached a new inclusive style of politics for the Assembly. But it has practised a closed and élite form of constitution making. Thus important parameters of the [devolution] scheme were set inside the [Wales Labour] Party. The people were invited to assent.

Similarly, Jones (2000: 191–2) asserts: 'it is difficult to avoid the conclusion that the exercise made little impact on the general public ... While the[y] ... might have been apathetic, organizations and interest groups seized the opportunity to have their say.'

Whilst opinions differ on the full extent of internal Welsh Labour Party influence on NAAG's work, Jones's assertion (2000: 191–2) is correct in respect of gender equality, for women's interest groups *did* seize the opportunity to influence the institutional blueprint. A chief link in this process was Plaid Cymru nominee Helen Mary Jones, future acting director of the Equal Opportunities Commission Wales and leading figure in the WWNC. Jones was one of the fourteen members of NAAG.[11] Contemporary minutes of a WWNC meeting conclude that, 'the NAAG is a very positive opportunity for women's organisations to influence the way that the Assembly would operate'.[12] In promoting women's issues and wider equality concerns in the NAAG recommendations, Helen Mary Jones was supported by other Advisory Group members, including Mari James (former national coordinator of the Parliament for Wales Campaign), Eluned Morgan MEP (Welsh Labour), Ray Singh (CRE Commissioner) and the future Welsh Liberal Democrat AM, Kirsty Williams, as well as, on the face of it, unlikely allies, such as the Tory peer, Viscount St Davids.

During the Advisory Group's consultations, which commenced on 17 April 1998, equality activists and women's NGOs lobbied to influence the final recommendations on how the future Assembly should operate. Thus, organizations such as Chwarae Teg and Business and Professional Women were amongst those that contributed to the total of 348 written submissions to the Advisory Group (NAAG, 1998: 59). In particular, a coordinated input was achieved through co-working between the statutory equality commissions and members of WWNC. Thus, the records of one WWNC meeting state that:

> A paper that has been prepared jointly by the EOC, CRE and Disability Wales for submission to the National Assembly Advisory Group was circulated. Indications are that the Advisory Group will recommend an equal opportunities committee [of the Assembly] and a programme approach to decision-making. Additional copies will be made available to Coalition member organisations to circulate so that, when the Advisory Group's consultation paper goes out in late March or early April, member organisations of the Coalition will have had an opportunity to consider their response in light of the suggestions made by the EOC, CRE and Disability Wales. It was agreed to schedule Coalition meetings to enable the Coalition to attempt to form a united response to the Advisory Group's consultation paper.[13]

Advisory Group members recall the institutional resistance to the promotion of equality that surfaced in the NAAG deliberations. One recalled:

> It's in all the *Yes Minister* textbooks! [A c]ivil servant brings an authoritative looking paper ... and says 'this is the *only way* it can be done' – or 'it *can't* be done it seems' ... You've got to have a bit of guts to stand up against that when it's a very confident person saying that ... So we decided *we* would have to rewrite some of these things ourselves. I think the only people who actually wrote papers were three of us women ... So it was a few of the women who decided we are going to have to write this ourselves and every now and then [we] started coming up with standing orders for the Assembly ... and they are still there.

Such accounts also reveal the origins of the Assembly's Standing Committee on Equality of Opportunity. One member of the Advisory Group recalls:

We looked at the operation of the cross-cutting committees. That was part of the plan that Jane Hutt and Jane Davidson ... were working on – how to address some of those fundamental issues such as equal opportunities. [Initially] ... the equal ops committee was a gender committee and then the equal ops committee became an equal ops committee with specification of the three main areas of gender, race and disability ... that came out of NAAG – and the women's groups, disability groups, the church groups, all sorts of groups, saying [during the NAAG consultations] 'specify what you meant by 'equal ops' – this [process] was very important because we became sophisticated enough and cynical enough to know that it wasn't enough to just have a [Parliamentary Devolution] Bill: it was about *translating* the Bill into 'bricks and mortar', into the structures of the Assembly in such a way that it *couldn't* be taken out. They became part of the structure of the Assembly so when you'd set up that vehicle you *had to do something with it*. That rolled it forward. We took a lot of views in consultation.

By July 1998, NAAG had sent its final report to the Secretary of State. The prevailing feeling amongst women activists was that they had succeeded in influencing NAAG's recommendations. Yet they were not about to become complacent. The minutes of a WWNC meeting held in late July 1998 record: 'the equality proposals, including EO committee, have remained in the advice ... but it was agreed that *the pressure needs to be kept on*'.[14]

When, later in 1998, the NAAG recommendations were published, they contained an extensive raft of equality-based recommendations that related to many aspects of the new Assembly's functions and procedures (Figure 3.2). They included proposals on family-friendly working hours, permitted language in debate, and securing gender-neutral titles.[15] Crucially, as noted, in order to meet its obligations under the Government of Wales Act, NAAG recommended that: 'a standing equal opportunities committee ... be established with a remit including the three strands of gender, race and disability as a minimum'. This development was consistent with the Secretary of State's own position. At the time he concluded:

> Not only do I accept the case for such a committee, I believe it should be chaired at the highest level by the Assembly's First [Minister]. From the outset it has been my conviction that the Assembly should be open and inclusive. Inclusiveness means giving active support to those groups who feel alienated from the political process. That's why I believe an Equality Committee should have a high profile at the Assembly. (Davies, 1998a)

In addition to equality concerns, women activists' lobbying also helped to underpin NAAG's 'support for a break from Westminster traditions ... [that are] based on outdated practices unsuited to a modern participative democracy' (NAAG, 1998: 7). Thus, the final recommendations also stated that the procedures of the new body should be 'democratic and inclusive, flexible and responsive, efficient and effective, and transparent and accountable' (NAAG, 1998: 3, section 0.24, 20).[16] Importantly, the NAAG report signalled a concern to engage women's

1.10 There was strong support for a break from Westminster traditions where they were seen as based on outdated practices unsuited to a modern participative democracy. There was support for a move to more family-friendly working practices, coupled with some scepticism about how achievable this will be in the face of the Assembly's demanding work programme.

2.14 We recommend that any titles used in Assembly proceedings or standing orders should be gender neutral.

2.22 We recommend that standing orders specify that: the official languages of the Assembly are English and Welsh; the Assembly conducts its business in accordance with the requirements of the Welsh Language Act 1993; Assembly Members are entitled to speak in English or Welsh in plenary sessions and in all committee sessions ...; Assembly Members are entitled to receive the papers for consideration at formal sessions in English and Welsh.

4.18 Additionally, we recommend that in standing orders the approval of the full Assembly is required for: [...] – the proposed equal opportunities arrangements and report (section 120).

4.20 We recommend that standing orders should require the Assembly to debate the following matters at least once a year: [...] the Assembly's equal opportunities arrangements and report – including as a minimum the three strands – race, gender and disability.

4.24 We recommend that standing orders set out rules governing the process of debate in plenary sessions which will promote the dignity of the proceedings and in line with the requirement placed on the Assembly by the Government of Wales Act to take account of the principle of equality of opportunity for all people in the conduct of its business. Racist, sexist and other discriminatory language should be forbidden by standing orders.

4.2 We are anxious that the Assembly should be as open and as accessible to the public as possible. We also recommend that ... in addition to a self-financing crèche providing a childcare facility for Members and staff, the Assembly should consider further whether it would be desirable to make crèche facilities available, on a drop-in basis, to members of the public wishing to visit the facility.

5.1 The Government of Wales Act requires the Assembly to establish the following committees: subject committees, regional committees, a legislation committee, and an audit committee. In addition, we recommend that standing orders provide for two other types of committee whose role would be to: coordinate policy development on issues which cross-cut subject areas [i.e. equality]; and, monitor and evaluate progress with implementing these cross-cutting programmes.

5.11 Each subject committee will need to ensure that it has regard to equality of opportunity in conducting its business and exercising its functions, in line with sections 48 and 120 of the Government of Wales Act.

5.13 The equal opportunities standing programme committee should develop an initial action programme lasting three or four years, with activities across all subject areas, designed to promote equality of opportunity in Wales; the equal opportunities standing programme committee periodically monitors progress on implementing the action programme in each area; the equal opportunities standing programme committee would be responsible for the annual report on the effectiveness of the Assembly's arrangements for promoting equality of opportunity required by sections 48 and 120 of the Government of Wales Act.

6.7 We also recommend that the Assembly's annual timetable should be arranged so far as possible to coincide with school term-times – so that the Assembly does not normally meet in formal session during the Christmas, Easter and summer vacation periods.

7.12 It will be for the subject committee and the Assembly [minister] to decide on the exact procedures to be adopted for each [public] appointment, in line with the framework of the Commissioner for Public Appointment's requirements – that is appointment on merit, independent scrutiny, [and] equal opportunities.

7.27 Requir[ing] the Assembly to make appropriate arrangements with a view to securing that its functions are exercised with due regard to the principle that there should be equality for all people, and to publish a report each year on how successful its arrangements were.

Figure 3.2 Setting the institutional prerequisites for the promotion of equality: selected National Assembly Advisory Group recommendations (NAAG, 1998).

NGOs and other parts of civil society through its call for 'an inclusive, cooperative approach to developing and implementing policies' (NAAG, 1998: 7, section 0.23) (see chapter 7 for an analysis of the political participation of women in civil society). The NAAG report concluded that: 'the themes of ... inclusiveness and participation were strongly endorsed ... there was a strong desire for effective mechanisms for consulting and listening to people in Wales and for them to influence the Assembly, especially at an early stage in developing new policies' (NAAG, 1998: 7).

Importantly, there was no backtracking and, as noted, the majority of NAAG's recommendations, including the equality-based recommendations shaped over previous years by the lobbying of key gender activists and women's NGOs, were subsequently framed into the National Assembly's internal procedural law by the Standing Orders Commission of the National Assembly (Figure 3.3).[17]

WOMEN'S ROLE IN SHAPING THE POLITICAL AND INSTITUTIONAL BLUEPRINT

Overall, the history of the 1990s Welsh devolution campaign is one where 'strategic' women equality activists and women's NGOs acted to shape the institutional blueprint of the National Assembly. This scenario broadly parallels the

GOVERNMENT OF WALES ACT (1998)

S.47 (1) The Assembly shall in the conduct of its business give effect, so far as is both appropriate in the circumstances and reasonably practicable, to the principle that the English and Welsh languages should be treated on a basis of equality.

(2) In determining how to comply with subsection (1), the Assembly shall have regard to the spirit of any guidelines under section 9 of the Welsh Language Act 1993.

(3) The standing orders shall be made in both English and Welsh.

S.48 The Assembly shall make appropriate arrangements with a view to securing that its business is conducted with due regard to the principle that there should be equality of opportunity for all people.

S.120 The Assembly shall make appropriate arrangements with a view to securing that its functions are exercised with due regard to the principle that there should be equality of opportunity for all people.

NATIONAL ASSEMBLY STANDING ORDERS

5.2 Motions under paragraph 5.1 shall be tabled having regard to any advice offered by the Business Committee under paragraph 13.1(i). Wherever possible, motions shall be framed having regard to the family and constituency or electoral region responsibilities of Members, and their likely travel arrangements; and in any event shall seek to avoid programming business before 9.00am or after 5.30pm on any working day.

6.5 Time shall be made available in each 12-month period for the following categories of Assembly business: (viii) debate on the annual report on the [Assembly Government's] equal opportunity arrangements.

6.6 The Assembly shall ensure that time is made available for consideration either in plenary meeting or in committee of the reports of the Equal Opportunities Commission, the Commission for Racial Equality and the Disability Rights Commission.

6.7 Any documents relating to business taken in plenary shall be made available in English and Welsh.

7.1 Members called by the Presiding Officer to speak shall address the chair. Members may speak in English or Welsh.

7.2 Members shall not use language which the Presiding Officer considers to be disorderly, discriminatory or offensive or which may detract from the dignity of the Assembly. The Presiding Officer may direct a Member who has used such language to withdraw it.

7.8 The Presiding Officer shall maintain order in the Assembly and shall call to order any Assembly Member who: (v) is using disorderly, discriminatory or offensive language.

14.1 There shall be a Committee on Equality of Opportunity, which shall audit the Assembly's arrangements for promoting in the exercise of its functions and the conduct of its business the principle that there should be equality of opportunity for all people. The Committee shall also have particular regard to the need for the Assembly to avoid discrimination against any person on grounds of race, sex or disability.

14.2 The Committee shall submit an annual report to the Assembly on those arrangements and their effectiveness. It shall also review and report to the Assembly its conclusions on the Annual Reports submitted to the Assembly by public bodies concerned with the promotion of equal opportunities.

14.46 Without prejudice to paragraph 8.14, the [Equality] Committee shall, from time to time, appoint such advisers as it requires to enable the views of minority or disadvantaged groups to be put before it.

14.57 The [Equality] Committee may report to the Assembly from time to time in addition to submitting its annual report.

Figure 3.3 Legal equality instruments integral to the National Assembly's institutional structures and procedures.

contemporaneous processes in Scotland and Northern Ireland. Yet, as noted in the previous chapter, it lacked the broad-based mobilization seen in the other two countries. This, in part, reflects the longer-standing history and, arguably, greater impact of administrative integration with England (see Williams, 2005). When compared to Scotland and Northern Ireland, this, in turn, resulted in: less overall support for constitutional reform (a fifth of the population were English-born); weaker Welsh-focused networks of women's NGOs; and less identifiably *Welsh* civil society organizations and institutions. Nevertheless, in these challenging circumstances, women's NGOs supported by women activists, key political 'insiders', and importantly, 'strategic women' (see previous chapter) all played a significant role in securing equality mechanisms in the new 'Welsh constitution', one that has begun a transformation in the nature of national Welsh politics. As we have seen, this was not a uniform, linear process. Rather, it was the result of the convergence of a number of sometimes parallel, sometimes interrelated, processes that involved women in various networks, organizations and political parties. Importantly, several of these had overlapping memberships and key activists were able to spread, and maximize, their influence, as they belonged to several interrelated associations.

One 'strand' in this complex history is the actions of gender equality activists within the left-of-centre political parties (see chapter 4). Foremost, in terms of overall impact, were women (sometimes supported by male colleagues) in the Welsh Labour Party, who, partly in reaction to similar developments in Scotland, secured, in the early 1990s, a commitment to equal representation for men and women in the new Assembly. As noted earlier, this was accompanied, in

May 1996, by a WLP undertaking to include an equality clause in the future devolution statute, one requiring that the National Assembly promote equality. Interconnected with these developments, the broadening of the Parliament for Wales Campaign's membership and, albeit late in the day, the development of cross-party working in the 'Yes For Wales' campaign saw renewed commitment to gender equality in the context of devolution. Significantly, this was reinforced by the development of the campaign group 'Women Say Yes'. In turn, and related to the foregoing, the development of the Wales Women's National Coalition and its co-working with the Equal Opportunities Commission in Wales were further vital aspects of women's lobbying activities. The WWNC also gave greater democratic legitimacy to the actions of 'strategic' women activists, who ensured that gender equality remained a priority issue. Importantly, a working partnership between the WWNC and the EOC in Wales made certain that the Welsh Labour Party honoured its 1996 commitment to the inclusion of equality clauses in the devolution statute.

Subsequent lobbying and participation by women in the National Assembly Advisory Group ensured that the Standing Orders Commission codified a full range of mechanisms to promote equality in the Assembly's internal procedural law, or standing orders. International processes were also salient here, most notably in the work by women's NGOs on the Welsh responses to the UN Global Platform for Action (or the 'National Agenda for Action Programme for Wales'). This was both shaped by, and in turn influenced, the new devolved arrangements. In addition, whilst legal developments meant the abandonment of earlier proposals for a statutory requirement for gender balance amongst elected representatives, the various lobbying processes undertaken by women did secure an unparalleled advance by *requiring* the National Assembly to promote gender and other modes of equality, in both the exercise of its functions and the conduct of its business.

Speaking at the annual conference of Chwarae Teg in 1999, Val Feld reflected upon women's history of shaping the blueprint for the Assembly:

> It seems to me we are uniquely lucky people because we live in a time where what we do can really make a difference to our country and to future generations and particularly to future generations of girls and women in Wales ... I think if we look at what we have achieved now in the establishment of the Assembly and, particularly, at the extent to which we have been able to integrate equality into the foundations on to which the Assembly is built and the foundations in the way in which it's working, I do believe very strongly that we must all take credit for this. We have, all of us, in a number of different ways, different areas, and different activities, pushed very hard over the recent years to try to achieve some real change in Wales. A lot of the time it's felt as if we've been banging our heads against stone walls, glass ceilings, solid wood doors: that we are pushing and pushing and getting nowhere. But I do hope like me, you feel that we have turned a real corner. It's my belief and main message for today that we are through stage one. I do think we have hammered so

hard on that door and pushed enough to get through it and we are now actually 'in there', on the agenda and part of the game.[18]

As Feld's assessment suggests, at the time of the first Assembly elections, in May 1999, it was increasingly apparent that the political climate for gender equality had shifted significantly from the earlier exclusive and discriminatory practices of administrative devolution. Nevertheless, as the Assembly was about to begin its business, it was far from a foregone conclusion that these changes alone would automatically translate into future gender equality outcomes. This was the line taken by Val Feld in her key Chwarae Teg address. She continued by posing a series of crucial questions: 'What matters now is ... How we deliver? How we interact? And, how we effect change in the long term?'

The opportunities and challenges posed by post-devolution politics and institutions, and the way in which women have responded to them, are the issues that concern us in the second half of this volume. First, we finish the pre-devolution story in chapter 4 by returning to the struggle for women to take an equal place in the Assembly (descriptive representation), and to the respective role played in securing substantial gains by party activists, political parties and wider systematic factors.

4

Women and the Political Parties in Wales: Victories and Vulnerabilities

INTRODUCTION

Having discussed the role of the women's movement and 'strategic' individual women in the devolution debates, we now move on to examine women and the political parties. This chapter has a broader time-span, the period from 1979 until 2003 – from the first referendum on devolution, which registered an overwhelming vote against the government's devolution plans, to the second elections, in 2003, to the National Assembly for Wales that had been established in 1999, after a narrow majority in a second referendum in 1997 (see McAllister, 1998). Our principal focus is on the political parties and their roles as 'carrying agents' for gender equality initiatives. We concentrate on changes in candidate recruitment and selection processes and their relative success in delivering more women politicians. Specifically, we examine the mechanisms used by the four main parties in Wales to improve the number of women AMs elected in the first two Assembly elections. More generally, we consider the ways in which devolution has offered new opportunities for women as elected politicians. Devolution, in its modern incarnation, was designed to bring government closer to the people, to strengthen democracy by remedying democratic deficits and to provide a layer of added accountability (Burrows, 2000; Bogdanor, 2001). As we have seen, in Wales it became intertwined with a new, value-based, political lexicon, promoting the goals of equality, inclusiveness, power-sharing, participation, transparency and consensus. The White Paper that preceded the Government of Wales Act 1998 (which established the Assembly) was forthright in its challenge to the parties: 'the government attaches great importance to equal opportunities for all – including women ... The government also urges all political parties offering candidates for election to the Assembly to have this in mind in their internal candidate selection processes' (Welsh Office, 1997: 24, para 4.7).

Here we explore the ways in which the profile of women in the four main political parties – the Welsh Labour Party, Plaid Cymru: The Party of Wales, the

Welsh Liberal Democrats and the Welsh Conservative Party – has changed, and the ways in which each party has responded to the challenge of involving more women in the new devolved arena.

Opinion has wavered as to the very validity of women's involvement in conventional party politics. Early campaigns for women's franchise were based on the assumption that equality could be achieved only by political representation (see Beddoe, 2004). The second wave of the 'women's movement' in the 1960s and 1970s challenged the idea that political representation and constitutional changes would bring about gender equity, focusing instead on extra-party involvements as mechanisms for improving equality. In the last two decades of the twentieth century, there was a return to the priority of party politics, as the campaigns for adequate childcare, specialist health care, equal pay and working conditions for example, were seen to require structured access to public policy-making in order to enact change. This, in turn, precipitated a reappraisal of the internal operation of political parties, with issues such as manifesto policy commitments, internal and external candidate selection and the establishment of special internal structures for women brought to the fore. The growth of party women's sections and women's committees in local councils, together with strategies for the promotion of women to internal decision-making positions within parties, as election candidates for democratic bodies and to public appointments, are all indicative of the newly acknowledged gender context for politics. All of this further legitimizes the academic exercise of searching for the 'distinctive female political experience'. Work in the UK within this broad field of enquiry has so far concentrated upon the impact of women politicians on the institutions to which they are elected (recent work includes Norris, 1996; Bochel and Briggs, 2000; Childs, 2001, 2002, 2004b; Mackay, 2001b; Cowell-Meyers, 2003; Lovenduski and Norris, 2003; Mackay, et al., 2003; Lovenduski, 2005), as well as some considering the position of women in each of the main British political parties (for example, Maguire, 1998; Lovenduski, 2005). Longitudinal information about candidates for the Scottish Parliament and National Assembly for Wales elections has also been collated, highlighting issues surrounding the selection of women candidates (Russell et al., 2002), but much of this has been part of a broader examination of candidate-selection procedures (Bradbury et al., 1999). Whilst all of this offers valuable background to our analysis, our principal aim is to assess changes in party politics in Wales.

This chapter has four specific objectives: to consider the impact devolution has had on the position of women in political parties; to measure the success of the different measures of interventions or 'positive actions' used principally by two of the parties, Labour and Plaid Cymru, to promote women within their internal structures and as party candidates; to evaluate the separate organization of women in each party and, where appropriate, how they have helped change women's roles and status; and, finally, to evaluate the relative 'security' or permanence of achieving or exceeding what would normally be defined as 'critical mass' in the Assembly, alongside other significant and visible enhancements of women's input to the political process.

By way of theoretical background, we continue to draw upon theories of equal opportunities and equality, paying particular attention to debates over the causes and symptoms of gender disadvantage. In our examination of the political parties, we pose the specific question: to what extent do limited forms of positive action address the symptoms of gender inequality, rather than its root causes? By distinguishing between positive (or 'add-on') measures that are usually specific and time-limited, and mainstreaming (or 'built-in') approaches that seek to institutionalize and routinize equality, we predict the likely sustainability of the measurable successes in women's representation in Wales to date.

This chapter completes the story of women in the pre-devolution period, whilst also moving us a stage further. In so doing, it offers an early assessment of the likely sustainability of larger numbers of elected women politicians since 1999. Part of this involves judging the extent to which the numerical gains reflect the beginning of a cultural shift, or merely the outcome of alterations in party rules. Answers to this will, of course, help determine the security of improvements in descriptive representation.

BACKGROUND

Women have always made significant contributions to the political parties in Wales. Their input at grassroots level, whilst difficult to quantify, is widely acknowledged by all parties, although largely undervalued. Despite this involvement, there has been no serious representation of women at leadership level in any of the main parties. One of the key factors behind this is the operation of parties and modes of control over candidate-selection processes. Generally, the parties' reactions to shifts in political culture have been slow and hesitant. There are a number of reasons for this – male hegemony within each party leadership, a small power-base in three out of four cases (Labour, as the traditionally dominant party in Wales, being the exception), which means that men would have to relinquish power and office for women to gain significant access, and disagreements as to how better representation of women might be achieved in practice.[1]

Prior to the establishment of the Assembly in 1999, elected women politicians were a rare breed.[2] Set against generally much lower levels of political representation for women compared with many European states, there have only ever been twelve women MPs elected in Wales since women won the right to vote in 1918. At the 1997 General Election, Labour held thirty-four (85 per cent) of the forty parliamentary constituencies in Wales, but only four of its MPs were women (and three of these were selected as Labour candidates through all-women shortlists). None of Plaid Cymru's four MPs, nor either of the Welsh Liberal Democrats' two was a woman. In total, this meant 10 per cent of Welsh MPs were women (in 1997, the Conservatives had no MPs returned from Welsh constituencies). Despite the 2001 General Election seeing the first fall in the number of women MPs since 1979 (with 118 women elected, 18 per cent of the total), in Wales, the position was unchanged, the balance of seats remaining exactly the same, as did the number of women MPs. In 2005, this altered, with a generally more volatile electoral map. Labour won twenty-nine seats (seven women, three of whom – Madeleine Moon in Bridgend, Nia Griffith in Llanelli and Siân James in Swansea East – were selected to replace sitting MPs through the still-controversial, reintroduced all-women shortlists policy (Beddoe, 2004; Campbell and Lovenduski, 2005; Childs et al., 2005), the Liberal Democrats four (one woman), Plaid Cymru three (all men) and the Conservatives three (all men), plus one Independent MP, Peter Law in Blaenau Gwent. This meant Wales had its highest ever complement of women in Parliament – eight MPs, or 20 per cent in total.

Despite these comparatively minor improvements in representation at Westminster, it is at the devolved level that there has been the most significant increase in the number of women politicians. In the first Assembly, elected in May 1999, twenty-five (or nearly 42 per cent) of the sixty Assembly Members (AMs) were women. There were sixteen Labour women AMs (from a group of twenty-eight)[3] and six Plaid Cymru women (from a party group of seventeen). Three of the Liberal Democrat group of six were women. The first Labour Cabinet contained four women ministers,[4] whilst the Labour/Liberal Democrat coalition administration which governed from October 2000 had five women in its nine-strong Cabinet (55 per cent), making it one of the few executives in Europe with a larger proportion of women ministers than of men.[5] This was almost double the level of women represented at Westminster and 'thrust the National Assembly for Wales into the international limelight' (Mackay, 2003: 140), placing Wales a close second in international rankings for gender parity behind Sweden with 42.7 per cent (Beddoe, 2004).

In the second Assembly, elected in May 2003, the position of women improved further (again, largely through the incumbency factor, with Labour's women AMs successfully securing their constituency renomination, although not without challenge, as we shall see). Thirty women in total were elected, meaning women formed exactly half of the Assembly. Women comprised 55 per cent of the forty constituency seats and 40 per cent of the twenty regional list seats. Almost two-thirds of Labour AMs were women. As well as women making up 44 per cent of the Welsh Assembly Government, women also chaired more than half of the subject and standing committees (an increase from 40 per cent in 1999).

How, then, did we reach a position in 2003 where exactly half of AMs and four of the nine Welsh Assembly Government's Cabinet ministers were women, which has led to the Assembly being heralded as the much-vaunted inclusive politics in practice (Richardson, 2003)? As part of the search for answers, this chapter charts some of the landmarks in the process of enhancing women's *descriptive* representation. It concentrates on progress made within the principal political parties since discussions on devolution began, and offers some explanations for these shifts. There have been important breakthroughs, and the significance of impressive levels of formal (or descriptive) representation of women should not be underestimated. However, claims of an equality panacea in Wales, together with suggestions that the hard work has been done, need serious qualification. Whilst acknowledging the major breakthroughs made to date, our analysis looks beyond the public profile and bald statistics, examining, first, the ways in which improved representation has come about, and, second, the security of the gains made so far. We recognize some significant breakthroughs, whilst offering a more sober assessment of the processes and permanence of women's political representation in Wales.

STRUCTURAL OPPORTUNITIES FOR CHANGE

We have already described the opportunities provided by the relatively blank political slate of a new system of governance. In chapters 1 and 3, we discussed 'strategic agency' and 'system-level' explanations of changes in women's representation. In tracking how the political parties manoeuvred within, and adjusted to, devolution's new terrain, we assess here the robustness of mechanisms taken to safeguard and promote women's representation – both descriptive and substantive.

Devolution offered a unique potential for radically changing women's representation. Two specific factors helped bring about the seismic shift underlying the increase in women in the Assembly: one is systemic, the other political or organizational. First, a more proportional electoral system – the Additional Member System – was used for Assembly elections. Second, different forms of positive action were taken by the Welsh Labour Party and Plaid Cymru (and to a much lesser extent, by the Welsh Liberal Democrats) to ensure greater numbers and a higher profile for women candidates.

The new electoral system
A system of proportional representation (PR), the Additional Member System (AMS), was used for the first elections to the devolved institutions in Wales and Scotland. This is a hybrid and limited form of PR; in Wales, AMs were split into forty, who were elected for constituencies paralleling the existing Westminster seats, using the traditional first-past-the-post method, and the remaining twenty members, who were elected using a regional 'top-up' party list, four being

elected for each of Wales's then five European Parliament regions (using the d'Hondt formula to ensure that votes cast in this second ballot help balanced the distribution of seats already achieved via the first constituency ballot). Whilst AMS is far from proportional (and the Welsh version is less so than the same system used for the Scottish Parliament), it does provide opportunities for ensuring better representation of different groups. Specifically, it allows parties more power in the management of candidate selection than do some other PR systems. This reinforces the importance of our focus on the parties.

Nevertheless, it is worth reminding ourselves that, despite the demands made during the passage through Parliament of the Government of Wales Bill (see chapters 3 and 9), no formal mechanism for ensuring equal gender representation was set out in the Government of Wales Act. Instead, it was a non-compulsory recommendation for parties to implement as they saw fit. This is not to underestimate the importance of the White Paper's rhetoric, such as, 'It [the Government] believes that greater participation by women is essential to the health of our democracy' (Welsh Office, 1997: 24). Given that there is limited usage of constitutionally mandated positive-action measures in the UK (Childs et al., 2005), even a recommendation should be regarded as a step forward. However, as we shall show, like most non-statutory recommendations, the challenge was taken up with differing levels of enthusiasm and commitment. The unprecedented numbers of Labour (and, to a lesser extent, Plaid Cymru and Liberal Democrat) women AMs in the first two Assemblies were clearly not the result of a natural or organic trend towards fairer representation. Rather, they were the direct outcome of measures taken to ensure better women's representation. In Labour's case, this was through its controversial 'twinning' policy, and in Plaid Cymru's, through a less contentious and less expansive policy of prioritizing or 'zipping'[6] women candidates on the regional lists. The other two parties took fewer, or no, hard formal promotional actions. They did, however, use other, softer, measures, such as training, soft quotas in terms of shortlisting policies, and the incorporation of some equal opportunities measures in job criteria.

We begin by examining two important 'add-on' mechanisms to support and promote women: first, some of the specific positive action measures taken by the parties to date. We look at how far these measures have made concrete contributions to improving women's position and also assess their capacity for overcoming institutionalized discrimination. We then examine women's organizations (variously called 'sections', 'forums' or 'committees') within the Welsh parties. In structuring this discussion, we concentrate on the Welsh Labour Party and Plaid Cymru, as developments in the two parties have often mirrored each other. Furthermore, of the four main parties, it is these two that have given most serious consideration to implementing firm strategies for enhancing equality.

POSITIVE ACTION TAKEN BY THE POLITICAL PARTIES

In terms of measurable outputs, easily the most significant initiative that boosted this dramatic increase in the number of women represented in the Assembly were the procedures introduced by Labour and Plaid Cymru in the selection and prioritization of candidates for the two Assembly elections, in 1999 and 2003. This underlines the importance of political parties as agents, particularly their internal management of candidate selection, as a stimulus for better gender representation.

It was clear to the Wales Labour Party that most of its Assembly seats would be won from the first-past-the-post or constituency ballot, as in Scotland. After much debate, the party adopted a system of 'twinning', which created pairs from the forty Welsh constituencies and resulted in sixteen women and twelve Labour men being elected in 1999, and nineteen women and eleven men in 2003. In order to understand the wider processes of change at work in the party, we should first explore briefly the background to twinning. The debate on the promotion of more women candidates is inseparable from general party disagreement as to how all candidates were to be selected (see Morgan and Mungham, 2000). In 1997, a

Table 4.1 **Numbers of women candidates and elected AMs in the 1999 and 2003 National Assembly elections.**

National Assembly election 1999				
Political Party	*Women candidates (FPTP constituencies)*	*Women candidates (regional lists)*	*Women AMs elected (FPTP constituencies)*	*Women AMs elected (regional lists)*
Welsh Labour	20	11	16	0
Plaid Cymru	8	14	2	4
Welsh Conservatives	12	18	0	0
Welsh Liberal Democrats	13	20	3	3
Independents/other parties	1		0	
National Assembly election 2003				
Political Party	*Women candidates (FPTP constituencies)*	*Women candidates (regional lists)*	*Women AMs elected (FPTP constituencies)*	*Women AMs elected (regional lists)*
Welsh Labour	23	24	19	0
Plaid Cymru	8	18	1	5
Welsh Conservatives	8	8	0	2
Welsh Liberal Democrats	13	11	3	3
Independents/other parties	9	45	0	0

network called 'Twin to Win' was formed, comprising senior Labour women offi-cials and politicians,[7] together with key male supporters from the modernizing wing of the party. They began to lobby Labour members to endorse positive action (Russell et al., 2002; Mackay, 2003). Whilst women's sections in the Wales Labour Party were relatively weak and less organized than their counterparts in Scotland (Russell et al., 2002), pressure was, nevertheless, maintained on the party leadership for positive action in candidate selection. It is interesting that campaigners used unfavourable comparisons with Scotland – and the politics of 'catch-up' – as a means to spur reform (Mackay, 2003). This reinforces the import-ance of intra-party dynamics – between Wales, Scotland and the Labour Party centrally. Once twinning had been endorsed for Scotland, the party centrally was anxious that a uniform approach was adopted in both countries. Comparisons with Scotland thus became powerful tools in arguments for twinning in Wales.

The twinning debate was extremely acrimonious in Wales (Brennan, no date; Gill, 1999; Edwards and Chapman, 2000). Candidate selection for the first Assembly elections had become enmeshed in a wider fallout from the Welsh Labour leadership contests (see Morgan and Mungham, 2000; Flynn, 1999; McAllister, 2000). Although the twinning policy was agreed in January 1998, the exact form of its operation was still to be confirmed some months later. By now, opponents had organized in the form of the internal party 'Campaign against Twinning'. Two options for implementing twinning were presented to the Welsh party conference in May 1998; one was the executive's twinning formula, the other a so-called 'Ponty Option', devised by the Pontypridd party, whereby a shortlist of one man and one woman would be drawn up by each constituency, with a selection panel interviewing both candidates before making its recom-mendations. Pro-twinning campaigners argued that constituencies would probably choose mostly male candidates under this system. The 'Ponty Option' was narrowly defeated (by 51.95 to 48.41 per cent), meaning that the straight-forward twinning of constituencies into pairs, with one male and one female candidate in each pair, was accepted by the narrowest of margins (see Morgan and Mungham, 2000; Edwards and Chapman, 2000; Edwards and McAllister, 2002). The debate had been highly polarized, and twinning was grudgingly accepted as a time-specific, once-only measure. One member later claimed, 'As far as I know it's [twinning] over. The guarantee was given to those constitu-encies which were against it, of which mine was one, that this was a one-off and it wouldn't happen again.' Yet, as Morgan and Mungham revealed: 'While the decision may have been historic, the row rumbled on … Labour's twinning battle had helped sap the Party's energies, seriously delayed candidate selection and left many Party activists disaffected and demotivated' (Morgan and Mungham, 2000: 170–1). This added a layer of vulnerability to an important equality device.

Like Labour, historically Plaid Cymru's representation at every electoral level has been overwhelmingly male. Prior to 1999, the party had never had a woman

MP or MEP, and only around one in five of the party's councillors were women. The Assembly and European elections, held within a month of each other in 1999, marked major advances for Plaid: six of its seventeen AMs were women (over a third) and one of its two MEPs elected in June 1999 was a woman, underlining the scale of the breakthrough, albeit less striking than Labour's. How then did Plaid Cymru improve its representation of women so dramatically, and what was the background to this? The party had established a Gender Balance Commission in 1993, whose most significant recommendation had been that Plaid 'should commit itself to the aim of ensuring that 50% of its candidates for the Welsh Parliament are women, and 50% men by the time of the first Welsh Parliamentary elections' (McAllister, 2001a). Yet, when it came to party discussions on candidate selection for the first Assembly elections a few years later, there was little specific reference to this tacit commitment, which offers further illustration of the temporary nature of many of Plaid's initiatives and utterances on gender equality. Nevertheless, Plaid Cymru compares favourably with its 'sister' nationalist party in Scotland, the SNP. In the run-up to devolution, the SNP had no gender commission, and its Women's Forum was relatively weak. This may, in part, explain why women activists in Plaid were more successful in pressing for formal positive action than were their counterparts in the SNP.

A paper to Plaid Cymru's National Council (its supreme, sovereign decision-making body between annual conferences) in November 1997 offered two options for ensuring more women were elected; constituency twinning (on a similar basis to Labour), and 'top-up' prioritization, or 'zipping', on the party's regional lists for the PR part of the ballot. As in Labour, there were stormy debates about how best to proceed. These encapsulated both gender-based and wider power-battles in the party as it prepared for the new challenges of devolution. Eventually, it was decided to defer the decision to the party's National Executive Committee, which settled for the latter option, with women guaranteed first and third places on each of the five regional party lists (with a similar method employed for the European elections, held a month later). The claim was that this would see the election of at least five Plaid women AMs which would, in turn, help balance the four males expected to win in its target seats of the constituency ballot. A basic underestimation of the prospect and extent of Plaid's likely success meant that unanticipated gains in the first part of the ballot in 1999 ensured that the gender composition of the eventual Plaid group in the Assembly was not, in fact, balanced. This was clearly an important and unexpected factor, but the outcome also underlines that a zipping approach is considerably less effective at ensuring a balanced representation for women than twinning, especially in an electoral system in which the proportional element is so limited. This point was frequently made in the debates on positive action options, so why, then, did Plaid Cymru not follow Labour's lead and use twinning? There were many political subtexts to Plaid's decision: heated discussions had taken place between the party's

Director of Elections, Janet Davies, its Director of Equality, Helen Mary Jones (both former women's section activists who became AMs and gained senior positions within the new Plaid group in the Assembly), and the party's chair and president (both male), in which there were alleged threats of resignation and accusations of blackmail. Both women judged that their party leadership's commitment to zipping was based on pragmatism, rather than principle. Yet most women activists were also pragmatic about the decision to 'zip' women on the regional lists, admitting that this was the only option that would not have divided the party at leadership and grassroots level at a vital juncture in its political history. Davies claimed that twinning was 'never a reality' in terms of the crucial National Council vote, for fear of undermining potential gains in the first devolved elections. Reflecting the wider mood concerning gender equality in the party, others commented that it would have been impossible to carry the grassroots of the party along in a pre-election consensus, had twinning been adopted. Others acknowledged the (predominantly male) leadership's role in rejecting twinning. This is important, given that it had already proved so divisive an issue for Welsh Labour. Unsurprisingly, the successful candidates – Plaid's women AMs – were unanimously relieved at not having to contend with the level of local opposition that Labour had to its 'twinning' selection policy, with a clear majority of this – albeit unrepresentative, as they had clearly benefited from the alternative system – group justifying zipping as the 'best pragmatic option available at the time'.

The internal debates underline just how significant scarce power-resources are in smaller parties like Plaid Cymru, as well as the concomitant difficulties this may bring for selecting women candidates, when leading males may lose out as a consequence. One woman AM also highlighted the additional difficulties associated with twinning in a small political party, where contests are 'instantly personalized'. This emphasizes how the intellectual and equality rationale for positive actions can easily be muddied by personality issues. This became a particular issue in the composition of the South East Wales regional list for the first Assembly elections, where a prominent, long-standing party activist, the late Professor Phil Williams, looked likely to lose out to Jocelyn Davies, who, according to the gender-zipping scheme, would take pole position on the party's list. Plaid expected only the first candidate on the list to be elected, and there was long-running pressure to make an exception to the 'women first' strategy in this region. Suggestions were made (by the then party president, Dafydd Wigley MP, a close ally of Williams, amongst others) that, in this region alone, local members should be allowed to decide whether they wished to have a man or a woman at the top of their list. One woman candidate confessed she felt compelled to stand up to the leadership, who seemed happy to bend an important principle to ensure that a 'favoured son' or a 'vital man' be allowed a better chance of becoming an AM. Interestingly, some candidates we spoke to also suggested that several former leading members of the party's women's section failed to offer support to those arguing for consistent application of the gender prioritization policy in all five regional lists. Facing the prospect of real electoral gains for the first time, it would appear that Plaid was starting to behave like a traditional political party, in terms of candidate selection at least.

Although some leading women in Plaid confessed to some unease regarding zipping, others, like Janet Davies AM, confessed to being 'as happy as she could be'. Other women AMs reiterated their support for twinning as a more expansive mechanism, even if they had been elected without it. Yet the unease within Plaid at the minimal mechanisms for promoting women continued. There were highly vocal criticisms of zipping, alongside acknowledgements that, as a policy, its impact did not go far enough, especially when juxtaposed with the obvious success of Labour's twinning. There were similar concerns about the absence of guarantees of continuity in employing this policy over a series of elections. This raises issues of sustainability once more. Several women candidates suggested the party's leaders might jeopardize the fragile consensus around procedures for promoting women candidates, especially when it was felt a leading man might miss out in future (we have evidence of many 'off-the-record' claims that this was a major factor in the twinning option not gaining more popular support in Plaid). In terms of further outcomes from zipping, it is interesting that one AM claimed that the concentration of Plaid women elected from the regional ballot had brought with it specific difficulties, especially in terms of establishing a natural political base for those AMs without an identifiable and manageable constituency. Given that many elected women were new to national politics, this meant they struggled to develop a sufficiently high profile. However, the counter-argument to this is that women were thus able to adopt broader and more thematic approaches to policy initiation, including those related to gender. It would seem that, in both Labour and Plaid, there remain serious tensions as to the ongoing application and development of its equalities strategies, both add-on and build-in, underlining the vulnerability that often follows gender victories.

THE WELSH LIBERAL DEMOCRATS

There is rather less to document in the other two main parties' internal debates on improving their numbers of women candidates and AMs. The Liberal Democrats have long supported equal representation, but their promotion of women candidates had been limited, and tied in with the case for a more proportional electoral system. Historically, the party's record of women's representation is no better than that of the other parties. Moreover, they have consistently shied away from the kind of positive action taken by Labour and Plaid Cymru. Underlining the thrust of many Liberal Democrat debates on this subject, the party's spokesperson on women's issues, Diane Maddock, claimed 'we want equal treatment for women, not special treatment. Our aim is equality of opportunity, not equality of outcome.'

Founded in 1988, the Welsh Liberal Democrats are a quasi-autonomous organization within the larger party's federal structure, with responsibility for local organization and membership, candidate-selection processes, and country-specific policy and election manifesto matters. It is largely in the context of wider equal opportunities that the Welsh Liberal Democrats debated positive action and the role of women in the party. Linked, one assumes, to its libertarian traditions, the party has preferred to try to extend recruitment to broaden the type of member it attracts, and thus the variety of election candidates it fields.

Enthusiastic advocates of devolution, the Welsh Liberal Democrats identified opportunities for promoting a new politics with the advent of the Assembly. In his foreword to the party's 1999 Assembly election manifesto, the party leader, Mike German, asserted: 'I am determined to make our historic new Assembly work. Liberal Democrats are the Party which has campaigned for devolution for more than 100 years. We will make devolution work for ... new, open politics where people's voices get heard.' Yet, the party pursued no formal positive action in its selection procedures for the first Assembly elections. It used informal methods of encouraging more women to put their names forward, ran a limited number of women-only training days for prospective candidates and insisted on equal numbers of men and women on the candidate selection shortlists. However, this method, of course, has no guarantees of increasing the number of successful women candidates. In practice, the party fielded high-profile women candidates to fight two of their key target seats – Brecon and Radnor, and Cardiff Central – both of which were won in 1999 (and retained in 2003). Women were placed top on two regional lists in 1999 and second on three others. This meant that of the six seats the Welsh Liberal Democrats won, three (or half) of its AMs were women (two successful on the constituency ballots, and one from the regional lists). So, whilst avoiding the acrimonious debates that surrounded positive action in Labour and Plaid, it would seem that an equal number of Liberal Democrat women AMs was achieved, more by luck than by design, which poses further questions of sustainability. More widely, the central party set up a Gender Balance task force, chaired by Baroness Harris of Richmond, to maximize the participation of women throughout the party and in politics more widely. In Scotland, a separate women'a organization, Scottish Women Liberal Democrats:

> encourages, advises and trains women to participate fully throughout the party and attain public office; influences party policy by taking a leading role in debates and seeking to set the agenda on issues that effect women; and actively campaigns for equality of opportunity both locally and nationally.

THE WELSH CONSERVATIVES

Of the four main parties, the Welsh Conservatives have easily the worst track record in terms of formal women's representation. In line with its UK party, the Welsh Conservatives have historically opposed all measures of positive action. The 1997 General Election saw a record number of women elected to Parliament – 120 in total – although only 13 of these were Conservatives (compared with 101 for Labour). This represented 7.8 per cent of the parliamentary party.[8] Due to the Welsh party's limited degree of independence, it has been difficult to trace separate or distinctive debates on gender equality, or even to determine their existence. We are therefore largely reliant on the wider arguments in the Conservative Party on this issue. What is clear is that the party has no formal policy on equal opportunities, nor any firm mechanisms for promoting women election candidates, other than ongoing training sessions, initiated and run by its women's organization.

In 2004, Theresa May MP, the party's spokesperson on women's issues, told a special 'women's session' at the annual conference (the first ever held at a Conservative conference) that the party rejected positive 'discrimination' as it 'had never been a party to ghettoise' people.[9] She argued: 'In the Conservative Party we have always taken the view – and women have as well – that they do not want to be selected on that basis of positive discrimination, but there is a long way to go. I accept that there is a lot of work to do.'

In September 2005, May addressed the Fawcett Society, acknowledging that gender-specific targets were a 'painful' issue for some in the party: 'Looking at its elected representatives, you will see a predominantly white, male party. Given that we now see an ethnically diverse society, where women increasingly play a major role, the Conservative Party just doesn't look like the people that it is claiming to represent.'[10] Whilst arguing that they would not pursue positive discrimination, May stressed five reasons why the party needed more women candidates:

> Firstly, women make good MPs. Their skills of listening, and delivering are ideally suited to what an MP's role increasingly requires. Secondly, if we are seeing a shift of salience in British politics to a feminisation – a less macho form of politics, a move away from the 'ya-boo' tone, the car bore obsession with mind-numbing details, and the focus on traditional, big political issues that characterise the old macho approach – then surely it makes sense to have more women MPs. Third, a party seeking the most talented and able candidates should not ignore 50% of the population and their talents. Fourth, women have different experience sets to men – they know first-hand about things that most men don't. Finally, and perhaps fundamentally, we need more women to vote for us, but as things stand, the modern Labour Party is far better than we are at speaking the language of the woman voter.[11]

The advent of devolution exposed the poor status of women in the Welsh (and Scottish) Conservatives, which, at the very least, resurrected the issue on the party's internal agenda. At the same time, it offered a lifeline for a party which currently had no elected representatives from Wales at Westminster. At the first Assembly elections in 1999, the Welsh Conservatives did not employ any promotional measures for selecting women candidates. The party eventually fielded eleven women, but none was successful, with all nine of its AMs in 1999 men. In view of this and the large number of women AMs elected from the other parties (thus underlining the theory of 'contagion' between rival parties), several prominent party members called for changes to be put in place ahead of the second Assembly elections in 2003.

In April 2002, one of its Assembly candidates, Dianne Rees, called for radical changes to give more women a chance to forge a career in front-line politics: 'We had a lot standing in 1999 but it is not the number of candidates, it is the number that are elected to the Assembly.' Welsh Conservative Party leader, Nick Bourne AM, responded: 'I would hate women to turn round and feel they are only here (in the Assembly) because of quotas' (quoted in Hazelwood, 2002). Another AM, David Melding, proposed an element of positive action to promote women candidates for the second Assembly elections in 2003. The South Wales Central AM called for places on the five regional lists to be allocated specifically to women. This limited proposal – which would have seen women guaranteed at least the third slot in each of the lists and, in one region, a woman placed second – was rejected by the party's board of management. Nevertheless, limited intervention from the party leadership meant that, in four of the five regions, whilst women were not allocated the top position on the list, the second place went to a woman – guaranteeing that at least some Conservative women were returned to the Assembly. Thus, in the second Assembly elections, the Conservatives again returned no women AMs from the constituency ballot, but two from the regional lists – Lisa Francis in Mid and West Wales, and Laura Ann Jones in South Wales East – meaning two of the party's eleven AMs were women. Yet, there has been little real appetite in the Conservative Party to use positive action on a similar basis to the other parties, although the women's organization chair, Gloria Lumley, told us: 'The success of these two Assembly members will ... be encouraging for other women who are putting themselves forward for selection'. She repeated the arguments for a 'meritocracy': 'the Conservative Party does not put pressure on constituencies/selection committees to ensure they adopt women – each candidate whether male or female is selected on their own merit as being the best person for the job'. There is no indication that the women's organization has challenged traditional male-based definitions of a 'meritocracy' or engaged in campaigns for positive action, although it was suggested that 'the "mood" within the women's organization on this is good'. The best one can say is that the Welsh Conservatives have shown ambivalence towards positive action; the worst, that there has been downright opposition, with many activists (including women themselves) claiming that they wanted 'to be treated on merit alone', and some even calling for the abolition of their party's women's committees, which were seen as a barrier, rather than a boost, to more women becoming MPs.

As well as gaining its first two women AMs in 2003, there were some signs of improvement at the 2005 General Election, when the party fielded nine candidates in the forty Welsh seats, one more than in 2001 (although none was elected). Given that these very limited improvements were achieved largely without any positive action, it left those arguing for more strategic or radical action in a somewhat weakened position.

WOMEN'S SECTIONS OR ORGANIZATIONS

Welsh Labour Party
Separate constituency-based women's sections were formalized in the 1918 Labour Party constitution and have existed ever since. However, until the party's restructuring in 1999, women's sections in the Welsh Labour Party were branch-based and patchy in their existence, created largely in response to demand.[12] As one party worker put it: 'How it used to work here was there was a women's section for every ward, if they wanted it ... That was the telling phrase "if they wanted it".'

Women's sections were more popular in some parts of Wales than others. In the southern valleys in particular, whilst conditions of party membership were equal, the locations for branch meetings were patently not (and, in some cases, this remains the case). Baroness Gale, former general secretary of the party in Wales and now a life peer, suggested that wider attitudes in the party to women had required separate women's organizations in some areas:

> I always saw the women's sections as a door through which women could come into the party. A lot of women wouldn't want to come to mixed meetings especially if they were in pubs and remember, a lot of men wouldn't like their wives going to meetings where there were other men, but they were quite happy for them to go to the women's section because generally they wouldn't meet in a pub or club ... a lot of their meetings took place in schoolrooms or community centres, that sort of environment ... Nowadays, of course, things are completely different – the young women, especially, are not worried about going into a pub for a branch meeting.

The early 1980s saw the rise of socialist feminism in the Labour Party as a whole, epitomized by the Women's Action Committee (WAC), which was instrumental in promoting positive actions to increase the numbers of women candidates for election and also for the party's National Executive Committee. The Riverside women's section in Cardiff was one such highly politicized group. One of its members recalled:

> Ours ... was one of the most active wards in the constituency ... There were ten of us and we all had common ideas ... you need a catalyst to keep these things together,

and when three of us became councillors and we were very overtaken by the agenda, we were all very busy. Now all three of us are Assembly Members, Sue [Essex] Jane [Hutt] and myself, and I was the junior ... they were very much my mentors to me as well.

This suggests that, whilst small branch-based women's sections might be successful in promoting women to positions of power, this was the exception, rather than the rule. Nevertheless, these women went on to become Cardiff City councillors, responsible for initiating women's/equal opportunities committees in local government, before becoming AMs and ministers. In this case, one local party actually provided several of the core 'strategic women' who played so important a role in 'gendering' constitutional change in Wales (see chapters 2 and 3).

In 1999, the Labour Party reorganized, abolishing branch-based women's sections and replacing them with constituency-based women's forums. The timing of this reorganization was inopportune in Wales, coming, as it did, so soon after the hugely acrimonious 'twinning' debate. There have been suggestions that reorganizing branch-based women's sections into constituency-based women's forums at this time may also have led to manipulation of the elections for the post of Women's Officer, in order to sustain support for anti-twinning caucuses (see Edwards and Chapman, 2000). Evidence suggests that this change made it easier for men to gain (and sustain) control over their constituencies, particularly in small communities, where the social status and political influence attached to the job might be disproportionately large. One woman activist, for example, claimed that the women's section was manipulated by the male-dominated executive to condemn the candidature of the prospective woman candidate for the Assembly. Clearly, women challenging the legitimacy of other women was seen by some as having added weight.

Delegates from the local forums meet annually at the All-Wales Women's Forum, itself heralded as a strategy for mainstreaming women's policy-making within the party as a whole, thereby avoiding separate women's conferences and designated representation at the annual party conference, which had been criticized by some. But the fact that a separate route for women's voices was preserved in the All-Wales Forum suggests that the party was well aware of the dangers of demands for separate representation for women being drowned out at constituency level.

Not all constituencies established a women's forum after 1999. There seem to be two reasons for this: first, finance, and second, the lack of replacements for women's officers who became AMs in the first Assembly elections. Party regulations require that every woman member in the constituency has to be informed, in writing, fourteen days prior to a women's forum meeting. As one women's officer said:

there, I think, is where you would come up against male opposition, because they will say well, hang on now, it will cost ... £200 to send letters out four times a year so could not this money be spent better than on women's (matters) ... you know?

This echoes reports that women had already experienced difficulties in getting funding from their constituencies to be delegates to women's conferences under the old system. There were assumptions that women had the time to organize fund-raising, not only for their constituencies generally, but also for political skills training for their own conference delegates. Although one local women's section saw three of its most prominent women members eventually promoted to Cabinet positions in the Assembly, more generally there have been few clear links between Labour women AMs and local women's sections. About half of Labour's women AMs had previously been members of women's sections. However, some doubted their relevance:

> Some of the wards which had women's sections – and they'd be very much fund-raising sections – people used to go along, have a nice time and a natter and they were gradually dying away. But my generation were content to have ward meetings rather than have women's sections in the branches, but I've nothing against them ... I think they are useful from a confidence-building perspective, but I'm not a big fan of separate structures, to be honest with you.

> Now as regards the women's section ... at the time I got back from college there wasn't one and then there was a brief attempt to revive the one that had been and I went to the first meeting and to tell the truth it was awful. I mean, they were telling me about how they used to have these linen parties ... I assume it's like a Tupperware party and I said I didn't think that was what it was going to be about; I thought it would about more political things and issues to do with women you know? So I knocked that one on the head and it didn't actually revive anyway.

Of course, the very existence of women's political organizations that prioritize social activities may reveal a wider problem, namely, the general lack of social spaces for women to meet and debate, particularly in the valleys and rural parts of Wales. The responsibility for caring, or organizing care, for dependants still largely falls to women in families, whatever positions they may have achieved in work or politics. It does, however, challenge the idea that the principal political function for women's organizations has to be electoral or even conventionally political in the first instance.

The pattern of development of these separate processes and structures for women was largely unsupported by party resources and authority, suggesting an ambivalent attitude towards equality by Welsh Labour. There was little routine monitoring of local constituencies and branches to tackle examples of institutionalized sexism, largely because the Women's Officer was not a full-time post with a dedicated budget. Many Labour women reported feeling marginalized in their party, suggesting separate structures had to be constantly defended, even within their own party, and overall had made limited impact.

Plaid Cymru: The Party of Wales
The operation of separate women's organizations in Plaid Cymru has some clear parallels with developments in Labour. Since its establishment in 1925, Plaid

Cymru has always had some form of official women's section (*Adran y Menywod*, in Welsh). However, the role and status of the section in the party have fluctuated considerably. During its early years, the women's section was largely a fund-raising organization, providing a general support role for elections and campaigns. The section was resurrected in the early 1980s by a small group of younger women who were part of general moves to radicalize the party, following the severe blow dealt by the 'No' vote in the devolution referendum of 1979. The section's approach and organization were heavily influenced by the wider women's movement, and by the development of feminism especially (McAllister, 2001a, 2001b). From 1979, the women's section adopted a more overtly political role. This peaked during the 1980s when the section drove the equal-representation agenda forward – within the party internally, at least. It simultaneously pursued specific positive actions alongside wider mainstreaming strategies. First, it pushed various promotional measures designed to achieve better representation for women, both within the party's own structures and as election candidates. Second, it highlighted examples of institutionalized sexism within Plaid, focusing on discriminatory policy suggestions at the party confer-ences, for example. The section also concentrated on cooperation with the Plaid Cymru Youth Movement, since, as one activist put it: 'there was a better chance there ... of educating younger, male members'.

The section developed a broader training and educational role, holding sessions before annual conferences to assist women delegates and potential speakers. It organized the party's policy discussions to help delegates to National Executive and National Council (Plaid's principal decision-making bodies). The women's section was run on a relatively informal basis but functioned successfully, due to a high level of commitment amongst activists, especially new women members. Its relative success led to some of its leading women being elected to the Assembly (Helen Mary Jones and Janet Davies, for example), and to the European Parliament, (former party chair and current MEP Jill Evans). Many of these women have since attributed their own self-confidence as politicians to the informal political education and wider support-networks provided by the women's section. They also recognized that whilst the section had benefited a few women dramatically, its influence 'did not spread much beyond that to other women in the party'.

The section's most important contribution to the development of equality strategies came during the 1980s, when it helped initiate what proved to be a long-running debate over the issue of equal representation, both within Plaid's internal structures and in the selection of candidates for external elections. In 1981, the party embarked on its first experiment in positive action, with space for five women representatives (rather than the single one to which each official section of the party – women, youth and trade union – was entitled) on the party's National Executive Committee for a trial period of five years. Upon the trial's completion in 1986, the party ended this positive action, pointing out that, at one-third, the proportion of women members of the executive was higher than ever before. The women's section was the leading advocate of this measure and argued for it to be continued. When the policy was rescinded in 1986, the section accused Plaid of short-sightedness and a lack of sincerity in its professed commitment to redressing gender imbalance. Specifying a fixed time-span for such measures would seem to be a recurring feature of the party's approach to promoting equality and a major source of frustration for women activists. Jill Evans MEP suggested: 'We do need to look again at the painful subject of the representation of women within the party which is not improving ... I am inclined to suggest drastic action, such as threatening to boycott elections for all senior posts in the party' (quoted in McAllister, 2001a: 196). As well as underlining the vulnerability of such initiatives, as we shall see, there was a danger of this being repeated in the party's policy for prioritizing women on regional lists in the Assembly elections.

Little meaningful progress was made on the equality agenda subsequently, which was as much to do with the election of several prominent women to leadership positions within Plaid as with the long-standing stubborn resistance of the leadership to supporting radical, innovative and lasting internal reform (see McAllister, 2001a; Chaney and Fevre, 2001a). It is fair to say that the leadership felt they had made the effort to improve equality through specific, short-term measures, but, in a small party, were unprepared to concede further scarce resources and influence. Moreover, as in Labour, some key 'strategic women' were quickly caught up in wider party business, diluting their role in the gender debate.

After this first experiment in positive action, little attention was paid to the gender issue until 1993, when Plaid Cymru established an internal Gender Balance Commission, with a remit of proposing necessary constitutional changes to address the issue of gender balance. This initiative came from the party's leadership at a special conference in September 1993 and reflected pragmatism, as much as principle. As we have seen, the women's section was scarcely operating, and the party leadership was embarrassed by its all-male presence at Westminster (which, incidentally, it still has) and its few visible women politicians elsewhere. The commission made recommendations under five headings – policies, presentation, resources, elections and monitoring/review. There was some scepticism about its likely impact (two members of the eight-person commission claimed it largely reiterated what the party already knew, in terms of improving procedures for ensuring better equality and presenting more equitable images). Nonetheless, its wide-ranging report outlined various ways of redressing the imbalance between the sexes in Plaid Cymru's structures and elected representatives; in this way, it added legitimacy to the criticisms of internal discrimination against women members and to the calls for further positive action. Some also felt that it had prompted the party to take the issue far more seriously, with the leadership committed to at least some improvement, even if the motivation was largely pragmatic. This was later reinforced by women candidates for the Assembly elections, who claimed Plaid's commitment to equal opportunities was based on trying to be 'seen to be better than the other parties'. It is certainly true that Plaid has traditionally enjoyed adopting the halo of radicalism, seeing it as a way of setting itself apart from an increasingly moderate Labour party and further distinguishing itself from an essentially symbiotic relationship with its electoral opponent (see McAllister, 1995, 2001a). However, as we have seen, Labour's adoption of the radical and expansive policy of 'twinning' challenged Plaid's self-image, for the policy was a more radical and far-reaching one than the party had seen fit to introduce itself.

The 1990s saw the role of the women's section decline dramatically. From a central and powerful role within the internal equality debates of the 1980s, one leading member described the section as 'virtually defunct' in 1999. It maintained its representation on the party's executive but met irregularly, with low-key agendas and generally poor attendances. This is significant for, at a time when Plaid's representation of women in elected tiers was at its highest level ever, the party's women's section was relatively inactive. The virtually moribund status of the section has been acknowledged as a potential problem: one female member observed: 'women are just not coming forward: that might well be because there is no women's section to fulfil the training and preparatory function'.

What had caused these shifts in the status and authority of the women's section? Basically, there was a feeling within the section itself that it had 'run out of ideas', having tried most options for positive action and mainstreaming equality, without sustainable success. It was also a case of high expectations having been shattered by the sudden abandonment of the first positive action measures.

It is fair to say that Plaid has since suffered from the decline in the 'ginger-group' role of the women's section, that is, in setting a radical agenda for mainstreaming equality, towards which the party might then make gradual, incremental progress. More importantly, without an ultimate goal or ambition, it was harder to push for staged, 'add-on' improvements in the position of women. We will return to this issue of pursuing positive action and main-streaming strategies simultaneously.

The Welsh Liberal Democrats
Whilst there is no separate women's organization as such within the Welsh Liberal Democrats, at a UK level there is a functioning women's section, 'Women Liberal Democrats'. This describes its role

as a supportive organization which aims to:

- Lobby for better representation within the party;
- Organise seminars, fringe meetings and workshops;

- Campaign on issues which affect women's lives;
- Encourage women to become and remain active members of the party.;
- Ensure high quality Liberal Democrat candidates locally, nationally and internationally;
- Provide training to develop political expertise, at all levels.[13]

The Welsh Conservative Party

There has been limited separate organization in the Welsh Conservative Party, based, one assumes, on a lack of enthusiasm for all forms of positive action. The Welsh party does now have a women's organization, called 'Conservative Women in Wales', which is estimated to have around 300 members, active on regional and constituency committees. However, the independence of this organization would appear limited, and there is no real indication that measures to improve the numbers of Conservative women AMs are under way. This is despite the gains made by the other parties, and thus challenges theories of party 'contagion'.

WOMEN IN THE SECOND ASSEMBLY ELECTIONS

After the second elections in May 2003, exactly half of the sixty AMs were women. Women comprised 63 per cent of Labour AMs, 50 per cent of both the Plaid Cymru and Liberal Democrat groups and 18 per cent of Conservative AMs. Women AMs represented 55 per cent of constituency seats and 40 per cent of the regional list seats. In these elections, once more, only two of the four main parties used formal positive mechanisms for promoting women.

Welsh Labour was the first political party to use the new enabling legislation passed by the Westminster government permitting all-women shortlists. These were used in six constituency seats (Russell et al., 2002). The *Western Mail* newspaper had predicted that the party's decision to extend positive action discrimination in candidate selections for the 2003 elections meant,

> that three selections in a group of constituencies that comprise three Assembly seats where sitting AMs are retiring and the Party's five most winnable seats must now be from all-women shortlists. Conwy and Islwyn are two other seats Labour hopes to reclaim from Plaid Cymru, they selected women candidates. A further six constituencies are using women-only shortlists, meaning if Labour does well at the poll, as many as 19 female Labour AMs could take up seats in Cardiff Bay.[14]

Women were also selected to fight four key marginal constituencies without resort to specific 'add-on' measures. Replicating some of the arguments over twinning in 1999, all-women shortlists engendered enormous controversy, causing considerable discontent amongst constituency activists, who felt their autonomy over candidate selection was being compromised. It is significant that only one of the constituencies that used all-women shortlists volunteered to do so.

Other research has highlighted cases of both existing female AMs and new female candidates experiencing antagonism, dirty tricks and obstruction by disgruntled local members (Edwards and Chapman, 2003). The relatively young profile of sitting women AMs on the constituency ballot, helped by their incumbent status, challenges our vulnerability arguments somewhat, as it shows the potential for sustaining levels of women's representation, in the right circumstances. Interestingly, it is the first-past-the-post part of the ballot that has offered the best incumbency protection for Labour's women AMs.

Plaid Cymru's approach to the 2003 elections was slightly different to that of 1999. With incumbent men contesting seven of the nine first-past-the-post seats that the party was defending from 1999, it was the allocation of the regional list positions that was always to be critical. In 2002, the party's chair and Ceredigion AM, Elin Jones, had stressed:

> Plaid Cymru is keen to maintain and increase women representation in the National Assembly and to build on our party's achievements in the 1999 elections. It is important that we do not slide back in relation to the number of female candidates and potential members that we have in the Assembly.[15]

The party's National Executive duly considered four different options to promote equal representation of women, the most radical reserving the top *two* positions for women on each of the regional lists. Other options included the same system that had seen four women elected via the lists in 1999, with women allocated the top position in each. Other options included open lists, with no guaranteed places for either sex; another suggested considering the nature of each separate regional list in tandem with the predicted first-past-the-post results for that area. The latter proposal would, of course, have resulted in inconsistencies between regions, with some safeguarding the top position for women and others operating a more open process. The party's executive finally decided to use the same system of list-zipping as it had in 1999, whilst also permitting local parties to go further in some regions and promote women in the top two positions. This meant that in two regions – North Wales, and Mid and West Wales – women took both first and second position on the list. This was based on a decision to allocate the first two slots to women in regions where the woman in the top list slot was also fighting a winnable first-past-the-post seat. In regions like South Wales Central and South Wales East – where the sitting AM, Pauline Jarman, stood down and Jocelyn Davies did not contest a first-past-the-post seat – this left the second slot on the list open to a man or a woman. This marked a departure from 1999, when men were automatically allocated the second place, with women third, in the characteristic manner of 'zipping'. Ultimately, Plaid fielded thirty-four male candidates and only six female in the constituency ballot. On the regional lists, it fielded thirteen women candidates. The elections saw one woman AM elected from the constituency ballot and five from the regional lists.

Whilst still rejecting formal positive action mechanisms like zipping (which the party in England had employed for the 1999 European elections), the Welsh Liberal Democrats took a slightly more proactive stance towards candidate selection in 2003. This came via better enforcement of the shortlist rule, whereby all candidate shortlists had to include at least one woman and one man. Confusingly, the party stated that 'at least one-third of seats in any list will be made up of either sex'. However, there was no sex promotion at the final stage of selection. The party's candidate committee operated an informal rule of thumb to try to ensure a gender balance on both constituency shortlists and regional lists, with committee members re-advertising candidate selections, and targeting and directly encouraging new candidates to come forward where there was a shortfall of either female or male candidates (Mackay, 2003). The Welsh Liberal Democrats fielded twenty-seven male and thirteen female candidates in the constituency ballot and only six women in the lists. However, women topped three of the five regional lists in 2003. As in 1999, the party returned 50 per cent of women AMs, although, this time, it is fair to say slightly more by design than chance.

Despite having no women AMs in the first Assembly, the Welsh Conservatives operated no formal measures to promote women candidates in 2003. There were loud complaints from some leading Conservative women, spurred on, no doubt, by the profile of women AMs representing the other parties. North Wales women's chairman [sic] Felicity Elphick criticized the party's constituency selections, which saw just seven women chosen and none in winnable seats for the Conservatives: 'People like me see there's no point in putting their names forward because they know there's no chance of getting a seat that's remotely winnable ... There's a feeling that the party want women but just as token candidates.'[16] There was only one Conservative constituency AM – David Davies in Monmouth – and the party's best chance of gains came via the list, thus offering the best opportunities for women to be elected, too. The Welsh Conservatives selected eight women to contest the constituency ballot and eight on the regional lists. However, there was no systematic or consistent promotion of women candidates on the lists, which meant women had to compete straightforwardly with men. There was added competition, as the lists were the Conservatives' best hope of electoral success for *all* its candidates, men and women. An examination of the party lists shows that women were generally placed towards the upper middle of most lists. The party performed better than expected in the regional ballot, thus bringing its first two female AMs, meaning women comprised 18 per cent of the party group.

ANALYSIS OF THE CHANGES AND THEIR SUSTAINABILITY

In assessing the robustness of the changes in women's representation and the contribution of the political parties to this, it is useful to return to our equality framework. Much work to date has concentrated on attempts to explain institutionalized sexism in employment selection and recruitment procedures more generally (Jewson and Mason, 1986; Cockburn, 1989; Rees, 1999c), although insights related to political recruitment and selection can be drawn from these. More relevant is Campbell and Lovenduski's exploration of the rather odd combination of 'fast track' and 'incremental' strategies for equality in the UK. They have developed a three-pronged framework for equality strategies: 'equality rhetoric' or 'public acceptance of claims for representation'; 'equality promotion', which 'attempts to bring those who are currently under-represented into political competition'; and 'equality guarantees' that 'require an increase in the number or proportion of particular types of candidates' (Campbell and Lovenduski, 2005).

There are acknowledged to be two principal strategies to promote gender equality and to overcome institutionalized sexism:

- *add-on:* various specific, often detailed, policies that offer extra support for or promote disadvantaged groups, like women;
- *build-in:* policies that incorporate or mainstream equality of opportunity by 'integrating equality into all policies, programmes and actions, from the earliest stages of their formulation to their implementation and review' (Rees, 1999c: 165; see also Edwards and McAllister, 2002).

The two principal areas of add-on strategies, liberal and radical, are often confused (Jewson and Mason, 1986). The former provides only for equality of *treatment*, whereas the latter seeks to ensure equality of *outcome* (and, as such, is not legally enforceable in the UK). Cockburn (1989) has observed that both types of add-on approaches provide some assistance, usually in the form of positive action, to the relevant person or group, but can do little to change the discriminatory procedures, policies or practices that disadvantage these groups in the first place. In the political arena, add-on strategies mask the hidden biases that have historically privileged certain groups. As such, strategies can deal with the symptoms of disadvantage, so women are trained to compete with men for selection as candidates for party or external office, the essential characteristics of the job having originated in male-defined norms. Positive action in terms of political representation may include all-women shortlists for election candidates, as well as the twinning and list-prioritization strategies. Unlike positive discrimination, 'positive action stops short of tampering with the decision-making process itself [and] selection for posts remains based on individual attainment or technical

qualification' (Jewson and Mason, 1986). It is concerned with equality of opportunity in the stages leading to elections, rather than within the due processes of
the election itself.

Meanwhile, build-in strategies focus on discriminatory practices, rather than
on their recipients – the disadvantaged individuals or groups. Such strategies aim
to mainstream equality by challenging existing cultural, social and political
norms, such as assumptions that women are better suited to childcare and
domestic labour, whilst men are better politicians and managers, and has been
labelled 'a paradigm-shift in thinking' (Rees, 1999c: 4). In this way, promotional
activities become integral to the political and policy process, rather than simply
dwelling on distinctive elements of current representations. In the political
context, build-in strategies uncover hidden biases that benefit the existing elite,
such as public perception of politicians, the structure of selection conferences,
sitting hours for political bodies, evening and weekend party meetings, whilst
also challenging the assumptions of add-on strategies that women need training
to compete equally with men. In focusing on the commonality of experiences to
challenge these accepted norms, build-in strategies, largely based on mainstreaming equality and managing diversity, also emphasize the differences
between women; that is, they avoid treating women as a homogeneous group.
The build-in approach focuses on discriminatory or non-gender neutral practices,
rather than on disadvantaged groups. It also clarifies the distinction between institutionalized (unconscious) discrimination and personal (conscious) prejudices.

Macpherson's definition of institutionalized racism can equally be applied to
sexism, in order to demonstrate how organizations like political parties fail to
consider how their policies and practices (or processes, attitudes and behaviour)
discriminate against women:

> The collective failure of an organisation to provide an appropriate and professional
> service to people because of their colour, culture or ethnic origin. It can be seen or
> detected in the processes, attitudes and behaviour which amount to discrimination
> through unwitting prejudice, ignorance, thoughtlessness and racist stereotyping
> which disadvantage minority ethnic people. (Macpherson, 1999)

Whilst it can take both anticipatory and participatory forms (McCrudden, 1996),
it is fair to say that a mainstreaming approach applies most effectively to new
contexts (it would be unrealistic, for example, to rebuild all public buildings to
ensure full accessibility). This underlines a synergy between the two approaches,
as some add-on actions are necessary to rectify institutionalized discrimin-
ations, whilst simultaneously working towards mainstreaming equality for all.
In light of devolution's 'blank slate', it is likely that both build-in and add-on
measures are necessary to sustain and develop better representation for women.
Without robust, build-in measures to tackle the institutionalized sexism within
their structures, it is unlikely political parties will be able to achieve genuine and
sustainable equality for women, whatever course of add-on action they take now

or in the future. This conceptual framework adds another layer of analysis to this examination of women and the political parties.

CONCLUSIONS

The advent of the National Assembly in 1999 presented immeasurable new opportunities for promoting women in the political parties. In Scotland, public debates on wider representation for women in the Scottish Parliament had begun with the Constitutional Convention in 1991 and developed considerable momentum by the advent of the Parliament. In Wales, the likelihood of an elected Assembly remained uncertain until the narrow victory in the 1997 referendum. This left very little time to debate either electoral procedures or systemic opportunities for promoting women (see chapter 2). Yet, whilst there was no equivalent to the Scottish Constitutional Convention, debates around Welsh devolution had at least incorporated an equal opportunities agenda, set within the broad lexicon of more inclusive and participatory politics. However, this was conducted at a loose, overarching level, rather than one specifically related or conducive to women's enhanced involvement. This engendered a top-down, rather than a bottom-up approach, meaning the framework for women's participation has been statutory, rather than voluntary.

Although the much higher proportion of women politicians post-devolution – especially in the two largest parties, Labour and Plaid Cymru – is a major step forward, it is based less on systemic and secure processes, or on definitive cultural changes, than it is on the pressure of short-term campaigns by women in the parties themselves. Whilst some parties took advantage of the unique opportunity provided by devolution and a more proportional electoral system to promote women candidates, others did not. Labour and Plaid selected different positive measures to help ensure women featured prominently within their eventual Assembly groups, albeit with differing levels of success. These measures brought immediate and visible improvement in the representation of women in both cases. However, the reality is that the two parties have faced serious struggles both to sustain and to develop further positive action. We offer a number of reasons for this.

First, continuing arguments within the political parties as to the merit and legitimacy of positive action measures underline their essential fragility. Criticisms still focus on the issue of merit versus systemic or institutionalized discrimination, that is, that both women and men should be selected as candidates purely on merit. It is claimed that any mechanisms used to promote women undermine a meritocracy in candidate selection. Yet, as the Fawcett Society reported, the problem is not that women cannot win on merit alone; discrimination means 'women are rarely given the opportunity to try' (Fawcett Society, no date: 2). This is often because definitions of a 'meritocracy' use male-favouring criteria. It seems that equality and merit have been seen, not as complementary, but as contradictory.

Secondly, there are fears of, and actual evidence of, a backlash from party members – male and female – to positive action, largely because of scarce resources, particularly in the form of winnable seats. This continues to influence debate and decisions on improving representation of all under-represented groups – in smaller parties even more than in larger ones.

Thirdly, there are issues of vulnerability and the danger of complacency or lack of will to sustain positive action for further election candidate selection (in the case of Westminster general elections, the 2005 election saw an overall reduction in the 119 women MPs elected in 1997, albeit with the largest ever number from Wales, although the lion's share of these came from Labour's controversial use of all-women shortlists. Nevertheless, improvements in the number of Labour women MPs elected are impressive at an election where the party lost seats).

This chapter has examined women in the political parties, tracing the background to the various measures adopted by some to promote women politicians. We have identified obstacles that continue to restrain women. Given the constraints on access to internal and external power in the parties, women have traditionally been forced to organize separately to overcome structural obstacles. Separate organizations for women have thus become institutionalized within most political parties, and offer a crucial support function in the face of discrimination within the processes, attitudes and behaviours of parties. However, despite their value, separate women's sections, particularly in Labour and Plaid Cymru, have been only partially successful in promoting women as candidates and representatives. In both parties, most internal procedures and practices continue to be designed for the dominant group (the scheduling and location of meetings, perceptions of appropriate political behaviour, and the selection of election candidates). This means that, if women's sections, councils and conferences are merely add-on positive actions to educate 'deficit women' into traditional politics, then such actions, whilst enabling some women to achieve status within their parties, also serve to reinforce male-defined styles of politics as normal.

We have also seen evidence here of the symbiotic relationship that exists between parties, Labour and Plaid Cymru in particular (McAllister, 2001a). This is validated in an examination of the treatment of gender issues within the two parties. It also further reinforces the importance of the concept of 'contagion' in influencing rival parties' engagement with women's representation (see Matland and Studlar, 1996). Most significantly, they have adopted formal and informal measures, such as the organization of women's committees or sections, and positive measures in candidate selection, on the assumption that, once women are elected to positions of power, they will demonstrate their ability to perform equally with men. There has been little acknowledgement that positive actions should not be time-limited to prevent a boom-and-bust approach to equality. Such measures usually form part of the solution, as they leave institutionalized sexism untouched, of which there remains firm evidence across the parties.

It is a further irony that, whilst AMs are taking seriously the mainstreaming of equality at every level of the policy-making process in the Assembly, their parties are less enthusiastic about taking a similarly formal approach to mainstreaming gender equality within their own parties. Without additional formal protection or longer-term commitments by the parties, there are inevitable dangers to the security of equal representation actions pursued to date. We would dispute the claim, after the 1999 elections, from one prominent woman Labour minister that 'twinning' would not be necessary again, since the objective of equality had been achieved and its impact on the culture of the institution was likely to be permanent.[17] The mechanisms discussed here are essentially fragile strategies, and almost entirely dependent on goodwill and the support of leadership and members for their continuance. Their vulnerability is, in part, due to their implementation as top-down strategies, rather than organic bottom-up ones planned after prolonged and rational discussion (for which there is more evidence in Scotland, where there is a lasting consensus on women's representation amongst political elites with respect to the Scottish parliamentary level, at least).[18] If either elite or membership withdraws goodwill at any stage, such strategies become almost impossible to implement.[19]

Women politicians have enjoyed a vastly enhanced profile in Wales since 1999. Clearly, incumbency, public awareness and familiarity all help root and protect women's position. However, we suggest there is a greater degree of fragility in women's status in the Welsh political parties than elsewhere. This is largely based on a failure to mainstream equal representation in a way that would prove difficult to challenge or undermine. Gill's research suggested that women's involvement in the establishment and formulation of the National Assembly and the Scottish Parliament ensured that both conducted business in considerably more flexible ways than Westminster, which encouraged and enabled women to take a larger role. Yet, Gill also pointed to hostility towards women in both institutions and evidence of negative reporting of women politicians by the media (Gill, 1999). For equality to be entrenched inside and outside the political parties, it will need to be embedded in cultural change, rather than in temporary alterations to party rules.

Next, we examine women and the ballot box, specifically the dynamics of women's distinctive electoral behaviours and attitudes, and how these differ from those of men. This is important, for proof of differentials between women and men in the electoral arena might further spur parties to advance descriptive *and* substantive representation.

5

Women and the Ballot Box

This chapter looks at women's political behaviour in relation to devolution. Specific attention is focused on: voting patterns, party identification, interest in politics, attitudes towards political parties, constitutional preferences, and opinions on public policy issues. As the following discussion will reveal, the party manifestos for the first two Assembly elections in 1999 and 2003 evidenced a determination to influence women's political behaviour. For example, they referred to: 'promoting equal opportunities and participation by women'; 'specific support to women ... entrepreneurs'; 'introduc[ing] a range of "family-friendly" policies'; 'promot[ing] women in sport at all levels'; and 'invest[ing] additional resources in tackling domestic violence'. Against this limited background of electoral competition around gender equality issues, we explore whether post-devolution electoral politics is characterized by gender differences in political behaviour, and whether voting patterns are shaped by gendered responses to political factors, such as party ideology and party leadership style, as well as by intra- and inter-gender differences based on ascriptive and non-ascriptive characteristics, such as language, age, class and national identity. Accordingly, we first examine women's political behaviour in the Assembly elections by exploring attitudes to politics and policy, as well as towards constitutional and governance arrangements for Wales. Subsequent attention is then placed on the main parties' Assembly election manifestos and the manner in which gender equality was an arena of electoral competition, as parties attempted to engage women voters through targeted policies and programmes.

The impact of gender on electoral behaviour, including voting patterns and turnout, is often overlooked, since any differential gender dimensions can be difficult to decipher once electoral behaviour is aggregated, as occurs in most studies. Having said that, most research suggests that there are more similarities than differences between men and women, with more significant differentials being generated by the merger of gender with age. This suggests that women's political priorities (and hence, their electoral behaviour) change incrementally as they age and this affects their views on many areas of public policy, such as health, child care, education, social policy and pensions. There are also suggestions that women differ most in terms of the weight they give to political issues, rather than their position on them, with, for example, women more likely than men to prioritize health and education (Campbell, 2004). We explore here whether these conclusions can also be drawn in post-devolution Wales.

WOMEN'S POLITICAL BEHAVIOUR: ELECTION STUDY DATA 1999 AND 2003

Our discussion is based upon analysis[1] of two secondary data sources: the Welsh Assembly Election Study 1999 (WAES)[2] and the Welsh Assembly Election Study conducted as part of the Wales Life and Times Study 2003 (for a discussion of the technical aspects of these surveys, see Thomson, 2003).[3] These studies will be used to examine the perceptions, opinions and resulting voting patterns of female and male citizens at the time of the Assembly elections. Principal attention here is placed upon the data relating to the 2003 election, for these relate to women's (and men's) voting decisions, as informed by individuals' understanding and experience of the first term of directly elected devolution.[4] As such, they provide greater insight into voters' engagement with the new system of Welsh governance. Discussion of differences in attitudes and the voting behaviour of different groups of women (defined, for example, by age, social class, national identity or language) is shaped by two factors: tests of statistical significance (that is, a technical measure that tells whether emerging patterns in the data are more than coincidence); and, for the present purpose, the adequacy of the secondary data-sets (*inter alia*, that different sub-groupings were included in the coding of the original respondent data; that an adequate-sized sample was taken in order to allow meaningful inferences to be drawn from these data; and that appropriate questions formed part of the original research instruments).

Attitudes to politics and policy
The Election Study data underline the challenge facing the main political parties in attempting to overcome their former exclusive practices in order to engage women electors. In response to the question, 'how much interest do you generally have in what is going on in politics?' women expressed less overall interest than men. Just 5.4 per cent of female respondents, compared to 10.2 per cent of men, answered 'a great deal'; and 16.5 per cent responded 'quite a lot', compared to 22.3 per cent of men. In respect of the mode response, 29.9 per cent of women and 32.3 per cent of men said they had only 'some interest in politics'.[5] When asked the strength of their identification with a political party (Table 5.1),[6] just over a third (35 per cent) of women said that they had either a 'very strong' or 'fairly strong' identification with a political party, compared to 42.2 per cent of men. For both sexes, the highest proportions of those with no party identification were to be found amongst those aged eighteen to thirty-four.

Table 5.1 **Strength of identification with a political party:**
disaggregated by sex and age (*c*.2003).

	Age band (years)	No party identification	Very strong	Fairly strong	Not very strong	Don't know	Not answered	N
Female	18–24	28.6	10.2	12.2	46.9	0.0	2.0	49
	25–34	22.1	3.2	24.2	49.5	0.0	1.1	95
	35–44	16.5	6.3	24.4	52.0	0.0	0.8	127
	45–54	12.2	12.2	28.0	47.6	0.0	0.0	82
	55–59	10.9	8.7	30.4	47.8	0.0	2.2	46
	60–64	2.5	22.5	20.0	52.5	0.0	2.5	40
	65+	11.8	16.4	27.3	41.3	0.9	1.8	110
	All	15.9	10.4	24.6	48.0	0.2	1.3	549
Male	18–24	33.3	0.0	23.1	43.6	0.0	0.0	39
	25–34	25.0	2.6	28.9	43.4	0.0	0.0	76
	35–44	5.7	8.6	32.9	51.4	0.0	1.4	70
	45–54	7.6	16.5	30.4	44.3	1.3	0.0	79
	55–59	5.6	5.6	41.7	41.7	0.0	5.6	36
	60–64	2.4	14.6	24.4	58.5	0.0	0.0	41
	65+	6.8	21.6	34.1	34.1	0.0	3.4	88
	All	11.9	11.2	31.0	44.2	0.2	1.6	429

Note: Figures in percentages, to be read by rows. Each row displays the proportion of each age–grouping selecting respective answers (as set out in column headings).

In both Assembly elections, women showed a slightly greater propensity to vote than men. In 1999, 55.6 per cent of women voted, compared to 48.8 per cent of men.[7] In 2003, 49.6 per cent of women and 48.9 per cent of men voted.[8] The data also indicate that parties' attempts to engage women voters need to be tailored to different groups of women, for the Election Study findings show gender differences in political behaviour to be more pronounced along lines of age and language. For example, younger women aged eighteen to twenty-four and twenty-five to thirty-four were significantly more likely to vote than men of the same age (30.6 per cent, compared to 20 per cent, and 27.7 per cent, compared to 21.1 per cent, respectively).[9] In addition, Welsh-speaking women were more likely to vote than Welsh-speaking men (thus, they constituted 11.7 per cent of voters in 2003, compared to the 6.4 per cent made up of Welsh-speaking men).[10]

In both the 1999 election[11] and the 2003 election[12] there were statistically significant contrasts in women's and men's reasons for *not* voting (Table 5.2). Once again, the data underline the challenge faced by the parties in engaging women electors better and highlight the potential need for more flexible voting arrangements (such as web-based schemes, extended periods of polling, and the use of 'non-traditional' voting facilities, such as retail centres). Overall, when compared to men, women were more likely to say: that they were prevented from voting through 'lack of time/other commitments' (in 2003, 18 per cent of women,

Table 5.2 Cited reasons for not voting in the 1999 and 2003 National Assembly elections: by sex of respondent.

Reason for not voting	*Female*		*Male*	
	1999	*2003*	*1999*	*2003*
Deliberately abstained	6.9	0.4	8.9	0.5
Work prevented me	6.3	8.5	13.6	18.0
Away on election day	6.9	8.5	12.6	9.0
Other commitments/no time	12.7	18.0	7.8	12.6
Couldn't be bothered/not interested	20.2	27.0	18.8	19.8
Couldn't decide between parties/ candidates	3.5	8.9	0.5	7.2
Vote wouldn't have affected who won	0.6	0.0	4.2	0.9
Don't believe Welsh Assembly should have been created	5.2	2.8	6.8	4.5
Not eligible to vote	5.8	4.3	5.2	3.6
Other reason	31.9	21.6	21.6	23.9
N	173	282	191	222

Note: Figures in percentages; each discrete column (sex/year) summarizes the proportion selecting respective reason for not voting.

compared to 12.6 per cent of men); or that they were 'not interested/could not be bothered to vote' (in 2003, 27 per cent of women gave this response, compared to 19.8 per cent of men).

There are no statistically significant gender differences in respect of the parties for which electors voted.[13] Most women said that the reason why they voted for a given party in the constituency seats was simply because they felt it was 'the best party' (42.9 per cent). Traditional party allegiance was far more evident than tactical voting in explaining women's voting behaviour. Over a third said 'I always vote that way' (38 per cent), compared to just 4.5 per cent who said: 'I really preferred another party but it had no chance of winning in this constituency.' Unfortunately, the Election Study data provide no direct insight as to whether women electors were more inclined to vote because a women candidate was standing for election. Interestingly, however, given the battles over achieving gender balance amongst candidates in Assembly elections (see chapter 4), just 4.1 per cent of women respondents said that they 'voted for the candidate rather than party'. The data also suggest that only a minority of citizens' voting intentions were swayed by the parties' campaigning in the immediate lead-up to the Assembly elections.[14] Just 34.3 per cent of women and 27 per cent of men decided who they would vote for during the election campaign. Almost a half, 48 per cent of women and 53.6 per cent of men, reported that they had decided 'a long time ago'.

A gendered dimension to public policy emerges from the election data. Thus, for citizens who did vote, there were significant gender differences[15] in the responses given to the question: 'in deciding how to vote in the Welsh National Assembly election [2003], which issue mattered most to you?' Overall, and reflecting the design of the original survey instrument used to gather the data, the disparate nature of responses is a defining feature of these data. Nevertheless, when compared to men, marginally greater proportions of women decided how to vote based upon a concern with education, promoting the Welsh language, and 'local issues' (Table 5.3). This is important, for it further highlights the salience of women's substantive representation in post-devolution politics. That is, enhanced substantive representation may be achieved only through the wider institutionalization of women's distinctive political choices and their integration within the broader policy machinery.

Further contrasts exist in the basis on which women cast their vote in the Assembly elections.[16] The data reveal that domestic Welsh political issues determined the voting behaviour of the majority of women. Once again, this indicates the potential significance of the devolved policy agenda in shaping the voting behaviour. Just over a half of women respondents (50.5 per cent)[17] cast their vote 'mostly according to what was going on in Wales', and a further tenth (11.9 per cent)[18] based their vote equally on Welsh and British matters. Just a third (30.7 per cent) of women[19] voted 'mostly according to what was going on in Britain as a whole'.[20]

The salience of the devolved policy agenda to understanding gender differences in political behaviour was further evidenced by contrasting attitudes between women and men on a range of political issues. For example, in 1999, more women (12.6 per cent) than men (7.7 per cent) said that the Welsh or UK government should 'get rid of private education'.[21] In 2003, in respect of the public sector, women appeared to be more in tune with the putative 'clear red water' (see Morgan, 2002) between Welsh Labour and the Blair government's embracing of the private sector in the delivery of public services. Fewer women (22 per cent) than men (31.3 per cent) were in favour of the idea that 'semi-independent "foundation hospitals" be introduced into the NHS in Wales, as they have been in England'.[22] Significant gender differences also emerge in respect of how government should prioritize taxation and public spending. Fewer women than men said that the government should keep taxation and spending rates unchanged (31.8 per cent, compared to 38.3 per cent). Rather, more women (56.7 per cent) than men (51.3 per cent) said that the government should increase taxes and spend more on health, education and social benefits.[23]

Despite, as noted, the absence of significant gender differences in party support in the Assembly elections, interesting contrasts do emerge in respect of electors' preferred type of governing administration in the National Assembly. These findings suggest a nuanced and complex relationship between gender, party and

Table 5.3 Principal cited issue determining how individuals voted in the 2003 National Assembly election: by sex of respondent.

Most important issue determining vote	Female	Male
Education	13.0	9.0
Health/hospitals/NHS Wales	12.3	16.1
Immigration/asylum seekers	0.7	3.8
Law and order	1.4	1.4
Economy	0.4	3.8
Care of elderly	1.8	2.4
Against devolution in principle or practice	1.0	3.8
Welsh language	1.4	0.0
Local issues	2.9	2.4
Rural issues/farming	2.5	4.7
Don't know	6.5	5.2
Other[24]	56.1	47.4
N	211	277

Note: Figures in percentages.

preferred type of devolved executive. In 2003, a greater proportion of the women surveyed were supportive of having a coalition government (47.4 per cent, as opposed to 42.1 per cent), whereas more of the men supported single-party government (47.4 per cent, compared to 37.3 per cent).[25] With regard to party preferences for coalition government, more men backed the (then) prevailing arrangement of a Welsh Labour–Welsh Liberal Democrat alliance (59.4 per cent, compared to 51.3 per cent), whereas more women than men favoured a Welsh Labour–Plaid Cymru coalition (33.5 per cent, compared to 26.1 per cent).[26] This evidence also challenges one of the principal arguments against a PR voting system – that it is unpopular because it normally produces coalition government.

The election data also reveal subtle gender differences in attitudes towards the political parties. When respondents were asked how they 'felt about' the four main parties (see Table 5.4), fewer women than men said they were strongly in favour of the Welsh Conservatives,[27] and more women claimed to hold a disinterested viewpoint, saying that they were 'neither in favour [of] nor against' the Tories[28] (43.5 per cent, compared to 36.6 per cent), a pattern also replicated in the case of the Welsh Liberal Democrats (60.6 per cent, compared to 49.7 per cent).[29] Similarly, fewer women than men said that they were 'against' or 'strongly against' Plaid Cymru.[30] These findings suggest more subtle potential associations between gender and party ideology. This then becomes important to an understanding of gender and voting behaviour because, as Lovenduski asserts (2005: 59), 'political parties institutionalise ideas about politics that have gendered implications'. Whilst there is continuing and powerful resistance to gender

Table 5.4 Citizens' views of the political parties: by sex of respondent (*c*.2003).

How do you feel about the respective parties?	Welsh Labour[31]		Welsh Conservatives		Plaid Cymru[32]		Welsh Lib Dem	
	Female	*Male*	*Female*	*Male*	*Female*	*Male*	*Female*	*Male*
Strongly in favour	12.2	12.8	3.0	5.8	5.4	4.2	2.9	3.5
In favour	35.5	34.0	16.1	15.6	27.2	21.1	18.6	22.0
Neither in favour nor against	28.7	28.6	43.5	36.6	40.5	40.8	60.6	49.7
Against	14.9	14.7	22.4	22.6	16.5	20.6	12.9	17.6
Strongly against	8.1	8.6	14.2	17.9	7.2	8.4	2.7	5.1
Don't know	0.5	0.9	0.7	0.9	3.2	4.2	2.3	1.6
Not answered	0.0	0.5	0.0	0.5	0.0	0.7	0.0	0.5

N 557 (female), 430 (male)

Note: Figures in percentages, to be read in columns. Proportion of women and men respectively, selecting respective answers (left of table), grouped in relation to the four political parties.

equality by influential sections within all four political parties, across the political spectrum clear ideological differences operate between the right and left-of-centre parties. Broadly, these can be characterized on the left by the advocacy of egalitarianism, social reform and interventionist measures to further notions of 'social justice' (see Leach, 2002); in contrast, the right-of-centre Conservative and Unionist ideological position has been characterized as one seeking 'to protect the established social, political and economic order … [through] a set of dispositions that includes the rejection of the ideas of abstract rights and the effectiveness of social engineering' (Lovenduski, 2005: 59; see also Webb, 2000). The Election Study data point to the salience of party ideology in understanding gendered patterns of voting, yet the extant data are insufficient to offer a full understanding of such a relationship in the post-devolution context. What it does indicate is that attempts to garner 'the women's vote' might have to take on subtly different characteristics from general electioneering.

Gender differences are also apparent in respect of respondents' view of the potential competence of the various parties as governing administrations.[33] For example, when asked whether Plaid Cymru would 'be able to deal with all the day-to-day problems of running the government of Wales', more women than men thought the party would be as capable, or more capable, than the other parties (43.6 per cent, compared to 34.1 per cent).[34] Gender differences also extend to attitudes towards the leadership of the parties during the Assembly's first term. For example, more women than men were undecided about how they rated Welsh Labour leader (and First Minister) Rhodri Morgan,[35] whereas marginally more men than women gave Morgan a positive rating.[36] In turn, when asked 'how good or bad a job' they felt that the Plaid Cymru leader, Ieuan Wyn Jones, would do if he became First Minister, more women than men were, once again, undecided (43.4 per cent, compared to 33 per cent). Overall, marginally more women than men gave Wyn Jones a positive rating.[37] As noted, these differences suggest the emergence of post-devolution electoral politics that are characterized by subtle differences between the sexes in respect of political behaviour, in turn shaped by gendered responses to party ideology and leadership style. Whilst further research is required to gain a fuller understanding of these processes, their salience should not be underestimated in a devolved polity where, in two successive terms of the Assembly, the executive has struggled to achieve a working majority.

Attitudes towards constitutional and governance arrangements
In 2003, women were slightly more cautious than men in their assessment of whether, after four years of existence, the National Assembly had improved the way Britain as a whole was governed. The majority view was that, thus far, it had yet to make a difference, a statement supported by 64.1 per cent of women and 59.2 per cent of men.[38] One-fifth (20 per cent) of women thought that it had improved it a little (compared to 22.7 per cent of men). When age as well as gender is considered in relation to this question (Table 5.5), further significant differences emerge.[39] Amongst younger age-groups, a lower proportion of women than men said that devolution had improved the way that Britain as a whole was governed (for example, 22 per cent compared to 30 per cent of those aged eighteen to twenty-four; and 21.9 per cent compared to 34.3 per cent of those aged thirty-five to forty-four). Conversely, in the older age-bands, significantly higher proportions of men compared to women said that devolution had made governance in Britain worse (for example, 16.2 per cent compared to none of those aged fifty-five to fifty-nine). Self-defined national identity is also revealed as an important factor in explaining attitudes to devolution. The Election Study data show, for example, that a higher proportion of women identifying themselves as Welsh state that the advent of the Welsh Assembly has improved the governance of Britain (58.3 per cent, compared to 34.8 per cent of women non-Welsh identifiers).[40] A further significant difference to emerge from the findings was that a greater proportion of women (55.5 per cent) compared to men (47.7 per cent) said that the National Assembly gave Wales a stronger contemporary voice in the UK.[41] Overall, these findings provide further evidence of the more nuanced nature of women's political behaviour post-devolution and the way in which it is shaped by the individual's ascriptive and non-ascriptive characteristics, including gender, age, language and national identity.

The latter point is reinforced by responses to the question 'which government institution do you think ought to have most influence over the way Wales is run?' The majority of both sexes said that they felt that the National Assembly ought to exert most influence (54.9 per cent of women and 52 per cent of men). A minority, just over a fifth of women (22.4 per cent), said that Westminster should

Table 5.5 Gender/age split in respondents' answers to the question: 'Do you think that so far creating the Welsh National Assembly has improved the way Britain as a whole is governed, made it worse, or has it made no difference?' (c.2003).

	Age band (years)	Improved it a lot	Improved it a little	Made no difference	Made it a little worse	Made it a lot worse	Too early to tell	Don't know
Female	18–24	4.0	18.0	58.0	2.0	2.0	2.3	2.0
	25–34	1.1	25.3	60.0	7.4	1.1	1.2	1.1
	35–44	0.8	21.1	68.8	4.7	0.0	2.2	2.3
	45–54	3.6	15.7	68.7	4.8	1.2	0.0	1.2
	55–59	0.0	21.7	67.4	0.0	0.0	2.0	2.2
	60–64	2.4	17.1	70.7	4.9	4.9	2.0	0.0
	65+	7.3	18.2	62.0	7.3	3.6	19.0	1.8
N 412								
Male	18–24	7.5	22.5	57.5	5.0	5.0	0.0	0.0
	25–34	1.4	25.7	63.5	1.4	1.4	5.4	5.4
	35–44	0.0	34.3	52.9	7.1	0.0	1.4	1.4
	45–54	1.3	23.1	62.8	3.8	7.7	1.3	1.3
	55–59	5.4	18.9	54.1	8.1	8.1	0.0	0.0
	60–64	0.0	19.0	66.7	4.8	9.5	2.3	0.0
	65+	9.1	14.8	56.8	6.8	9.1	2.0	2.3
N 557								

Note: Figures in percentages, to be read by rows. Each row displays the proportion of each age-grouping selecting respective answers.

Table 5.6 Gender/age split in respondents' answers to the question: 'Which [government body] do you think ought to have most influence over the way Wales is run?'

Age band (years)	National Assembly	UK Government	Unitary authorities	European Union	Don't know
Female					
18–24	69.4	8.2	14.3	0.8	0.8
25–34	54.7	18.9	13.7	0.0	7.2
35–44	52.3	23.4	22.7	0.0	11.1
45–54	57.8	22.9	12.0	0.0	2.5
55–59	46.7	28.9	13.3	0.0	8.1
60–64	62.5	27.5	7.5	0.0	0.0
65+	49.5	25.2	16.2	0.9	4.6
N = 551					
Male					
18–24	42.5	30.0	20.0	0.0	7.5
25–34	57.9	25.0	11.8	2.6	2.6
35–44	57.1	32.9	7.1	0.0	2.9
45–54	39.7	46.2	12.8	0.0	0.0
55–59	50.0	33.3	11.1	5.6	0.0
60–64	69.0	16.7	7.1	7.1	0.0
65+	51.1	40.9	4.5	0.0	0.0
N = 439					

Note: Figures in percentages, to be read by rows. Each row displays the proportion of each age-grouping selecting respective government bodies.

have greatest influence, compared to over a third of men (33.6 per cent).[42] Again, further significant gender differences are apparent between different age-groups. Thus, in respect of the eighteen to twenty-four age-group, 69.4 per cent of women compared to 42.5 per cent of men said that they felt the National Assembly ought to have most influence over the way Wales is run (Table 5.6).

In addition, further contrasts are revealed when social class is factored into the analysis (Table 5.7). For example, fewer women than men in social class I[43] (2.6 per cent, compared to 9.1 per cent) and social class II (17.9 per cent, compared to 30.3 per cent) said that their preferred constitutional choice was independence for Wales within the European Union. In contrast, greater proportions of women than men in the unskilled occupational classes (IV and V) favoured greater autonomy for the country. Thus, for example, in class IV 23.1 per cent of women compared to 18.2 per cent of men said that they preferred Wales to be independent within the EU. Also, again in occupational class IV, 18.4 per cent of women compared to 9.5 per cent of men said that they favoured a Welsh parliament with primary law-making and tax-raising powers. With approximately a fifth of the residents of Wales born in England, self-defined national identity is once again shown to be important here. These data show, for example, that a significantly higher proportion of women identifying themselves as Welsh state that their constitutional preference is for increased levels of self-government. Thus, for example, 64 per cent of women Welsh-identifiers, compared to 51.8 per cent of women non-Welsh-identifiers, would prefer to see a Welsh parliament with primary law-making and tax-raising powers.[44]

When asked to project forward ten years to answer the question 'which government institution ought to exert most influence on the way that Wales is run?', proportionately more women (43.3 per cent) than men (39.5 per cent) felt that, in 2013, the National Assembly will have greatest influence. In contrast, a greater proportion of men (41.6 per cent) stated that Westminster will have most influence, compared to just over a third of women (33.6 per cent).[45] The answers to the foregoing question also reveal significant generational differences between the sexes (Table 5.8).[46] In all but two age-groupings, proportionately more women than men believed that, in ten years' time, the National Assembly will have most influence over the way Wales is run (for example, 47.2 per cent of women aged thirty-five to forty-four took this position compared to 35.7 per cent of men). In contrast, in the majority of age bands, higher proportions of men stated that they felt the UK government would exert greatest influence (for example, 48.1 per cent of male respondents aged forty-five to fifty-four compared to 36.8 per cent of women in the same age-band). Differences are also evident when this question is analysed by the gender and class of respondents (Table 5.9).[47] Greatest contrast emerges between the views of class III (manual) and class III (non-manual). In the former, a greater proportion of male manual workers (37.4 per cent, compared to 7.4 per cent of women) believed that, in ten years' time, the National

Table 5.7 Gender/class split: respondents' constitutional preferences for the way that Wales should be governed.[48]

Registrar General's social class	Independent outside EU[49]	Independent inside EU[50]	In UK, Welsh Parliament with law-making and tax-raising powers[51]	In UK, Welsh Assembly with limited law-making powers[52]	In UK, no assembly[53]
Female					
I	0.0	2.6	3.2	4.6	1.0
II	18.8	17.9	26.3	24.4	27.3
III (non-manual)	18.8	17.9	24.9	32.8	33.3
III (manual)	18.8	7.7	9.2	12.2	10.1
IV	15.6	23.1	18.4	9.9	9.1
V	3.1	5.1	1.8	3.8	5.1
N	32.0	39.0	217.0	16.0	99.0
Male					
I	3.4	9.1	2.9	6.7	5.9
II	10.3	30.3	27.7	24.2	35.3
III (non-manual)	6.9	3.0	21.2	8.3	7.8
III (manual)	27.6	39.4	34.3	41.7	31.4
IV	20.7	18.2	9.5	8.3	13.7
V	20.7	0.0	1.5	0.8	2.9
N	29.0	33.0	137.0	50.0	102.0

Note: Figure in percentages, to be read by rows. Each row displays the proportion of each age-grouping selecting respective answers (as set out in column headings).

Assembly will have most influence over the way Wales is run. Conversely, a higher percentage of women (32.1 per cent, compared to 11.7 per cent of men) in class III (non-manual) occupations foresaw the Assembly having the greatest influence.

Lastly, gender differences were also evident in the levels of trust placed in the different government institutions that influence the way Wales is governed. Thus, women were more sceptical than men as to whether the UK government could be trusted to work in Wales's long-term best interests. Over a quarter (25.1 per cent) of men thought the UK government could be trusted 'most of the time', compared to just 16.8 per cent of women. A majority of 57 per cent of women thought that the UK government could be trusted to work in Wales's long-term best interests only 'some of the time'.[54] When it came to trusting the Assembly, 5.1 per cent of men, compared to 9.5 per cent of women, said 'just about always'. However, little difference between the sexes was evident in respect of the mode response: 54.8 per cent of women and 52.7 per cent of men said the Assembly could be trusted 'most of the time'. National identity is also an influencing factor here, for a greater proportion of women identifying themselves as Welsh (as opposed to other self-stated national identities) said that they trusted the National Assembly to work in Wales's best interests 'most of the time' (61.2 per cent, compared to 47.7 per cent of 'other' national identifiers).

APPEALING TO WOMEN VOTERS? THE PARTY MANIFESTOS

In order to further understand women's political behaviour, we now examine the main parties' manifestos for the first two Assembly elections. These are the formal party statements of policy that underpinned election campaigning in 1999 and 2003 and, in turn, influenced women's (and men's) voting behaviour. Examination of these documents is appropriate, for they reflect internal party negotiations on political priorities, reveal the openness of parties to external concerns, and provide evidence of parties' attempts to engage different parts of the electorate. As such, they provide a good indication of the position of gender equality on the political agenda (see Pelizzo, 2003), and an indication of the complex interactions between feminist and other competing (or complementary) ideologies and political representation.

Initial reference to parallel developments in Scotland and Northern Ireland underlines the trend of electoral competition around gender equality associated with constitutional reform in the UK. Thus, in their manifesto for the 1999 Scottish Parliament elections, the Scottish Liberal Democrats asserted that: 'we will ensure that in all the workings of the Scottish Parliament (and Executive) . . . the principle of equal opportunities will be upheld'. The manifesto continued, 'we will: seek new powers over . . . equal opportunities' (SLDP, 1999). In their rival

Table 5.8 Gender/age split in respondents' answers to the question: 'In ten years' time, which [government body] do you think will have most influence over the way Wales is run?'

Age band (years)	National Assembly	UK Government	Unitary authorities	European Union	Don't know
Female					
18–24	42.9	32.7	6.1	14.3	10.2
25–34	43.6	36.2	4.3	11.4	8.5
35–44	47.2	36.2	2.4	8.2	5.5
45–54	45.1	36.6	3.7	7.4	11.0
55–59	31.1	44.4	0.0	8.7	6.7
60–64	45.0	17.5	5.0	3.7	22.5
65+	40.9	28.2	8.2	17.8	16.4
N 551					
Male					
18–24	37.5	50.0	2.5	0.0	10.0
25–34	48.0	33.3	2.7	12.0	4.0
35–44	35.7	41.4	4.3	12.9	5.7
45–54	40.3	48.1	3.9	3.9	3.9
55–59	42.1	28.9	2.6	21.1	5.3
60–64	42.9	40.5	0.0	14.3	2.4
65+	33.0	44.3	2.3	11.4	9.1
N 439					

Note: Figures in percentages, to be read by rows. Each row displays the proportion of each age-grouping selecting respective government bodies.

Table 5.9 Gender/class split in respondents' answers to the question: 'In ten years' time, which [government body] do you think will have most influence over the way Wales is run?'[55]

Registrar General's Social Class	National Assembly	UK Government	Unitary authorities	European Union	Don't know
Female					
I	3.7	3.2	4.2	0.0	1.7
II	25.9	22.3	20.8	28.9	15.3
III (non-manual)	32.1	21.8	29.2	33.3	18.6
III (manual)	7.4	11.2	4.2	13.3	16.9
IV	12.3	16.5	16.7	17.8	18.6
V	2.9	4.3	0.0	2.2	3.4
N 551					
Male					
I	3.5	7.3	7.7	2.2	8.3
II	23.4	25.7	30.8	39.1	50.0
III (non-manual)	11.7	13.4	15.4	6.5	4.2
III (manual)	37.4	35.8	38.5	34.8	16.7
IV	14.6	11.7	0.0	17.8	8.3
V	3.5	2.8	7.7	2.2	0.0
N 433					

Note: Figures in percentages, two sets of discrete columns (one for each sex). Proportion from each class selecting respective government bodies.

manifesto, the Scottish National Party (SNP) asserted that: 'the SNP will put equality at the heart of government' (SNP, 1999: 29). In turn, in its 2003 manifesto, Scottish Labour asserted: 'Labour will make sure that all our legislative, policy and resource decisions have equality at their heart' (SLP, 2003).

Similarly, equality was a core theme in Northern Ireland. For example, Sinn Féin's 1999 Assembly election manifesto asserted: 'our vision of the future is based on equality, [and] respect for difference ... a fair society where there is equality for all citizens [and where] all public sector spending in the Six Counties must be "equality proofed"' (Sinn Féin, 1999: 1–3). Likewise, in its manifesto, the Northern Ireland Women's Coalition referred to the fact that: 'the principles of equality and transparency and openness must apply to all budgetary decision-making ... clear equality targets [must apply] within the civil service [and] 'we ... call for an ongoing emphasis on policies designed to produce equality of opportunity and results' (NIWC, 1998: 6).

Equality also featured in three of the four main parties' manifestos for the first Welsh Assembly elections in 1999 (Figure 5.1). To varying degrees, these set out specific measures to promote gender (and other modes of) equality. Thus, the Welsh Labour manifesto asserted that:

> Labour is also determined to ensure that the National Assembly is a modern polit-ical institution. We will ensure it is committed to ... equal opportunities ... Labour has ensured that the National Assembly for Wales has a duty to apply the principle of equal opportunity to everyone, especially women (WLP, 1999: 3).

Plaid Cymru declared that: 'the Assembly has a crucial statutory responsibility to promote ... equal opportunities and ... th[is] require[s] action in all policy areas'. Amongst its specific commitments, the Plaid manifesto stated that: 'we will urge the National Assembly to ... offer specific support to women and ethnic minority entrepreneurs' (Plaid Cymru, 1999). In their manifesto, the Welsh Liberal Democrats aspired: 'to build and safeguard a fair, free and open society, in which we seek to balance the fundamental values of liberty, equality and community' (Welsh Liberal Democrats, 1999).

The evidence of the manifestos for the 2003 ballot illustrates an important side effect of devolution, namely the unprecedented way in which equality matters have become a core feature of electoral competition in Wales. Overall, the parties devoted more attention to equality matters in their 2003 manifestos, compared to those of the first Assembly elections. Most also moved beyond generalities to set out specific policy details (Figure 5.2). Indeed, Welsh Labour went as far as to issue a dedicated mini-manifesto on equalities (see WLP, 2003b). Of particular note in this context is the increasing prominence of equality in the policy programme of the Welsh Conservatives. Whereas the Tories' 1999 Assembly manifesto made only a single reference to the fact that: 'Welsh Conservatives believe in working for all of the people of Wales ... working for non-Welsh speakers and Welsh speakers – working for the elderly as well as the young –

Extracts from the Plaid Cymru 1999 election manifesto

'The Assembly has a crucial statutory responsibility to promote sustainable development and equal opportunities and both of these require action in all policy areas. The same applies to the vital national task of revitalising the Welsh language and creating a truly bilingual society.'

'... the future Assembly economic plan needs to co-ordinate a wide range of new and radical approaches. We have identified the following ... promoting equal opportunities and participation by women ... we will urge the National Assembly to ... offer specific support to women and ethnic minority entrepreneurs ... we will ... encourage a greater range of members of society to be represented in local council chambers – particularly younger people and women.'

Extracts from the Welsh Labour Party 1999 election manifesto

'Labour is also determined to ensure that the National Assembly is a modern political institution. We will ensure it is committed to ... equal opportunities – the National Assembly must be accessible to everyone, regardless of gender ... Labour has ensured that the National Assembly for Wales has a duty to apply the principle of equal opportunity to everyone, especially women. We have already applied that principle by fielding more women candidates for the Assembly than any other party... Under Labour the Assembly will ensure that combating discrimination on the grounds of race, disability or sexuality will have a high profile... Labour will continue to develop a national childcare strategy for Wales ... Labour has already set NHS Wales ambitious targets to improve the health of the nation. These include:

- a reduction of at least 30 per cent in the number of breast cancer deaths of women aged 50–74 by 2002 ... a reduction of at least 50 per cent in the incidence of cervical cancer by 2002.'

Extracts from the Welsh Liberal Democratic Party 1999 election manifesto

'Principles and values: The Liberal Democrats exist to build and safeguard a fair, free and open society, in which we seek to balance the fundamental values of liberty, equality and community and in which no one shall be enslaved by poverty, ignorance or conformity'; 'Disability rights: Liberal Democrats will: adopt policies promoting equal citizenship, accessibility, a culture of equality, equal learning opportunities and equal access for employment and grants.'

Extracts from the Welsh Conservative Party 1999 Welsh National Assembly election manifesto

'Welsh Conservatives believe in working for all of the people of Wales ... working for non-Welsh speakers and Welsh speakers – working for the elderly as well as the young – working for businessmen and women.'

Figure 5.1 Extracts on the promotion of equality from the
four main parties' 1999 Assembly election manifestos.

working for businessmen and women' (WCP, 1999: 7), in 2003 their manifesto contained a dedicated section entitled, 'A fairer Wales'. *Inter alia*, this asserted that:

the Government of Wales Act 1998 placed a duty on the National Assembly to further the principle of equality of opportunity. [...] The Welsh Conservative Party has worked assiduously on the Assembly's committee on equality of opportunity. In the Welsh Conservative Party we believe that the right to access services and be treated without discrimination is fundamental to human dignity. (WCP, 2003: 9)

The Tory manifesto proceeded to identify equality reforms, in areas such as public appointments, and equality training for AMs that the party would implement if it were to form a government. In turn, in its manifesto, Welsh Labour asserted that,

Labour has demonstrated the strongest commitment to equal opportunities ... In our second term we will press ahead with policies to promote equal opportunities for ethnic minorities, the disabled, gay and lesbian people and women, starting with the abolition of home care charges for disabled people.

Further specific policy commitments from Welsh Labour included the following statements:

- We will design a sports curriculum to increase participation from girls and promote women in sport at all levels.
- [We will promote] education for all, regardless of age or circumstance ... equality of opportunity ... will be our guiding principle.
- Securing a broader representation on public bodies from across the community particularly from ... women.
- Supporting those with caring responsibilities who wish to engage in employed work and encouraging women to set up their own businesses.

Similarly, Plaid Cymru asserted:

we are committed to the promotion of equal opportunities. We will mainstream the promotion of equality across all aspects of government, including the work of ASPBs [Assembly-Sponsored Public Bodies], for which targets will be set and backed where necessary by appropriate sanctions. We will establish effective means of consulting traditionally excluded groups, ensuring that organisations seeking to represent those groups are accountable.

Plaid's manifesto proceeded to list specific policy promises. These included:

- the key priorities of our Labour Market Strategy will be: ensuring that the benefit of [economic] development policies reach disadvantaged areas and groups, including ethnic minorities, disabled people, and women.
- A Plaid Cymru government will further develop and support the Communities First initiative[56] ... People from ethnic minority and lesbian and bisexual people are often vulnerable, as are women and older people. Their needs merit particular attention.

It is difficult to ascertain whether these integrated manifesto equality commitments can be traced to the larger number of women AMs in all parties (bar the

Extracts from Plaid Cymru's 2003 election manifesto

'We are committed to the promotion of equal opportunities. We will mainstream the promotion of equality across all aspects of government, ... We will ensure that our economic policies will be geared to achieving greater equality ... the powers that we are advocating for a Welsh Parliament by 2007 include: powers for the promotion of equality and the enforcement of equality law, including the powers of the statutory equality commissions, with a view to establishing a single Equality Commission for Wales ... the key priorities of our Labour Market Strategy will be: ensuring that the benefit of development policies reach disadvantaged areas and groups, including ethnic minorities, disabled people, and women ... People from ethnic minority and lesbian and bisexual people are often vulnerable, as are women and older people. Their needs merit particular attention ... Violence in the Home We will also ensure that domestic violence is treated with the seriousness it deserves. We will provide resources to make it possible for vulnerable women and children to leave violent partners, find new homes and rebuild their lives ... Training programmes should aim to eliminate gender-based job segregation and contribute to the elimination of discrimination in the workplace.'

Extracts from the Welsh Labour Party 2003 election manifesto

'Equal Opportunities: Labour has demonstrated the strongest commitment to equal opportunities ... The Assembly cabinet is the only one in the world where women are in the majority, while Welsh Labour is the only party in the UK to take advantage of new legislation allowing women-only shortlists. As a party we have also ensured that black and Asian candidates are represented on all our regional lists. In our second term we will press ahead with policies to promote equal opportunities for ethnic minorities, the disabled, gay and lesbian people and women, starting with the abolition of home care charges for disabled people ... We will design a sports curriculum to increase participation from girls and promote women in sport at all levels ... We will boost childcare and long term provision to assist those looking after dependants. We will increase part time and job share opportunities ... And we will invest additional resources in tackling domestic violence.'

Extracts from the Welsh Liberal Democratic Party 2003 election manifesto

'Equal Opportunities: Welsh Liberal Democrats are committed to fighting discrimination in all its forms, whether it is racism, sexism, homophobia or discrimination against those with disabilities. Equal opportunities are essential to a liberal society in which people are enabled to fulfil their potential and make informed choices about their lives. Welsh Liberal Democrats will ... Develop comprehensive policies promoting equal citizenship, accessibility, a culture of equality, equal learning opportunities and equal access to employment opportunities, drawing upon existing best practice ... increase the numbers of affordable, accessible, quality childcare places in Wales, focused on the needs of children and families ... develop the "Close the Pay Gap" campaign, ensuring progress towards equal pay in the public sector in Wales and promoting the business case for equal pay in the private sector ... consider the diverse needs of men and women in providing public services.'

Extracts from the Welsh Conservative Party 2003 election manifesto

'The Government of Wales Act 1998 placed a duty on the National Assembly to further the principle of equality of opportunity. The Welsh Conservative Party has worked assiduously on the Assembly's committee on equality of opportunity. In the Welsh Conservative Party we believe that the right to access services and be treated without discrimination is fundamental to human dignity. We value the work of the Equal Opportunities Commission ... The Conservative Party has played a significant part in the transformation of social views that has occurred since the 1960s ... We celebrate the fact that in today's Wales other sources of discrimination are more readily acknowledged, including those on age, religious beliefs, and sexual orientation ... to promote the principle of equality of opportunity a Welsh Conservative administration would ... further develop the Equal Pay Campaign.'

Figure 5.2 Extracts on the promotion of equality from the
four main parties' 2003 Assembly election manifestos.

Welsh Conservatives), which would suggest evidence of substantive representation coming from the presence of a large number of women AMs. Alternatively, they might be attributed to more focused and bespoke election preparations and campaigning in the new devolved context, and a greater emphasis on organic or bottom-up manifesto development by at least three parties that had previously had to operate within a UK manifesto framework.

CONCLUSION

The evidence from both the Assembly Election Study data and election manifestos underlines the challenge faced by the political parties in overturning their long-standing exclusive practices and engaging more women electors. In addition, these data sources reveal an interesting development: the emergence of post-devolution electoral politics characterized by subtle differences in political behaviour of the sexes. This is seen in gendered responses to political factors, such as party-ideology and party leadership style – as well as electors' preferences for the way in which Wales is governed. In turn, this is further nuanced by intra- and inter-gender differences based on ascriptive and non-ascriptive characteristics, such as language, age, class and national identity. Importantly, such gender differences are apparent in respect of voters' attitudes to policy issues and the devolved policy agenda. This highlights the importance of the substantive representation of women, which, as subsequent discussion reveals (see chapters 6 and 8), is probabilistically linked to the presence of women elected representatives in the Assembly.

Having said this, it should be conceded that the extant data offer an incomplete picture. Further research is necessary to gain a fuller understanding of women's political behaviour post-devolution. In particular, future election surveys need to be constructed in a manner that facilitates such work and allows further analyses of gender differences in the political behaviour of electors. Data are needed that can, for example, be disaggregated by gender to focus on disabled people, or different ethnic or faith groups. As noted, the salience of gender differences in the political behaviour of citizens following devolution should not be underestimated. The first two terms of the National Assembly have witnessed an executive struggling to achieve a working majority in an electoral context where, as party manifestos attest, gender equality is increasing the subject of electoral competition; this points to the increased salience of the new levels of democratic accountability and political responsiveness afforded by elected devolution. Accordingly, as devolution develops and matures, it is likely that the parties will increasingly appreciate the significance of this new political context, in which women cast their vote in a manner informed by the extent to which their sex is marginalized or mainstreamed in the political and policy process.

6

The Gender Dynamics of the National Assembly

You are a bunch of white men and have a macho culture that requires you to debunk our new kind of democracy.[1]

The outcome of the 1999 Assembly election raised hopes that the direct, or 'descriptive', representation of women, who now comprised 42 per cent of the Assembly's total membership, would, in turn, translate into 'substantive' representation, whereby women's concerns and interests would be heard and taken into account in the policy-making process. Many also hoped that near gender-parity in the Assembly would result in a new style of politics, one distinct from the traditional male mode of politics at Westminster (see chapter 9). Whilst aspects of the institutional blueprint of the Assembly appeared to guarantee equality in its proceedings, it was not clear whether the prevailing hopes for a new, gender-equal phase of politics were well-founded. For example, it was uncertain as to exactly how the increased representation of women would impact both upon the political agenda and the nature of politicking. Here, the relationship between the descriptive and substantive representation of women in the Assembly has a wider resonance with the international literature on women's role in contemporary politics (see chapter 1). For example, according to Karam (1997 and 2002, unpaginated) there is a 'need to look beyond the often-asked question of how to increase the numbers of women in parliament, and move towards presenting examples and experiences of how women can impact on the political process while working through a parliamentary structure'. Similarly, Lovenduski (2002: 2) asserts that: 'the challenge to feminist political science is to produce empirical research that relates gender to political behaviour. This means disaggregating organisational processes into component acts to assess their masculine and feminine elements.' Overall, as Norris and Lovenduski (2001: 7) observe, 'while some studies suggest that women do make a distinct contribution to the policy agenda in legislatures, the evidence remains under debate'. Accordingly, this chapter engages with these issues through an examination of the gender dynamics of the Assembly's first term. Specifically, it explores the link between the descriptive and substantive representation of women in political debate. In so doing, it provides initial evidence of the extent to which women Assembly Members were able to: set and shape the political agenda; effect a qualitative change in parliamentary discourse; and meet general expectations that women would 'make a difference' to national politics in the wake of elected devolution.

THE GENDER DYNAMICS OF DEBATE

The present findings relate to the analytical framework advanced by Lovenduski (1997: 718). She states that in order to understand and demonstrate whether the presence of women representatives makes a difference to the substantive representation of women, research must determine three points: that there are distinctive women's perspectives and issues; that women parliamentarians share these perspectives and issue positions; and that women act decisively on the basis of these differences. Accordingly, the following discussion is based on analysis of the entire Official Record of the first term of the National Assembly, namely, the transcripts of the 327 plenary debates that took place between July 1999 and April 2003 (see Chaney, 2006a, 2006b).

In order to explore the gender dynamics of these debates, a series of topics was identified as being likely to reveal distinctive women's perspectives and issues. These topics were derived from existing equality research (for example, Pollack and Hafner-Burton, 2000; Beveridge et al., 2000a, 2000b; Breitenbach et al, 2002). The topics included domestic violence, childcare and equal pay for work of equal value by women and men. Using appropriate software,[2] the Official Record files were analysed to determine the extent to which women parliamentarians acted decisively in debate to promote gender equality in relation to these issues. The findings were recorded in a database that detailed all instances where these issues – or key terms – were referred to in debate.[3] Building on recent research in relation to Westminster (Childs and Withey, 2004), individuals' interventions in the Assembly debates were coded[4] as to whether they were deemed to be feminist, anti-feminist or neutral.[5] Earlier work (see Betts et al., 2001) suggested that the impact of the increased representation of women in the Assembly would not be restricted to these key terms, or to what might traditionally be regarded as 'women's issues'.[6] Rather, it concluded that women AMs would act to promote women's interests in political debate across the full range of policy issues. To test this, further examination was made of the nature, frequency and gender dynamics of political debate featuring the key terms 'equality', 'equal opportunities', and 'women'.[7]

Our purpose here is to develop an understanding of the propensity and manner in which female and male AMs participated in political debate on key equality topics. In turn, this will provide an insight into the connection between women's presence as AMs and the substantive representation of women in debate. In order to realize this aim, initial attention is focused on whether women AMs are more likely to engage in debate on gender equality issues. The role of ministerial interventions is then explored, as well as the actions of individual women 'equality champions' in advancing the substantive representation of women. Attention is also focused on the extent to which gendered, cross-party cooperation, or a putative 'sisterhood', may be seen to operate in Assembly discourse. Subsequently, we examine various qualitative aspects of the plenary debates studied. These include: the 'direction' of speakers' interventions (in other words, whether, as noted earlier, they are for, against or neutral in respect of gender equality); the breadth of policy areas covered by women AMs' interventions to promote gender equality; and whether women speakers draw upon their own direct, gendered life-experience to inform debate.

ARE WOMEN AMs MORE LIKELY TO INITIATE DEBATE ON GENDER EQUALITY ISSUES?

The gender-disaggregated incidence of key equality terms in political debate during the first term of the National Assembly reveals a significant difference between male and female AMs.[8] Women exhibit a greater propensity to engage in debate on 'women's issues', as well as on equality topics in general (Table 6.1). The sex split is most pronounced in respect of 'women's issues', where women made approximately two-thirds to three-quarters of all interventions using the key terms analysed. Less pronounced is the gender difference (below 5 percentage points) in respect of interventions identified by usage of the terms 'equality' and 'equal opportunities'. This can be explained as a likely function of the Assembly's statutory equality duty, which requires AMs of both sexes to promote equality for 'all persons' and in respect of all governmental functions (Chaney, 2004a).

As the latter finding suggests, the link between women's descriptive and substantive representation in political debate needs also to be viewed within the context of the Assembly's institutional and procedural framework. As

Table 6.1 **The incidence of key terms featuring in political debate recorded in the Official Record of the first term of the National Assembly for Wales 1999–2003.**

Debating term	*Female* *% all references to topic*	*Male* *% all references to topic*
Childcare	64.7	35.3
Domestic violence	70.2	29.8
Equal pay	68.0	32.0
'Women's issues'	77.8	22.2
Equality	52.2	47.8
All	59.8	40.2
N	532	358

Cowell-Meyers (2001: 61) explains: 'institutional constraints, norms, and pressures may operate to minimize the emphasis women legislators place on issues associated with women'. At the forefront of such institutional and procedural factors is interaction between governing and opposition parties. This follows because the relationship between the descriptive and substantive representation of women in political debate is not directly causal. Rather, it ultimately depends upon party-political aspects of power relations in a given legislative context, and thus the ability to secure outcomes. After all, as ministers in the Assembly Government were swift to assert, the responsibility for setting the post-devolution equality agenda is 'a matter for the executive'.[9] The fact that women comprised a (five to four) majority in the Assembly Government's Cabinet makes this aspect of the gender dynamics of Assembly plenary debates of further interest. As Table 6.2 illustrates,[10] women predominate in ministerial interventions in plenary debates on the key topics selected for the present analysis. Typically, they account for two-thirds to three-quarters of such interventions. This pattern underlines the key role of women ministers in advancing the substantive representation of women. The latter point was also identified in the findings of earlier analysis of the papers and minutes of the Cabinet meetings held during the Assembly's first term (Chaney, 2005: 123). This revealed how women ministers mainstreamed gender (and other strands) of equality into Cabinet policy-making and discussion in relation to, for example: funding for a Muslim women's centre,[11] policy initiatives to achieve equal pay for women,[12] promoting gender balance in public appointments,[13] and securing gender equality in the work of the Cabinet's Economic Research Advisory Panel.[14]

Initiating political debate on a given subject serves the principal function of innovation, or the introduction of new ideas into the formulation of public policy (see, for example, Fischer, 2003). Therefore, understanding of the link between the descriptive and substantive representation of women is further informed by AMs'

Table 6.2 Ministerial interventions in debate on key topics recorded in the Official Record of the first term of the National Assembly for Wales 1999–2003.

Debating term	Female % all ministerial interventions on topic	Male % all ministerial interventions on topic
Childcare	67.0	33.0
Domestic violence	76.5	23.5
Equal pay	77.3	22.7
'Women's issues'	77.4	22.6
Equality	60.5	39.5
All	66.2	33.8
N	198	101

Table 6.3 Gender split amongst those initiating political debate on key terms recorded in the Official Record of the plenary sessions of the first term of the National Assembly for Wales 1999–2003.

Debating term	Female % total each topic	Male % total each topic
Childcare	61.8	38.2
Domestic violence	74.2	25.8
Equal pay	65.4	34.6
'Women's issues'	77.8	22.2
Equality	51.1	48.9
All	59.5	40.5
N	308	210

role in initiating debate on gender equality issues and ensuring that such concerns remain the subject of Assembly plenary discussions. As Table 6.3 shows, during the Assembly's first term women had a significantly greater propensity to initiate debate on gender equality topics than men. Such cases comprised approximately two-thirds to three-quarters of all instances when such terms featured in plenary debate.[15] However, this pattern does not extend to debate identified by AMs' more general reference to 'equality' or 'equal opportunities'. Here, virtual parity exists between the sexes, with male AMs introducing debate on such topics in 49 per cent of all cases. Again, this pattern is likely to reflect the impact of the Assembly's statutory equality duty that, as noted, applies to both female and male AMs.

IS WOMEN'S SUBSTANTIVE REPRESENTATION DEPENDENT ON WOMEN 'EQUALITY CHAMPIONS'?

In respect of women's substantive representation, Dovi (2002) refers to the role of what she terms 'preferable descriptive representatives'. By this she means those individuals with greater awareness, skills and feminist conviction in pursuing gender equality. This is a key point. It suggests that it is not only the number of women elected representatives that is important to the substantive representation of women but also *who they are*. It is a perspective that prompts questions about the relative importance of 'equality champions' amongst the twenty-five women AMs; not least, whether such key individuals make dispro-portionately high levels of interventions to advance feminist and gender equality concerns.

The data in Table 6.4 show that when compared to male AMs, debate on women's issues is more 'mainstreamed' amongst women AMs. In other words, it involves greater 'dispersion of influence' – or the participation of a greater proportion of the total number of elected women representatives.[16] Overall, 67 per cent of all women AMs engaged in debate on the key terms analysed, compared to just 36.4 per cent of male AMs. However, interesting variations exist in the proportion of the female cohort of AMs engaging in debate on each of the respective gender equality issues studied. Approximately one-half participated in debate on domestic violence and equal pay, compared to over three-quarters in relation to childcare and other women's issues. A more modest difference (8.6 percentage points) is also evident in respect of the proportion of male and female cohorts referring to 'equality' in debate. When all references to equality and women's issues are combined, the gender difference remains pronounced, with 73.6 per cent of the female cohort of AMs engaging in debate on these topics, compared to 47.4 per cent of the male cohort.

Notwithstanding the engagement of between two-thirds and three-quarters of all women AMs in debate on 'women's issues', data on the total debating interventions made by the three most prolific debaters on each topic (Table 6.5) affirms the salience of preferable descriptive representatives – or equality champions – to an understanding of the gender dynamics of Assembly debates. Thus, the data show that a key role is played by individual women who intervene in debate much more frequently than most other female colleagues; these 'equality champions' account for between, approximately, a third and a half of all women AM's interventions.[17] This pattern is all the more striking, given that just 48 and 56 per cent of all women AMs spoke on the 'women's issues' of equal pay and domestic violence, making the overall contribution of such 'equality champions' particularly significant in relation to specific aspects of women's substantive representation.

Taken together, these data reveal marked patterns of polarization with regard to gender and political debate during the Assembly's first term: namely, *intergender polarization*, in that, when compared to male AMs, a higher proportion of

Table 6.4 Percentage of female and male parliamentarian cohorts engaging in debate on key topics recorded in the Official Record of the plenary sessions of the first term of the National Assembly for Wales 1999–2003.[18]

Debating topic	% of all elected women debating topic	% of all elected men debating topic
Childcare	80.0	54.4
Domestic violence	56.0	37.1
Equal pay	48.0	17.1
'Women's issues'	84.0	37.1
Equality	100.0	91.4
All	73.6	47.4
N	25.0	35.0

female AMs was likely to engage in debate on the issues studied; and *intra-gender polarization*. The latter was evident in respect of both sexes, and stemmed from the fact that a limited number of 'equality champions' made a disproportionately high number of interventions in debate in respect of the key equality terms examined. In sum, these findings emphasize the importance of having both high levels of descriptive representation *and* women equality champions in order to secure women's substantive representation. In the context of the Assembly, the presence of equality champions can be explained partly by some women AMs' former professional experience, for three of the most prolific debaters on each of the topics analysed held senior managerial posts with national gender equality organizations. In the case of male AMs, intra-gender polarization can be explained by allocated party roles in relation to equality topics. Thus, for example, the chair of the cross-party Working Group on Equal Pay dominated debate on this issue (making three-quarters of all references by male AMs).

Earlier work (see Betts et al., 2001) revealed that, during the initial months of the new Assembly, there were widely held hopes amongst women AMs for a future 'cross-party sisterhood'. This was an aspiration that feminist and gender equality matters would take precedence over party-political concerns, and that women AMs would unite across party lines in order to promote women's interests. In the wake of intense inter-party competition during the Assembly's first term, some women AMs revised their earlier views (see chapter 9). Yet the evidence of political debate reveals that the notion of a 'cross-party sisterhood' does constitute a minor, yet interesting, aspect of the link between descriptive and substantive representation (see Figure 6.1). Thirty-three examples of this phenomenon were identified in the Official Record of plenary debates.[19] However, the earlier study (Betts et al., 2001) also suggested that exclusive reference to plenary debates in the Assembly (with their frequently adversarial nature) was likely to

Table 6.5 Equality champions? Percentage of total debating interventions on key topics made by the three most prolific debaters on each topic.

	Female		Male	
Debating term	% all female contributions	% all contributions	% all male contributions	% all contributions
Childcare	40.7	26.3	44.8	15.8
Domestic violence	45.0	31.6	35.2	10.5
Equal pay	53.0	36.0	75.0	24.0
'Women's issues'	31.2	24.2	40.9	9.0
Equality	40.3	21.0	28.0	13.4
All	40.2	24.0	34.4	13.8
N	532	890	358	890

Jane Hutt (Welsh Labour): [speaking on promoting equality in public appointments] 'Our approach to this process represents a model for the public appointments process procedures in the future. We have shown how the National Assembly can be inclusive, imaginative and open, particularly in the involvement of children and young people.
Helen Mary Jones (Plaid Cymru): It was – as Jane Hutt said – a groundbreaking process. We must ensure that the National Assembly and the Government of Wales learns from that process and uses it again, not only with children and young people, but with many more users of services when we consider other public appointments. I strongly echo what Jane Hutt said about thanking the children and young people involved.'[20]

Helen Mary Jones: 'I second the Minister's thanks to Edwina Hart as the former [Equality] Committee Chair. She steered the Committee's work expertly. I am sure that we are all agreed on that. She was impartial and sincere, and her energy and commitment is a good example to the Assembly as to how we take forward the equality of opportunity agenda.'[21]

Helen Mary Jones: 'We have achieved broad cross-party support and often consensus on important issues and on approaches to government. We have enthusiastically embraced the Assembly's statutory duties to promote equality and sustainable development and have placed ending poverty at the top of our agenda ... There can be no doubt that the National Assembly has, at the very least, demonstrated that Wales has a distinctive political culture.'[22]

Janet Ryder (Plaid Cymru): 'The Minister for Finance, Local Government and Communities' [Edwina Hart] experience will be sadly missed by the Committee on Equality of Opportunity. I compliment her on her work in that Committee.
Edwina Hart (Welsh Labour): I thank you for your kind comments about my chairing of the Committee on Equality of Opportunity. I enjoyed my time on the Committee and I am delighted that we had such cross-party support for the work on equal opportunities across the Assembly, which I am sure will continue.'[23]

Edwina Hart: 'I enjoyed Helen Mary [Jones]'s contribution a great deal [she] raised some key issues about staff and childcare in the Assembly and Assembly-sponsored public bodies ... we must examine the invisibility of women in certain bodies and women's roles and functions. In some sectors, women are invisible.'[24]

Jane Hutt: 'Thank you for the supportive comments from across the Chamber. I thank Helen Mary Jones first for her supportive remarks. I am grateful for the opportunity to respond to some of the points that she and others have made on the appointment of the Children's Commissioner [for Wales].'[25]

Gwenda Thomas (Welsh Labour): 'Helen Mary Jones also spoke about hearing the voices of children and about childcare. I agree with her that there is a need to develop childcare, not only in the Assembly, but in many other public bodies. We need a change of attitude to ensure that this is achieved.'[26]

Helen Mary Jones: 'A spirit of partnership and co-working is not necessarily cosy and does not always mean that we agree with one another. I take Val [Feld]'s point that those of us who have worked together outside this Chamber and in another place ... want to continue in that spirit of co-operation and co-working.'[27]

**Figure 6.1 Selected examples of cross-party 'sisterhood'
in the Assembly's debates on equality issues.**

underestimate the prevalence of this phenomenon. This conclusion was supported by participant observation of the policy development work of the cross-party subject committees. This revealed a strong pattern of inter-party cooperation on gender equality issues (see Chaney and Fevre, 2002b). The latter point serves, once again, to highlight the salience of institutional factors in shaping 'gendered' deliberative practices and the substantive representation of women in post-devolution politics.[28]

QUALITATIVE ASPECTS OF DEBATE

Reflecting the legal equalities framework of the Assembly, as well as the oft-stated determination following constitutional reform to deliver a 'new politics' founded upon inclusiveness (see, for example, Davies, 1999), the overwhelming majority (84.2 per cent) of cases where reference was made to the key terms examined here comprised incidences when the speaker adopted a feminist or pro-equality debating position (see Table 6.6).

When these data are disaggregated, there is a significant difference between the sexes,[29] with female AMs being almost twice as likely to advance feminist and pro-equality interventions when compared to male colleagues (women made 64 per cent of all such interventions). The greatest difference was in respect of debate on women's issues, where women made 85.9 per cent of feminist inter-ventions, compared to just 14.1 per cent made by men. In addition, male AMs were more likely to make 'neutral' interventions[30] on the topics analysed (9.1 per cent of all interventions, compared to 5.4 per cent for women). Rare instances (six in total) of overtly anti-equality interventions in plenary debate came from three male members of the same political party (see Figure 6.2).[31]

Table 6.6 The incidence of feminist/pro-equality interventions in political debate around key terms recorded in the Official Record of the plenary sessions of the first term of the National Assembly for Wales 1999–2003.

Debating term	Female % all such interventions on topic	Male % all such interventions on topic
Childcare	67.6	32.4
Domestic violence	75.7	24.3
Equal pay	70.2	29.8
'Women's issues'	85.9	14.1
Equality	56.9	43.1
All	64.0	36.0
N	480.0	270.0

David Davies (Welsh Conservative): 'I am pleased to have the opportunity to express my grave concerns about one of the directions that the Assembly is taking, namely, its inappropriate slide towards political correctness... [namely] whether or not the aims and aspirations of organisations fit into a left-of-centre pattern of thought, which I refer to as political correctness ... We spent the whole afternoon debating a motion along the lines of "this Assembly notes that it is International Women's Day". We had all worked that out by then and I do not know why we had to spend the whole afternoon debating it. Many people were probably wondering why we were not discussing health, education, rising fuel taxes or any of the other matters that cause people concern ... Where is all this leading us? ... What are we best known for? We are best known for calling for family-friendly hours, finishing at 5:30 p.m ... I tell Members who disagree with me to go out into the streets and into the pubs and talk to people. You will not hear many people calling for family-friendly hours, supporting International Women's Day ... If this Assembly does not begin to listen to people and to allow views to be expressed, which do not necessarily fit in with the comfortable intellectual left-wing ideals of so many of its Members, it has no chance of success.

Val Feld: '... the culture of your group stems from the fact that you are a bunch of white men and have a macho culture that requires you to debunk our new kind of democracy.'[32]

Alun Cairns (Welsh Conservative): 'Do you agree that it is the obsession of some Assembly Members or individuals with political correctness that riles the vast majority of people? On a few occasions I have used the phrase "businessmen" ... I believe that "businessmen" is a generic phrase in the National Assembly. I have been corrected on its use. People's obsession with political correctness is detracting from the debate ... It is a generic phrase and the general public understands that. When people detract from the debate by making interventions to correct me and say that I should use the term "business people" that annoys the vast majority of people who would stand by many of your comments.'[33]

David Davies: 'Anyone who tries to pass constructive criticism of the burgeoning equality industry is usually accused of bigotry rather than engaged in constructive debate ... I am particularly concerned about two aspects of the report, which are typical of the politically correct agenda that is doing so much damage to our society. First, the Assembly is handing over taxpayers' money to facilitate the setting up and ongoing development of a body, which can represent the lesbian, gay and bisexual communities in Wales. I do not care what people do in the privacy of their bedrooms, but I do not see why we as taxpayers should be expected to fund other people's lifestyles.'[34]

David Davies: 'There is an NHS [Wales] equality unit that costs hundreds of thousands of pounds a year to run. What do these people do all day? Is there inequality in the NHS? I do not think that there is, particularly, but if there is, there are laws to deal with it. Yet these people get hundreds of thousands of pounds a year, and to do what? I do not know'.[35]

Nick Bourne (Welsh Conservatives): 'In terms of the running of the Assembly ... I am glad about the [proposed] relaxation of or flexibility on the family-friendly hours. It gives us some additional flexibility. I think that the people of Wales will welcome that because it shows that we are determined to make the Assembly work ...'[36]

Delyth Evans (Welsh Labour): I will speak on the recommendation to extend Plenary hours until 6 p.m., or sometimes until 7 p.m., on Tuesdays. I strongly oppose any change of this kind. This is an important point of principle for me and other Members, in the

Labour Party especially. We are trying to develop a system of modern, inclusive government that is suitable for the real world and the lives of normal people. The adoption of this change would send entirely the wrong message.

David Davies: Do you agree that we will send out a negative message if we are not ready to debate matters that are important to Wales?'[37]

Delyth Evans: 'Had you any idea of the difficulties of trying to balance work with family life in this place, you would not single out certain people as if they were odd, particularly Helen Mary Jones, who is a single parent. We ought to protect such people and make it easier for them to do this kind of work, not behave as you did. I suggest that you look to your own party and ask yourself why there are no female Members on your benches when you speak in favour of this kind of change.'[38]

Alun Cairns: 'I will not listen to any lectures from Val Feld on this. The reality is that she is always obsessed with one issue, equal opportunities. Rather than with regenerating the economy and distributing wealth, which would benefit the whole of the Welsh economy.'[39]

Figure 6.2 Selected examples of male AMs' resistance/ambivalence to equality reforms as recorded in Assembly proceedings.

Analysis of the Official Record of the Assembly's first term also provides evidence of women AMs drawing directly on gendered, personal experience in order to advance gender equality in debate. In all, and across the breadth of key terms explored, fifty-one such incidences were identified. These included interventions on the following topics: fighting a high-profile sex discrimination case against an employer;[40] setting up an organization to tackle domestic violence;[41] the challenges facing women working in agriculture;[42] mothers' struggle to obtain appropriate childcare facilities;[43] increasing the provision of information on parenting skills to new mothers;[44] the role of women business managers;[45] trade unions' attempts to tackle gender segregation in the public services,[46] and equality issues facing female schoolteachers and school governors.[47] This phenomenon of the deliberative effects of women's presence as elected representatives is further illustrated by the examples of debating interventions set out in Figure 6.3.

One woman Assembly Member captured the effect of such interventions, and summarized the difference that having 42 per cent women AMs had made to political debate, by highlighting an incontrovertible fact. She stated:

[W]ithout women taking part in decision-making, their views and needs are bound to be overlooked to a certain extent. It means that the life circumstances and perspective of 52 per cent of the population are inevitably ignored, played down or tackled inappropriately. This does not assume that all male politicians are chauvinist pigs ... It simply recognizes that one sex, however sympathetic, cannot fully and fairly represent the interests of the other.[48]

Childcare: 'I was director of *Chwarae Teg,* which was set up to expand the role of women in the Welsh work force. Lack of childcare was a major issue that we were tackling. I am also a working parent and a working politician ... I can assure you that it was wild on occasions trying to juggle home and family responsibilities with work ...'[49]

Social exclusion: 'Social exclusion leads to unequal education and occupational opportunities ... I can bear witness to that. For many years I worked with unemployed young people ...'[50]

Business: 'From my private sector background, I know the level of equal opportunities training that is undertaken to ensure that it is at the core of recruitment practices.'[51]

Education: 'My concern is that equal opportunities – I speak as someone who has served as a governor and a Chair of governors in a couple of schools – is often treated as simply an exercise in ticking boxes ... The issues are clear. There is much evidence of gender inequality in society.'[52]

Homelessness: 'We have to find ways of hearing what people need. I have spent many years of my life working with people who are homeless ...'[53]

Domestic violence: 'I helped to establish the first Women's Aid refuge in Wales over 25 years ago. It is sad that we have to discuss in the Chamber today the need for more support and funding for women who are subjected to violence.'[54]

Figure 6.3 The deliberative effects of women's presence as elected representatives: selected interventions made by women AMs as recorded in the Official Record.

Within the existing literature on women parliamentarians' legislative priorities some authors assert that:

> women are expected to be more concerned than men with women's rights, needs that affect children and families, and also related areas of concern, such as education, health care, social welfare, and the environment ... Conversely, women are expected to be less concerned with legislative areas that focus on topics related to traditional areas of interest to men, such as business. (Taylor-Robinson and Heath, 2003: 80)

The experience of the Assembly's first term reveals how such an assessment oversimplifies matters. The data from the plenary debates studied show that women's substantive representation, and the wider promotion of equality, is a matter that cross-cuts and informs a full range of policy areas.

There is broad parity between the sexes in respect of the range of policy areas in which AMs intervened in plenary debate to promote equality (Table 6.7). In contrast, key differences exist in respect of debate on women's issues. Here, women AMs advanced the substantive representation of women across a significantly broader range of policy areas than did their male colleagues (Table 6.8).

Table 6.7 Interventions in political debate to promote equality: by policy area.

Policy area	Male (N)	Female (N)
Agriculture	0	1
All (i.e. non-specific – the general promotion of equality in all policy areas)	98	102
Arts/culture	4	0
Asylum seekers	6	3
Carers	1	0
Children	5	4
Welsh language	10	15
Economic development	12	9
Education	31	26
Electoral process	2	1
Health	4	11
Housing	0	11
Local government/public sector	8	18
Policing	3	1
Procedural matters – government	8	7
Sport	4	7
Transport	3	5
Miscellaneous	32	42
N	231	263

Table 6.8 Interventions in political debate to promote interests of women: by policy area.

Policy area	Female (N)	Male (N)
Agriculture	2	1
Arts culture	0	1
Asylum seekers	1	0
Carers	1	0
Economic development	10	0
Education	3	2
Employment	4	4
Families	1	0
Health	22	6
Homelessness	2	0
Peace campaigners	1	0
Policing	3	0
Political participation	4	0
Political representation	4	0
Sport	10	4
Welfare	0	1
Women's rights	6	2
Miscellaneous	4	0
N	78	21

Val Feld: 'Point of order. This is in a similar vein, under Standing Order No. 7.8 (iv), on discourteous and unbecoming conduct. We have returned to this issue several times over recent weeks ... I ask you to take away and consider our statutory obligation to have due regard for equal opportunities in everything that we do, in relation to how this Chamber operates ... This afternoon was another occasion when there was a clear gender divide. Much heckling came from men in the opposition parties. I was sad to hear it also coming from men in my party. That is taking us down a road that is very much akin to Westminster-style politics.'[55]

Helen Mary Jones: 'Point of order. I am not sure whether this is additional. I request that both the Office of the Presiding Officer and the Business Secretary look at the impact on the Assembly's statutory duty to promote equality of opportunity of our regular habits of having our staff working way past 5.30 p.m. We might be subject to a judicial review because that is a breach of our statutory requirement to promote equality of opportunity.'[56]

Alun Cairns: '... the businessmen are the ones we want to be talking about – ...' [breaks off]

Ann Jones: 'Do you agree that we also have businesswomen in Wales and that we should be referring to both businessmen and businesswomen in the entrepreneurship debate?

Alun Cairns: You are absolutely right. Thank you for that comment.

Ann Jones: It was a telling off, not a comment.

Presiding Officer: Order. I support Ann.

Alun Cairns: Forgive me. When I say businessmen I am including businesswomen. [Later in the same debate ...

Alun Cairns: 'My experience from talking and dealing with businessmen – [Interruption.]

Jenny Randerson: What about businesswomen?

Alun Cairns: I apologise. My experience from talking with businessmen and women ...'[57]

Val Feld: 'I raise a point of order under Standing Order No. 7.8 (iv) and (v), relating to discourteous or unbecoming conduct, and disorderly, discriminatory or offensive language ... I also prefaced a question to Mike German with some political remarks about Margaret Thatcher and the Conservative years – we are, after all, a political institution – but, once again, I was shouted down, particularly by Members from the Conservative side of the Chamber ... I have no objection to debates in this Chamber on issues and differences between us, but I take strong exception to being shouted down in this fashion by Assembly Members no matter which party they are from. I asked you [*Llywydd*/Presiding Officer] two weeks ago whether this kind of conduct was conducive with our responsibilities to give due regard to equality of opportunity. You have not yet replied. I am not best placed to judge whether I am shouted down more than male members of my party who make similar remarks. I ask you to judge that, if you would.'[58]

Figure 6.4 Promoting gender equality: debating interventions by women AMs.

A further noticeable aspect of the plenaries held between July 1999 and April 2003 is the manner in which the Assembly's statutory equality duties both influenced and formed the subject of the political debate. This is evidenced by the fact that almost a fifth (18 per cent) of interventions on the topic of 'equality' or 'equal opportunities' cited the legislature's statutory duty to promote equality. Strikingly, in respect of the latter finding, women were almost twice as likely to refer to the duty in order to underpin their pro-equality debating interventions, when compared to male AMs (62.5 per cent, against 37.5 per cent of men). This finding, and selected extracts from the Official Record (see Figure 6.4), show that women AMs were inclined to cite legal equality instruments and procedural rules in order to overcome resistance and to 'normalize' the promotion of equality in the developing institutional culture of the Assembly.

A NEW KIND OF DEMOCRACY?

The experience of the first term of elected devolution in Wales supports the general observation by Knight and Johnson (1997: 309) that: 'political equality is ... a complex conception, consisting of both procedural and substantive requirements ... [it] entails a guarantee of effective participation and thus a concern for the capacity of individual participants to engage in the process of mutual persuasion'. The evidence of the first Assembly shows that the substantive representation of women involved both the actions in debate of a substantial portion of female AMs and the interventions of key women 'equality champions', defined by their feminist conviction, professional experience and gender equality knowledge. The evidence of the Assembly's first term shows that through these processes descriptive representation has translated into substantive outcomes. Strikingly, 47.7 per cent of all plenary debates included discussion of 'women's issues',[59] and just over a half of all plenary debates included references to equality.[60]

In terms of gender dynamics, the data reveal that women AMs had a greater propensity than their male colleagues to both engage in, and initiate, political debate on 'women's issues' in order to further the substantive representation of women. It is also evident that women AMs drew directly upon gendered life-experiences in order to inform debate. Furthermore, they acted to promote women's interests across a broader range of policy areas than did their male counterparts. Notwithstanding this, the propensity of some male AMs to engage in debate in relation to equalities underlines the need to conceptualize the substantive representation of women in terms of the gender dynamics of political debate, rather than as an outcome arising exclusively from the actions of women elected representatives. Importantly, the evidence of the Assembly's first years lends support to theoretical assertions that women elected representatives can be more trusted to promote 'women's interests' (see Gargarella, 1998, p. 97) and that they have different political priorities from male parliamentarians (see Taylor-Robinson and Heath, 2003).

Of particular significance in understanding the move towards more gender-equal politics is the fact that the National Assembly is a new political space. This has weakened the scope for resistance to the promotion of gender equality because, underpinned by legal duties and procedural rules, measures have been taken to establish it in the institutional culture from the outset. When male AMs have attempted to emulate traditional macho, 'yah-boo' politics seen elsewhere, three factors have been successful in countering such retrograde tendencies: the descriptive representation of women; recourse to the Assembly's legal duties and procedural rules; and the vigilance of key women 'equality champions'.

In summary, based on the evidence of the Assembly's first years, it is apparent that elected devolution has been accompanied by gender dynamics that support the substantive representation of women in national politics. However, this interim assessment requires a caveat. The Assembly is a young and developing institution; ongoing work will be necessary to ensure the continuance of gender-equal patterns of debate and representation. As one woman AM put it: 'it is very important not to be complacent, not to think that the fact that we got it right to begin with doesn't mean that we need to be vigilant'.

7

A Participatory Democracy?
Women's Engagement in Post-devolution Politics

The themes of . . . inclusiveness and participation were strongly endorsed . . . there was a strong desire for effective mechanisms for consulting and listening to people in Wales and for them to influence the Assembly, especially at an early stage in developing new policies.[1]

Proponents of participatory democracy observe that, if legitimacy is derived from the people, for a purportedly democratic institution to be truly representative it must secure the participation of all groups in society – as citizens, employees and as elected representatives. In this sense, elected devolution has increased democratic legitimacy over the earlier mode of administrative devolution, not least because, as the preceding chapters have outlined, it has overturned earlier patterns of marginalization and exclusion and given women an equal position as elected representatives. Women now have a core role in making political decisions and national budgetary allocations, as well as in framing legislation. However, as two axiomatic terms in the devolution lexicon – 'inclusiveness' and 'participatory democracy' – suggest, there is a further dimension to increasing democratic legitimacy. In this chapter we explore the links between the Assembly and women in civil (and civic) society. Specifically, we examine: the mechanisms through which women have engaged in policy-making; the development of the principal women's policy network as part of a nascent women's lobby; and the types of policy issues that characterize the engagement of women's NGOs with the Assembly. In sum: using the results of earlier research (Chaney et al., 2003; Betts and Chaney, 2004) – including interviews with members and managers of women's NGOs – the following discussion sets out an initial assessment of the effectiveness and challenges associated with women's political participation during the first years of devolved government. We begin by briefly reflecting back on the arguments for inclusive and participatory democracy that featured at the time of the devolution campaign. These effectively provide a benchmark against which to measure subsequent developments.

AN INCLUSIVE AND PARTICIPATORY DEMOCRACY

As noted in chapter 2, fostering greater citizen engagement in the structures and processes of government was one of the principal arguments for constitutional reform advanced during the post-1987 Welsh devolution campaign. In part, this was a reaction to the exclusiveness of the Welsh Office. Seldom did this institution fully interact with civil society in fulfilling its public administration functions. As Bogdanor (1999: 160) states, there were 'very few instances where the Welsh Secretary ... challenged an important [British government] policy presumption or worked out a major policy from basic principles dictated by specifically Welsh patterns of need'. Thus, by 1996,

> the Welsh Office was responsible for ... the great proportion of identifiable general government expenditure in Wales. Yet there was limited territorial autonomy. The standard view is of a [government] department tightly constrained by the British constitutional framework, engaged for the most part in the humdrum business of implementing policies decided elsewhere. (Rawlings, 1998: 466)

It was in order to address the exclusive administrative practices of the Welsh Office, as well as to tackle enduring social divisions in Welsh society, that pro-devolution campaigners promoted the idea that elected devolution would deliver 'inclusive' governance (Day et al., 2000: 29; Chaney and Fevre, 2001b). Indeed, 'inclusiveness' became the buzzword of the 1990s campaign to establish the Assembly. The former Secretary of State, Ron Davies, described the term as the 'foundation stone' of constitutional reform (Davies, 1999: 6). He outlined the development of 'inclusiveness' in the following way:

> A political system which w[ill] lead to pluralism. Now that's the starting-point. It isn't a big step then to say if you have a political system which leads to pluralism that you actually empower a whole range of 'other' people. That's a consequence of the politics. But the motivation was political change, and I knew that that would then open up access to power and influence to all these 'other' people [that is, those currently marginalized or excluded] through pluralistic and open politics. (Davies, quoted in Chaney and Fevre, 2001b: 26)

Following a suggestion by Davies, Tony Blair also used 'inclusiveness' to advance the case for government reform. Blair stated:

> a Welsh Assembly and a Scottish Parliament are good for Britain and good for Wales and Scotland. It will mean making people's vote count. It will bring government closer to the people, make our politics more inclusive and put power in the hands of the people where it belongs. (Blair, 1996: 9)

Reflecting the new emphasis on citizen empowerment, 'participatory democracy' became another key term used by advocates of constitutional reform. According to Hain (1999: 14):

> In place of the limited form of democracy inherent in the British system, the objective should be to create a 'participatory democracy' in which there is the greatest

possible involvement of citizens ... it is only through interaction with others in political activity and civic action that individuals will fully realise their humanity ... the objective of socialists should be to create not simply a participatory government but a participatory economy and a participatory society ... democracy should extend not simply to government but throughout society.

Following Labour's May 1997 General Election victory, these core principles swiftly found their way into the devolution White Paper. This stated: 'the Government is committed to establishing a new, more inclusive and participative democracy in Britain. Its proposals for a Welsh Assembly reflect these aims' (Welsh Office, 1997: 3, para. 2.1). Crucially, the document continued, 'greater participation by women is essential to the health of our democracy' (ibid.: 24, para. 4.7). Thus, in addition to the earlier campaign speeches and pamphlets, the UK government's formal legislative proposals provided further evidence that the intention was to modernize not only government, but also the prevailing mode of governance. As Paterson and Wyn Jones (1999: 193) concluded, realizing inclusive governance would require more than setting up a new government institution. In their words, 'the implications are that the civic culture into which the new assembly ... will be inserted will be crucial'. Thus, in order to engage civil society in the work of the new legislature, the Welsh devolution statute contained a raft of innovative, and sometimes unique, structural mechanisms designed to reach out to groups and sectors outside the Assembly. We now turn to examining these mechanisms and their impact on the development of a women's policy lobby.

MECHANISMS FOR PARTICIPATION IN THE WORK OF DEVOLVED GOVERNMENT: THE DEVELOPMENT OF A 'WOMEN'S LOBBY'

As noted earlier (see chapter 3), the Assembly's principal statutory equality duty has, either directly or indirectly, shaped many of the mechanisms that have facilitated women's political participation following devolution. A key example is the partnership between the voluntary, or 'third', sector and government in Wales. Whilst government–voluntary sector partnerships have become an increasingly common feature of European governance (Harris et al., 2001: 12), the terms of the partnership with national-level government in Wales are, within a UK context, singular, in that they are on a statutory footing, effectively obliging the Assembly government to work with voluntary organizations (Chaney and Fevre, 2001a). The major significance of the partnership is the way in which it attempts to institutionalize the participation of women (and other groups) in civil society in the work of government. It provides procedural channels through which women can advance their priorities and concerns, and thus further the substantive representation of women by influencing the policy process.

These new procedures for fostering participation were first set out in the devolution White Paper. It stated: 'the Assembly will be able to develop ... [a] partnership; the Government will encourage it to harness the special contribution which voluntary organizations can make in a wide range of policy areas' (Welsh Office, 1997: 19). From the outset, the official voluntary sector body in Wales, the Wales Council for Voluntary Action (WCVA), recognized that the non-profit sector was central to the process of constitutional reform. It observed that, 'if the Assembly is to fulfil the expectations of operating inclusively and in partnership with others, then it will need to work closely with voluntary and community organizations' (WCVA, 1999: 8). The terms of the partnership were subsequently codified in section 114 of the Assembly's founding statute. This provides a broad definition of the term 'voluntary organization' and states that:

> s.114 (1). The Assembly shall make a scheme setting out how it proposes, in the exercise of its functions, to promote the interests of relevant voluntary organisations. (2) In this section 'relevant voluntary organisations' means bodies (other than local authorities or other public bodies) whose activities – (a) are carried on otherwise than for profit, and (b) directly or indirectly benefit the whole or any part of Wales (whether or not they also benefit any other area).

The text of the Voluntary Sector Scheme, the contract drawn up in response to the statutory duty, reflects both the Assembly's equality duty and wider aspirations for inclusive governance. It sets out the future agenda for the inter-sectoral partnership by stating:

> The Assembly values volunteering as an important expression of citizenship and as an essential component of democracy ... the goal is the creation of a civil society which offers equality of opportunity to all its members regardless of race, colour, sex, sexual orientation, age, marital status, disability, language preference, religion or family/domestic responsibilities; [and] is inclusive and enables people to participate in all its economic, social and cultural activities. (NAW, 2000a: ch. 2, para. 2.7).

Crucially, the Scheme echoes the earlier White Paper and states: 'the Assembly recognizes ... the role they [voluntary organizations] play in formulating and delivering public policy' (ibid.: ch. 2., para. 2.10).

In response to the statutory Voluntary Sector Scheme, new consultative networks have been created. Collectively they comprise the Voluntary Sector Partnership Council (VSPC), a body that consists of twenty-one interest-based consultative policy networks, designed to reflect the breadth of voluntary activity in the country, from environmental issues to the arts. Within the 'gender strand' of the VSPC, women's voluntary organizations total 1,621, or 6.4 per cent of the sector in Wales (see Figure 7.1). It is most likely, however, that this figure underestimates the number of women's voluntary associations. This reflects the inherently problematic nature of such classifications. As Barnes et al. (2003: 5) explain:

the definitions of both voluntary activity and active citizenship often specifically exclude action within families. This ignores gender differences in the nature of the activity in which women and men engage: for example, the informal networks through which child care responsibilities are shared are 'invisible' in studies which seek to measure active citizenship.

Aside from such issues, and in common with representatives from all twenty-one networks that comprise the Partnership Council, managers with women's NGOs hold regular meetings with AMs, officials and WCVA managers. Furthermore, in another singular aspect of the new arrangements, they exercise their right to hold biannual meetings with Assembly Government ministers in order to raise issues of concern to their members.

In addition to the VSPC, women's organizations have gained further points of entry into the policy process as a result of elected devolution. The Assembly's statutory equality duty has prompted the Assembly Government to develop and/or fund a number of additional, consultative 'equality' networks. These are predominantly comprised of voluntary organizations that represent the interests of hitherto marginalized groups. They have been given Assembly Government funding to support dedicated staff, expand their membership and feed into WAG's policy consultations (see Figure 7.2).

These networks include the Wales Women's National Coalition (WWNC), an organization that was instrumental in pressing for gender equality considerations to be incorporated into the institutional blueprint of the Assembly (see chapter 3 for a discussion). Following the establishment of the Assembly, it has continued to develop as a policy network and comprises an alliance of women's NGOs. WWNC's development deserves specific attention here, as it illustrates both the impact of devolution on the women's movement and women's capacity for political engagement in the policy process. Moreover, examination of the WWNC and its member organizations provides an insight into the types of women's organizations that have participated in the work of the Assembly during its first years.

Throughout the first three years of its existence, the WWNC was run and funded entirely by its member organizations on a voluntary basis. Elected devolution had a significant impact on the WWNC. It has been given Assembly Government funding and support in order to expand and develop. In 2000, the WWNC secured funding from WAG's 'Promoting Equality in Wales Project Development Grant' in order to employ a part-time project worker. During this period, WWNC had a limited administrative capacity with neither bank account nor mechanisms in place to employ staff. As a result, Chwarae Teg[2] agreed to act as a 'proxy' employer and deal with all accounts and financial transactions on the WWNC's behalf. Following Assembly Government support, the WWNC developed apace, and during the first five months of 2001, several new organizations joined the WWNC. These included: Women in Agriculture; Royal College of

Forum heading	WCVA classification	A National	B Regional	C Local	D Branch	E Project	Total (number of orgs)	% of whole
Gender		52 0.2%	74 0.3%	1702 6.7%	14 0.1%	7 0.1%	1849	7.2
	Men	20 0.1%	15 0.1%	223 0.9%	2 0.1%	1 0.1%	261	1.0
	Women	45 0.2%	67 0.3%	1489 5.8%	14 0.1%	6 0.1%	1621	6.4
Ethnic minorities		58 0.2%	48 0.2%	223 0.9%	10 0.1%	15 0.1%	354	1.4
	Ethnic minorities	53 0.2%	48 0.2%	221 0.9%	10 0.1%	15 0.1%	347	1.4
	Refugees	14 0.1%	2 0.1%	7 0.1%	1 0.1%	1 0.1%	25	0.1
Disability		134 0.5%	197 0.8%	1188 4.7%	95 0.4%	76 0.3%	1690	6.6
	Learning disabilities	78 0.3%	108 0.4%	695 2.7%	66 0.3%	50 0.2%	997	3.9
	Physical disabilities	117 0.5%	161 0.6%	906 3.6%	52 0.2%	51 0.2%	1287	5.0

Figure 7.1 Voluntary sector organizations representing marginalized groups: analysis of all-Wales database of voluntary organizations c.1 April 2005 (total 25,509 organizations) (WCVA, 2005).

PLATE 1. Members of Welsh Women's Aid in 1978. © Welsh Women's Aid.

PLATE 2. Women march from Cardiff to Greenham Common to set up the Women's Peace Camp. © Women's Archive of Wales / Margery Lewis Collection.

PLATE 3. The Miners' Strike Maerdy Women's Support Group, 27 August 1984. © Martin Shakestaff.

PLATE 4. Women Say Yes for Wales march, 1997. © Peter Polish. Image reproduced courtesy of Leighton Andrews.

PLATE 5. Women Say Yes for Wales, Whitland, 1997. © Yes for Wales Campaign. Image reproduced courtesy of Leighton Andrews.

PLATE 6. Women Say Yes for Wales. © Yes for Wales Campaign. Image reproduced courtesy of Leighton Andrews.

PLATE 7. Helen Mary Jones plants tree, Women Say Yes, Whitland. © Yes for Wales Campaign. Image reproduced courtesy of Leighton Andrews.

PLATE 8. Women Say Yes for Wales at National Eisteddfod, Castell Nedd. © Mair and Hywel Francis. Image reproduced courtesy of Leighton Andrews.

Women of Wales - Have Your Say!

- The average weekly wage for women in Wales is £250. In Britain as a whole, it's £283.

- In Wales, there are far less child-care places than in the rest of Britain.

- More young people in Wales leave school with no qualifications than in England.

- Women in Wales are more likely to have breast cancer and heart disease, compared to women in England.

We are getting a bad deal! Our families, our health and our jobs are suffering, thanks to unwanted, unelected Quangos! And we've had no choice and no voice... until now!

On September 18th, we can change things. The Welsh Assembly will be able to speak up for Wales in Britain and Europe. It will mean that our voices are heard and we can set our own priorities on the services that matter most to women.

Voting "Yes" means:

 "Yes" to bringing investment to all parts of Wales. This will create more jobs and better working conditions.

 "Yes" to improving our schools and our child-care provision.

 "Yes" to making sure that money is spent on caring for patients, not recruiting more managers.

 "Yes" to bringing more women into politics and getting women's voices heard.

A new organisation brings the chance to build in equality right from the start. Working together, we can find solutions to the problems we face - the Assembly can use the talents and ability of **all** our citizens.

Please pass this message on to your friends, and ask them to tell their friends. **Remember, this may be our last chance. Let's make sure we take it!**

For more information, or to join a local group, contact: "Yes for Wales", 7 St. Andrew's Place, Cardiff, CF1 3BE, Phone: (01222) 343535.

Vote "Yes" for the Welsh Assembly!

Printed with support from USDAW.

PLATE 9. Women Say Yes for Wales Campaign leaflet. © Yes for Wales Campaign.

Val Feld with Swansea East MP
Donald Anderson outside the DVLA -
created by Labour,
run down by the Tories,
expanding again under Labour

Val Feld - Standing up for Swansea east
Yn gefn i ddwyrain Abertawe

The first ever Welsh General
Election takes place on May 6th.

Labour has honoured its promise to bring decision
making to Wales. Now we want
to create a better Wales by working in the
National Assembly to:

- **raise standards in our schools**
- **improve the health service by cutting waiting lists**
- **support Welsh businesses as well as bringing investors in**
- **develop a Childcare Strategy**
- **improve transport and give pensioners free bus travel**
- **protect our environment as the heritage of future generations**
- **provide decent housing for all**

The Watchword of Labour in the Assembly will be
partnership - with local government, Westminster,
Europe and with business, trade unions and the
voluntary sector.
Labour believes that by acting together we can
create a Better Wales.

*Mae Llafur yn credu mai drwy gydweithio'n unig y
gallwn newid Cymru er gwell.*

Swansea suffered badly under the 18 years of
Tory rule - Five times more jobs were created in
South East Wales in the seven years up to 1998
than in Swansea.

Your Labour candidate Val Feld has long experience
of working in Swansea and at national level in Wales
to tackle inequality and injustice. She is a tough
campaigner. The founder director of Shelter Cymru,
she now heads a public body, is a school governor
and involved with many local organisations.

Val has the skills and knowledge to make the
Assembly work for Swansea and for Wales.

Committed to working for Swansea / Ymrwymol i weithio dros Abertawe

If you can help Val Feld in her campaign or would like help to get a postal vote or to get to the polling station
on May 6th please ring the campaign office on 421701.

Published by M. Lodlam, 30 Robert Street, Manselton, Swansea SA1 9NB. Printed by Bryaymor Press, Darcy Business Centre, Llandarcy SA10 6EZ

PLATE 10. Val Feld, election campaign leaflet 1999.

PLATE 11. The late Val Feld AM, tireless campaigner for gender equality.
© *The Western Mail*

PLATE 12. Women Assembly Members, 2003. © *The Western Mail.*

Assembly-sponsored consultative network	Membership size
Wales Women's National Coalition (WWNC)	Approx. 100,000 individuals in 20 affiliated groups.
Disability Wales	400 affiliated groups.
The All-Wales Ethnic Minority Association (AWEMA)	300 individuals.
Stonewall Cymru (formerly LGB [Lesbian, Gay and Bisexual] Forum Cymru)	Approx. 500 individuals. Mixture of affiliated groups and individuals.
National Partnership Forum for Older People in Wales	Approx. 200 affiliated organizations.

Figure 7.2 Assembly government-sponsored consultative 'equality' networks set up in response to the statutory equality duty.

Nursing Wales; Carers National Association Wales; the domestic-violence support group, Black and Asian Women Step Out (BAWSO); North Wales Lesbian Line; Shelter Cymru; and the multicultural women's group, SHEKINA. This brought the total number of member organizations at this time to over a dozen.

From the outset of devolution, WWNC lobbied and engaged in the work of the Assembly. A typical example of WWNC's work is the seminar entitled 'Women in Public Appointments in Wales' that was jointly convened by the WWNC and held at the National Assembly in March 2001. The event was addressed by the Assembly Government Minister for Finance and the UK Commissioner for Public Appointments. Each member organization of WWNC invited five guests to the seminar. These invitees were women who, it was felt, might be persuaded to stand for public appointments in Wales. At the event, the Public Appointments Unit of the Assembly provided application forms and information packs to attendees. The WWNC's records lament that, 'numerous press releases were issued leading up to and during the week – the interest from the media was, however, minimal'.

In respect of the WWNC's continuing development, in July 2001 it submitted a formal application to the Assembly Government Equality Policy Unit and secured annual funding of £50,000 (with equal funding in kind from the WWNC). This money was to employ two part-time workers in order to: 'carry out consultation work, lobby the National Assembly and influence policy makers – and develop the work of the WWNC' (WWNC, 2001: 3) (see Figure 7.3).

WWNC documents of the time record: 'the future of the WWNC appears to be positive ... The WWNC must now decide on its priorities and work in partnership to consult with women within their communities and lobby the policy-makers on behalf of the women of Wales.'[3] Subsequently, the WWNC was registered as a company limited by guarantee with charitable status. The Memorandum of Association states that:

1. To 'comment on official National Assembly for Wales documents, to be co-ordinated by the Coalition Manager in consultation with representatives from the Coalition membership. The Coalition membership represents a wide range of women in Wales from all walks of life. The membership itself has a wealth of expertise, which will be utilised, and we will endeavour to extend the Coalition membership further and target groups where we are under-represented or lack expertise. This will be done by directly inviting organisations to become full members of the Coalition or work in partnership with organisations on individual projects.'
2. To develop … 'A programme of consultation meetings with women within their communities. This will be achieved via a field worker who will visit women within their communities. The field worker will visit a cross-section of women's groups at grassroots level and bring together groups of women for consultation. These groups will include current Coalition members and also groups that have stated that they are prepared to work in partnership with the Coalition to arrange and attend such consultations. The results of these consultations will be fed to the National Assembly for Wales.'

Figure 7.3 The principal aims of Wales Women's National Coalition (WWNC, 2001).[4]

The Company is established to promote the best interests of women in Wales by:-

(i)   Promoting understanding and co-operation between voluntary organisations representing women in Wales;
(ii)   Assisting such organisations to work together to promote the interests of women amongst policy makers at all levels;
(iii) Being a forum for the National Assembly for Wales and other bodies to consult with women;
(iv)   Promoting the participation of women in Wales in decision-making at all levels.[5]

By 2005, the WWNC had developed a membership of over twenty affiliated organizations, including two distinct women's networks in their own right, the Minority Ethnic Women's Network (MEWN) Cymru, and the Wales Assembly of Women.

One of these networks, MEWN Cymru, describes itself as 'a second tier, umbrella body representing ethnic minority (visible and non visible) women across Wales, regardless of their age, religious observance, ethnicity or life choices'. It was founded in 1994 with the assistance of Val Feld, at that time Director of EOC Wales. Details contained in MEWN's publications illustrate the underdeveloped nature of parts of the women's movement infrastructure. One document states that: 'the number of Black and Minority Ethnic (BME) women's groups/organisations in Wales is unknown, however early indications are that there are an estimated 25, most of them based in south Wales'. MEWN's membership includes a significant number of these NGOs, such as the Bangladeshi

Women's Association, Chinese Women's Group North Wales and East Cardiff Somali Women's Group. MEWN Cymru has also received part-funding from the Assembly Government. Either via the WWNC, or through direct lobbying and consultation, it has engaged in the Assembly's policy-making structures in order to fulfil its stated aims of: 'policy and representation ... provid[ing] a platform for the views of minority ethnic women in Wales', and 'building the capacity to respond effectively to selected consultations that may directly affect BME women'.[6] MEWN assert that:

> [T] he fundamental basis for successful inclusion of ethnic minority women in activities is to achieve equal opportunity and democratic participation at all levels in society ... [through] political lobbying and raising public awareness MEWN Cymru attempts to influence legislation concerning the rights of ethnic minority women as well as raise public awareness of these rights.[7]

In addition to MEWN Cymru, WWNC's affiliate membership includes organizations with federal structures of varying types. Welsh Women's Aid, for example, adopts an individual collectivist approach, with high levels of autonomy for its thirty-four local groups. The organization 'is the leading provider of services aimed specifically at helping vulnerable women and children who are experiencing domestic violence and abuse in Wales'.[8] WWA lobbies to advance the following rights for women and their children:

- a right to a life free from fear, violence and abuse;
- a right to define and own their personal experience;
- a right to control their own lives and determine their own future;
- a right to be listened to and believed;
- a right to have increased choices to make informed decisions;
- a right to social and legislative frameworks to enable them to exercise their rights within society.[9]

In contrast, the National Federation of Women's Institutes Wales (NFWI-Wales) operates more of a hierarchical structure, via a NFWI-Wales Committee and Wales Office, both based upon the support of the 13 Federations of Women's Institutes and 800 local WIs across the country. Another mass-membership affiliate organization belonging to the WWNC is Merched y Wawr. This women's NGO 'campaigns for Welsh language rights and the rights of women'[10] and has over 250 branches across Wales. In a manner that encapsulates the intricate and complex organizational structure of the nascent women's lobby following devolution, WWNC is also the representative for gender on the Voluntary Sector Partnership Council (VSPC), and is itself a member of the British state-funded women's organization, the Women's National Commission.

In respect of lesbian, gay and bisexual (LGB) representation, Stonewall Cymru was established in 2001. Its aim is to be 'a voice for LGB people at key decision-making bodies – such as the Welsh Assembly Government' (Stonewall Cymru,

2004: 1). The organization operates in partnership with approximately twenty LGB groups in Wales, and a further fourteen mainstream organizations who support LGB people within their work by providing specific LGB services (such as an LGB youth group, a trades union LGB group and an LGB housing project). Assembly Government funding was central to establishing this first, national organization for LGB people (initially called LGB Forum Cymru) and is a further example of the impact of devolution in attempting to create a participatory infrastructure. Notwithstanding such developments, Stonewall Cymru conclude that:

> the capacity of the LGB voluntary sector still does not begin to match the level of need … we will continue to strengthen the LGB voluntary sector by taking forward the community development plan to improve the quantity and quality of services available to LGB people. (Stonewall Cymru, 2004: 4)

In 2003, Stonewall Cymru was afforded permanent adviser status to the Assembly's Standing Committee on Equality of Opportunity. In addition to the VSPC, this committee has developed into a further, key institutional nexus of engagement between women activists, women's NGOs, politicians and policy-makers, a development that has been further reinforced by EOC Wales's role as permanent adviser to the Committee.

A further forum directly related to gender equality has been created by the Equality and Human Rights Coalition (EHRC) for the voluntary sector in Wales. The EHRC had its first meeting in July 2004, and:

> aims to act as a forum for voluntary and community organisations working on equality and human rights issues to discuss policy issues and, where appropriate, agree and present a common policy position. It aims to provide a focus for exchange of information, ideas and experiences between voluntary organisations, and to generally provide a supportive forum for organisations working on equalities and human rights.[11]

As the foregoing suggests, the women's lobby in post-devolution Wales is characterized by a high degree of complexity in relation to organizational structures. To a large extent, this has resulted from the historical underdevelopment of national Welsh policy-making capacity and the failure of the 1999 devolution settlement to allocate primary law-making powers to the National Assembly; as a result, women's organizations, in common with all NGOs, need to focus on both Cardiff and London for many of their lobbying activities.

Whilst organizational complexity is one of the defining features of the nascent lobby, nevertheless, the new mechanisms for women's participation in the work of government lend credence to Morgan and Rees's general assessment (2001: 152) that:

> [T]he new governance structures – the Assembly itself, the office of First Minister, the Cabinet, the Subject Committees and the Regional Committees – have created multiple points of entry to the policy-making system, in sharp contrast to the Welsh Office era, when political access – principally to the Secretary of State and his two

junior Ministers – was highly restricted, and it was the civil servants who were the key to influencing the bulk of decisions about policy development. Quite simply, the Welsh governance system now enables much greater accessibility, at least to those with the organizational capacity to capitalize on the opportunities which are newly available.

Thus, devolution appears to have created an unprecedented locus for lobbying and participation in government. The process of developing a more specifically Welsh-focused infrastructure amongst women's NGOs that was begun during the devolution campaign (see chapter 2) has continued apace, following the creation of the National Assembly. Recent research showed that almost a half (49.1 per cent) of 800 women members of WWNC surveyed said that their organization had lobbied the Assembly on at least one issue during its first term (Betts and Chaney, 2004: 173). We now examine the types of policy issues at the heart of such lobbying and assess the overall nature of women's engagement with the devolved government.

POLICY PRIORITIES

The lobbying activities and partnership working of women's NGOs merit attention here on a number of levels, not least because they provide an insight into the policy priorities of women and women's NGOs, for so long excluded or marginalized in the work of government during the earlier period of administrative devolution. In addition, they illustrate the strengths and limitations of the new governance arrangements in furthering the substantive representation of women.

In respect of black and Asian women, MEWN Cymru has engaged with Assembly Government initiatives to tackle social disadvantage, most notably in the £83 million Communities First programme (see Adamson and Johnston, 2003). Here, MEWN has overseen the creation of black and ethnic minority support teams (BEST) in order to gather data and offer support in respect of the needs of BME communities resident in areas of particular social disadvantage.[12] In addition, MEWN has engaged in Assembly Government initiatives, such as: mapping social inclusion in publicly funded libraries in Wales (commissioned by the Welsh Assembly Government's library and Information Services Council);[13] partnership working with the National Assembly and WWNC in order to increase the number of women and members of ethnic minority communities holding public appointments;[14] encouraging participation in the Enterprise Rehearsal Project, part of the Entrepreneurship Action Plan (a National Assembly for Wales initiative that puts particular emphasis on encouraging women to become the entrepreneurs of tomorrow');[15] and work to achieve 'greater participation by BME women in both sport and the arts in Wales'.[16]

The official records of the VSPC reveal how it, too, is operating as a lobbying mechanism for gender equality. A typical example is a position paper by Audrey

Jones of Wales Assembly of Women on 'gender [im]balance in unitary authorities in Wales'. This invited members 'to note the significance of this situation and
be aware of its potential for the disempowerment of women, thereby perpetu-
ating social injustice'.[17] It proceeded to recommend that:

> [T] he Welsh Assembly Government promotes still further its equal pay initiatives,
> by requiring Unitary Authorities to provide a gender audit of its staff appointments
> with classification by level of appointment and salary scale, and with information on
> the composition of the appointment panels. This audit should be published in each
> [unitary] Authority's Annual Report ... [and, that ...] the outcomes of policy decisions
> made by the Authorities be made subject to gender impact assessment, especially
> those dependent on financial allocations, and that such monitoring is undertaken
> within the Welsh Assembly Government's Equality Unit, which would appear well
> placed to undertake this significant responsibility.[18]

Other examples of gender equality issues raised via VSPC include: lobbying to
improving women's representation in the structures of the Assembly
Government's Communities First and community-led regeneration schemes;[19]
making representations to the chairs of the Local Government Partnership
Council (LGPC) about gender imbalance in local authorities;[20] and calls for
sustained focus on gender equality in WAG's 'Mainstreaming Equality in Public
Appointments Action Plan'.[21]

In addition to lobbying the Assembly Government via the new consultative
structures and networks, women's organizations have themselves directly
lobbied the Assembly Government. For example, the National Federation of
Women's Institutes Wales has been active in pressing for greater government
support for the economic and social infrastructure of rural communities, as well
as on the issue of sustainable development. The following is typical of its position
in lobbying and consultation responses:

> NFWI-Wales welcomes the statement that the Assembly will work in partnership with
> others ... Women are in the unique position of being able to directly influence many
> aspects of Sustainable Development. Agenda 21 recognises the critical role that
> women play in achieving fundamental changes that are necessary to bring about
> Sustainable Development ... NFWI-Wales would urge the National Assembly for
> Wales to recognise the important role that women can play in the process of
> Sustainable Development and to create more opportunities for women to participate
> effectively in economic and social development as equal partners in all sectors of the
> economy.[22]

In respect of education policy, Welsh Women's Aid (WWA) has worked in collaboration with ACCAC, the Welsh state schools' curriculum and qualifications body,
to produce learning materials, including lesson plans and resources, with regard
to advancing children's rights and addressing stereotyping, aggressive attitudes
and domestic abuse (see chapter 8 for further discussion of gender equality and
education policy).[23] Since 2002, WWA has also participated in the three-year
development of the Welsh Assembly Government's National Strategy on Tackling

Domestic Abuse through its membership of the Working Group on Domestic Violence and Violence Against Women. In addition, WWA has successfully lobbied the Assembly Government for the creation of a national all-Wales domestic violence telephone helpline, and for an increase in Assembly Government funding to tackle domestic abuse. The latter secured a £1.1 million increase in funding over three years and was announced in March 2003.[24] Coupled with these developments, the Assembly Government has legislated in respect of extending support for victims of domestic violence (see chapter 8).

The Wales Trades Union Congress (WTUC), via its Women's Committee, has also been part of women's engagement in devolved policy-making. This has covered a range of issues, such as the Assembly Government-sponsored 'Close the Pay Gap' campaigns that have sought to raise public awareness and press for action in order that women receive equal pay to men for work of equal value (see Chaney, 2004). Recently, the Women's Committee of the WTUC has lobbied to address what it sees as oversights in the development of the Assembly Government's National Strategy on Tackling Domestic Abuse by stating that:

> Whilst we felt that the report covered most of the issues associated with the issue, it is apparent that domestic abuse as a workplace matter has not been examined to any extent and included within the Strategy. The sub-Group believes that this is due to the lack of representation from the Wales TUC on the working group from the outset. Trade unions have a vital role to play to help and support working women who are unfortunate enough to suffer such abuse. The effects of domestic abuse can impact on a number of issues within the workplace. (WTUC, 2004: 1)

In respect of the new policy networks, WWNC has adopted a 'targeted' approach to policy consultations, choosing to focus on three core issues: encouraging women into public life, tackling violence against women, and women and poverty. In respect of the first aim, the Coalition's objective was to 'increase the numbers of women in Wales holding a public appointment ... to 50% by the end of the Assembly's second term' (WWNC, 2003). One of the WWNC's member organizations, Merched y Wawr, has continued a long tradition of campaigning for Welsh language equality. Further extensive lobbying has been undertaken by Stonewall Cymru, in respect of equality for lesbian, gay and bisexual people on a broad range of issues, including education, health and housing. For example, Stonewall has: engaged in consultations about progress and the future direction of the Assembly Government's health strategy 'Well Being in Wales';[25] worked with the Assembly Government in developing new guidelines for schools on teaching relating to LGB issues;[26] and informed Assembly Government housing research in respect of LGB issues. In addition, Stonewall has lobbied for: greater rights and support in respect of same-sex couples' adoption of children; pressed WAG to issue guidance to NHS Wales regarding the legal constitution of the term 'next of kin', in order to fully encompass the needs and concerns of same-sex couples; called for the Assembly Government to take measures to address the discrimination experienced by women, ethnic minorities and disabled LGB people; and called for measures to reduce the social exclusion of older LGB people from the major LGB social scene in Wales, by creating support groups and promoting positive images of ageing.[27]

WOMEN'S PARTICIPATION IN THE
WORK OF DEVOLVED GOVERNMENT

Based upon the new participatory structures, lobbying issues and consultation exercises that together constitute women's engagement in the work of the Assembly, what can be said of the nature and quality of this new political partici-pation? What have been the barriers and limiting factors applying to women's participation in the work of the Assembly? What challenges remain in furthering this engagement? We now draw upon a series of one hundred interviews with managers of women's NGOs and associated research findings in order to address these questions.

Over two-thirds of women interviewees welcomed the new openness and opportunities to work with government. They saw the development of women's networks and organizations as an attempt to create a locus for lobbying and participation in government in a way that did not happen prior to devolution. In the words of one, this process had encouraged new groups and individuals to 'come out of the woodwork'. Another said, 'there's been a lot of interest from people willing to join'. Such developments surprised some of those involved. One respondent concluded of the new system of governance: 'there seem to be a lot of open doors, people who want to hear what we have to say, a lot of the members are coming to us wanting to help in any way they can'. This was a view reinforced by a project worker with a women's NGO, who concluded that:

> I think it is user-friendly. They have made an effort to involve the voluntary sector which I think is quite important. My feeling, looking at it all, is that they do feel strongly about the voluntary sector and they do want to involve us and there are opportunities. It's certainly not a closed way of government compared to experiences that we may have had in England. I think my job is a lot easier to a certain extent and the amount of information I could find out is just absolutely phenomenal ... they are very open to making these links [with voluntary organizations].

A woman trade unionist also referred to the new levels of accessibility and the availability of information on the policy process, stating:

> I am very positive about this, it's excellent, it's a good move forward and what I like best about this is, it's not just the relationship that we have with the women Assembly Members but it's the whole openness of the Assembly. Any member of the public can – I don't think that we have told the public enough – and people in general in Wales – that they can actually go to the Assembly, walk in and actually sit in and listen to

the debates. It is such an open thing. Immediately after the debates they're put on the Internet so you can download it, so the information is there continually, day after day … it's like a breath of fresh air, that's the only way to describe it.

This new relationship with policy-makers was also described as a two-way process by interviewees. As one observed:

they want us to sort of reach out to the very disparate and varied lesbian and gay community across Wales and be a mechanism for inputting their views and reaction to Welsh Assembly policies and government. My feeling is that can be reactive and proactive. They are very open to us coming to them with ideas of things that we'd like to do to improve the involvement of the LGB community of Wales in the work of the Welsh Assembly.

Another interviewee underlined the importance of descriptive representation and having women AMs to work with. She said:

[T] alking about the women's side of it; that is the particular advantage that we have now got, so to push all these policies we are very pleased that we have got the high number of women there … we work well with them … we work with all the women in the Assembly.

The openness and opportunities to engage with government referred to in the foregoing comments by managers of women's NGOs is also acknowledged by the grassroots membership of WWNC organizations. For example, an extensive survey of 800 members of WWNC affiliate organizations found that the majority (58.2 per cent) said that they felt that the National Assembly was accountable to members of their respective NGOs (Betts and Chaney, 2004: 178).

However, the comments of interviewees also reveal contradictions and elements of dissatisfaction, as well as significant challenges in respect of political participation in devolved governance. Many widely held concerns amongst women's NGOs were captured in a policy document by MEWN Cymru (see Figure 7.4). Foremost amongst these is the need to develop the organizational, administrative and skills capacity of NGOs in order to engage more effectively with the Assembly and Assembly government. This priority stems both from the low, pre-devolution starting-point, when women's organizations were seldom involved in Welsh Office policy-making, and from the sheer volume of Assembly consultations. In total, 440 consultation documents were issued by the Assembly Government and Assembly committees during the first five years of the devolved governance (Richard Commission, 2004: 218), with a further 96 formal policy consultation exercises undertaken in 2005 (Chaney, 2006b: 8). The manager of a black voluntary sector women's organization voiced commonly held views about the challenges that the transition from administrative to elected devolution presented to her organization and others like it. She highlighted the way that the limited capacity of women's NGOs necessitated an 'executive' approach in responding to consultation exercises:

'WHAT ARE THE PROBLEMS AFFECTING THE BME WOMEN'S VOLUNTARY AND COMMUNITY SECTOR?

At several events over the past 18 months, BME women's groups have voiced concern that, despite BME women constituting over half of the BME population, "gender and race has fallen off the Government's agenda". It is given insufficient priority in both funding and policy. Under-resourcing continues to be the primary issue facing the BME women's voluntary and community sector – particularly the lack of stable, long-term core cost, organisational development and project funding. Subsequently, long-term project and strategic planning, developing the sector through partnership and engaging in consultation – all of which are necessary to building a sustainable BME women's voluntary and community sector – are not undertaken. Heavy reliance on Government contracts and grants, the three-year funding cycles and changes in funding priorities and funding policy has left BME women's groups in extremely vulnerable positions, especially since few other options for diversifying funding are available (and many organisations have closed in recent years). Developments in funding policy and priorities have included competitive bidding, the removal of ring-fenced/targeted funding for BME women's groups, and the emphasis on 'innovation'. Additionally, having to complete different monitoring and evaluation requirements for each funder diverts resources away from delivering on core aims. Recruiting and retaining paid staff is also difficult, usually due to low salaries relative to the specialist skills required of the position. Training volunteers is resource intensive. Most BME women's groups do not have a website, which limits their ability to publicise their services to other voluntary and community organisa-tions as well as potential service users, employees and funders. It is affects their ability to participate in Government moves towards ICT delivery of services and information. Office space in urban areas in Wales consumes a major proportion of an organisation's funding. A significant number of premises do not comply with the Disability Discrimination Act due to lack of funding to finance building costs. Many are also cramped and/or in need of repair. An organisation's premises can impact on staff recruitment if it is inaccessible or provides a poor environment.

WHAT DOES THE WALES BME WOMEN'S VOLUNTARY AND COMMUNITY SECTOR NEED?

(i) Funding. Despite the enormous contribution that the BME women's voluntary and community sector has made to gender equality, this has not been matched by Government commitment to secure a stable funding base for BME women's groups. Women's groups need long-term and ring-fenced/targeted funding for projects, core costs, premises, organisational development, recruitment, sector development, consultation and participation in local governance. Collaboration amongst funders to develop generic funding applications and monitoring and evaluation standards, and to ensure pots of funds are strategically aligned, would also benefit BME women's groups.

(ii) Research. Substantial investment into research is urgently required (including a directory of BME women's organisations in south Wales) to develop a comprehen-sive picture of the status, nature and scope of the BME women's voluntary and community sector, of which little is known. Research undertaken on the wider voluntary and community sector and data collected by funders must be disaggregated in order to identify trends as well as areas of need and good practice.

(iii) Consultation and Formal Structures. Many BME women's organisations, especially smaller groups, simply do not have the time, resources or capacity to attend consultations and other forums and therefore chances to influence public policy or planning, in both local boroughs and regionally, pass. Given the high volume of consultations and other meetings, attending these events places further stress on already pressurised resources. For Government and the wider voluntary and community sector, valuable opportunities are missed to gather information from organisations about how policies and strategies are affecting or will affect BME women. It is now widely acknowledged that attempts to regenerate and economically develop areas often fail because they do not involve and/or benefit local communities sufficiently. In order to engage meaningfully in consultation, BME women's groups must be funded to do so. Agencies undertaking consultation would also benefit from using models of good practice such as outreach. Reporting back on consultation responses is also well received by the BME women's voluntary and community sector.

(iv) Infrastructure Support. Infrastructure support, coupled with funding, allows groups to develop the skills to sustain their organisations. Infrastructure bodies provide training and support in governance, management, fundraising, planning, ICT, employment, policy, research and service delivery. It is vital that infrastructure bodies are adequately resourced to provide this support effectively.'

Figure 7.4 Problems and needs of the BME women's voluntary and community sector in Wales (MEWN Cymru, 2005).[30]

They [National Assembly officials] send us everything for comments. But again it's time isn't it? Some things come through in good time and you've time to respond. Some things come through like a week before and say 'please comment' and I feel I always have to comment otherwise they haven't got a view from the black voluntary sector, which is not fair; because sometimes I haven't got the time to comment. I've got about four papers here that need commenting on and it means sitting down reading it and taking it in – and then being able to make a decent comment on it and send it back. Where's the time? It's just mad! So I pass them on because we've usually somebody from the management committee who has skills and expertise in each of the different fields so – that's the way we are getting around it at the moment.

Elsewhere, the manager of another women's NGO observed:

They don't realize that with one full-time worker and four part-time workers, they expect you to be able to move a mountain ... if you had thirty workers doing that work then fine, we would be able to complete all of the paperwork; but it is just never-ending.

Aside from issues of capacity, other managers of women's NGOs questioned the appropriateness of some Assembly Government consultation documents. One observed:

I have mailed all Assembly Members, I was very pleased with some of the responses from the non-Welsh speakers, they all actually made an effort and did translate [into Welsh] the letters that they sent back. However, having said that, quite a lot of mail still comes out from the Assembly in mono English, especially to our regional district, I have been to quite a few local meetings [of my organization] where they have accepted a letter in English from some of the Assembly Members – and officials from the Assembly ... But, I have told them now to reject this and send them back and ask for a Welsh translation ... *I think it's worth campaigning for.*

The steep learning-curve associated with devolution was another strong theme that emerged from interviews with members of women's NGOs. It was evident in the comments of a manager of a women's cross-border NGO with headquarters in England. She said: 'our first priority of the last six months has been to really get the organization up to speed with [devolved] policy areas ... we're at the stage where we are gathering intelligence and really then determining how we will lobby'. Similarly, another interviewee described the impact of devolution in the following terms:

[W] e have decided, that we do have to become more 'political', but again with a small 'p'. We need to join these new alliances and networks. We are very geared-up now to kind of having a voice within, the new policy structure ... I mean it's a changing culture. Our organization's changed over the past year: it's now *very different*. So we're very much in a state of flux – but I think it's a very positive kind of change.

In the opinion of some informants, the infrastructure of women's organizations was not yet sufficiently developed to enable it to fully participate in the mode aspired to by devolution campaigners in the 1990s. As one interviewee put it:

you have got to *generate* that informed opinion as widely as possible. And that means developing ... these forums that take responsibility for pulling groups of people together, so you get groupings of people working on a specific issue, once they start meeting together, once we've found them, we can start feeding other issues in.

In this respect these research findings are encouraging, for a significant proportion of the survey of 800 women members of the WWNC who had yet to engage in lobbying or policy consultations said that they would welcome information, training and meetings in order to aid their future involvement in the work of the National Assembly. Thus, 43 per cent said that they would like better information on Assembly Government policies; almost a half (49 per cent) said that they would welcome opportunities to meet Assembly Members locally; and 26 per cent would welcome broadcast media advertising 'on how to get involved in the Assembly's work'. In addition, a third of WWNC members said that the Assembly Government should 'organize local "workshops" or training sessions for organizations advising on how to get involved in the Welsh Assembly Government's work' (Chaney et al., 2003: 23).

The comments of members of women's NGOs also reveal a tension between what the gender-mainstreaming literature describe as 'participatory' and 'expert–bureaucratic' approaches to policy (see chapter 8 for a discussion of mainstreaming): in other words, whether the engagement of women's NGOs in the policy work of government is based upon thorough consultation of the NGO's grassroots membership, or founded on a selective strategy of engagement that uses experts and managers to represent the diversity of women members' views and interests. The words of a senior civil servant suggest that parts of the Assembly bureaucracy are more at home with the latter mode of interaction. He described the role of the Assembly-sponsored policy networks such as the WWNC as 'find[ing] the *right* people ... to actually be able to put an input in from experience, through their own knowledge of a policy area'. Balancing reliance upon expertise and technocratic solutions with the need for broad-based engagement with the ordinary members of the women's organizations is a key issue. This was highlighted in a VSPC publication that stated:

> the numbers, independence and diversity of those involved of volunteering makes it both very important and very difficult to present a 'volunteering' perspective on issues. It can be particularly difficult to reflect the voice of the volunteer as distinct from that of the volunteer manager or the organisation itself. (VSPC, 2001c: 3)

This point was emphasized by a manager of a women's umbrella organization, who stated that:

> [W]ith the decision-making, first of all, we are still working on it, but ultimately the executive committee is where the decisions are taken. They're responsible for what we do and what we prioritize. But we hope to ensure that that is as legitimate and as responsive as possible through regular consultative meetings or mailings with the wider membership, to ensure that those views are taken on board ... we hope to ensure we're as responsive as possible to the grassroots. But a lot of that will be down to ensuring that grassroots organizations and individuals are able and in a position to feed into our work. It will be about 'capacity building' in a way, in enabling that two-way process to take place in certain areas that haven't been possible in the past.

During the Assembly's first years, many women's NGOs have faced this practical dilemma between adopting affordable 'executive' decision-making on behalf of the organization's membership, or more democratic, extensive, grassroots consultation of members, something that is often prohibitively expensive for NGOs with limited budgets. The internal correspondence of one women's organization provides a further insight into these issues and how they impact upon the way some consultations are currently being conducted. A document entitled 'Consultation Process' states that:

> [Our] organization in Wales, like many organizations, is on a steep learning curve! The reality is that consultation responses are often staff-led with little member input. Nonetheless, we do try to achieve member input. The format at the moment is to mail out a [Assembly government] consultation document to as many members as can be identified as being 'interested' or have expertise on that particular topic ... It is often difficult to identify who the experts are ... [we are] currently developing a

database and collecting information from members about their areas of expertise and their willingness to respond to consultation documents.

A further associated challenge that continues to face managers of women's NGOs is achieving appropriate organizational structures. In turn, this impacts both upon the administrative efficiency of women's NGOs, and their lobbying potential. The often-complex organizational and administrative structures of women's NGOs means that developing effective and democratic decision-making processes is a particularly difficult task. The minutes of one Voluntary Sector Partnership Council meeting highlight this point. They state: 'consensus is difficult when the structures to achieve it do not exist' (VSPC, 2000: para. 2.8). Managers with some cross-border women's organizations, in particular, acknowledged that devolution has implications for their organizational structures. As one noted:

> we're much more keen to have a particular presence in Wales. As an organization I think we could be criticized as being very 'English-focused' and we're conscious now that in Wales and Scotland we need to address that. In terms of restructuring and re-developing as an organization we are, every organization is, doing that.

Another manager referred to the increased levels of independence afforded to their activities in the wake of devolution:

> our organization has taken a view, I think, that it is happy for the Welsh operation to have quite an autonomous existence. To set priorities in Wales for what it wants to achieve and for ... [the British tier of the organization] to bring its expertise and help facilitate that in any way it can.

Other cross-border women's NGOs saw funding as a further reason for greater engagement with devolved government. In the words of one manager:

> we have a large [UK] government grant, which now, very clearly, is for England only. Yes, as an organization we need to find new ways of funding and I think the funding aspect is one reason why we need to better develop those links with WCVA – and with the Assembly as well.

The skills-base within women's organizations is also of key importance in fostering participation in government (Rubenson, 2000). Again, both the historical weakness of a Wales-specific policy process in many areas of government and the legacy of women's marginalization and exclusion in Welsh politics mean that, in some cases, women's organizations are currently suffering a skills deficit. New skills in areas such administration, leadership, lobbying, consultation and publicity will need to be developed in order to overcome this problem. This point was acknowledged by a number of interviewees. One said:

> it's a whole new set of skills and experience and understanding that we need to develop. To engage properly and put something useful into the policy process we have got to educate, we have got to give people the experience; we have got to build up that knowledge-base. *Then* we can do something useful. But it's not happening that quickly.

New information technology offers the potential to address some of the challenges facing women's NGOs. Thus, the first Annual Report on the Voluntary Sector Scheme (NAW, 2001a) contained an action plan on 'consultation and participation' that advocated technocratic solutions to fostering consultation, such as 'a web-based consultation template', a 'central database of potential consultees', and 'push technology ... so that organizations or individuals can select information in which they are interested' (WAG, 2001b: 14, para. 31). The danger here is that technology is seen as a replacement for, rather than an aid to, genuine broad-based consultation and participation. The director of a mid-Wales-based NGO said:

> at the end of the day not many of our members, and not many women in general, have access to a computer and the internet and email and all of those facilities. People in the Welsh Assembly seem to feel that everybody has direct access to internet and email and all of these other services, they don't. At the ground level people just don't have that sort of facility available to them.

In a structural sense, the evidence of the first years of devolved governance supports the assessment made by the manager of a women's NGO that 'perhaps the most significant aspect of the recent reforms is the way that the Assembly has given us impetus to lobby and created more opportunities'. The manager of another women's organization concluded that: 'the advent of the Assembly has meant that the focus is on Wales rather than on London. The very fact that I could attend a meeting with the Minister for Education in Wales, I mean that sets up new opportunities that didn't exist before.' Another added, 'we have good contacts now ... they're more open, the idea that a group like ours would meet with ministers would have been laughed at when things were still based in London'.

In addition to underlining the importance of the new consultative structures for women to engage with the National Assembly, many managers with women's NGOs also emphasized the value of descriptive representation in the Assembly and developing personal contacts with women Assembly Members. Such networking and co-working is a significant development for, in a sense, it effectively extends the descriptive representation so as to include women from civil society. This is apparent in the comments of interviewees. One noted: 'I mean for a start-off, our local AM is a member of our organization and through her we voice our feelings and one thing and another; that is our direct link with the Assembly.' Another spoke of the 'need to get to know personally the Assembly Members and those key contacts ... we are targeting specific Assembly Members now who have got an interest in our work'. Similarly, another said:

> we are obviously in close contact with all of the Assembly Members, and in particular the women Assembly Members. In fact many of them are members of this organization anyway. So we feel as though we have got quite an input; and a direct input because we know them all very well, and I think that will be good.

In other respects, not all women's organizations have been satisfied with the way that the new policy process is working. In particular, they were often unaware of whether their comments had influenced matters until the finished policy documents emerged, at which point it was too late to comment or influence them further. Amongst those interviewed, short notice and unrealistic submission deadlines for policy consultations were also areas of concern. This general point was acknowledged by the Minister responsible, who stated that officials were: 'increasingly accepting the need to engage with statutory and voluntary sector bodies at the outset of initiatives rather than playing catch-up at the end' (Hart, 2000: unpaginated). As a result, 'developing and implementing procedures that allow voluntary organizations sufficient time and resources to participate in consultation exercises' was prioritized in the Voluntary Sector Scheme Implementation Plan associated with the voluntary sector partnership with WAG (VSPC, 2001b: section 3). This set out a minimum eight-week time-frame for consultation exercises and offered the assurance that the 'voluntary sector [will be] engaged in the formative stages of policy development'. Despite this commitment, political expediency and ingrained working practices mean that women's organizations continue to complain about both the time-frame and volume of consultation requests.

Gaining sufficient resources to enable greater participation in the work of government is also a central issue. A 'Summary Activity Report' of one women's organization states that: 'for the fieldworker [charged with developing the network's membership] there is a tension between the range of groups "out there" and the constraints of the budget'. That a dearth of funds limits the capacity of women's organizations to respond to Assembly Government consultation exercises was affirmed in the words of a project worker who conceded that, 'we're just going to have to take a selective approach, there's a flood of paper, we can't possibly respond to everything; we'll just have to pick and choose'.

Other aspects of the new arrangements were also of concern to interviewees. A number indicated ill ease when asked about the dual role that the new participatory structures required them to perform. In this respect, women's organizations, in common with many third-sector bodies, found themselves at once 'acting for' the Assembly Government as (WAG-funded) coordinators of policy consultation exercises *and* operating as independent champions of members' interests as lobbyists of Welsh government. Such a dual role has the potential to undermine the autonomy of voluntary sector organizations (see Taylor and Bassi, 1998, for a discussion). This point is further illustrated in Charles's work (2004) on domestic violence. She shows that whilst aspects of devolved governance 'provid[e] a real opportunity to influence the development of policy', the new political engagement of women's NGOs in the policy process is also conditioned by a potential need to fit in with the norms associated with the power-structures of policy communities. In the case of developing the Welsh

Assembly Government's National Strategy on Tackling Domestic Abuse (*c*.2005), Charles observes that: 'in the process of ensuring that domestic violence be taken seriously, it has been reframed and depoliticised ... having the effect of marginalizing more radical feminist voices' (2004: 308).

In the face of such a stark warning, it is clear that members of women's NGOs and policy networks need to be vigilant against the spectres of neo-corporatism and co-option which may operate to compromise women's political participation. As the policy literature warns, the former is characterized by: 'the exclusive relationship between a handful of privileged groups and the state[, i]nstead of the multiplicity of relevant interest groups predicted by pluralism' (Wilson, 1990: 69).

Away from such concerns, a further issue highlighted by some managers of women's NGOs was the 'fine line' that they had to tread, for whilst members had very strong opinions on many key social issues, they were simultaneously highly resistant to the idea that they were engaging in 'politics'. One manager summed up this dilemma:

> I think some of our members get a bit anxious because they keep spouting 'you know we are a *non*-political organization and we shouldn't be talking to them' [that is, Assembly Members]. They get a bit confused about the fact that as an organization that lobbies and campaigns we *have* to talk to them because they are the people making the decisions at the end of the day. And, if we want to influence that decision, *we have to talk to them*.

Notwithstanding such challenges, earlier research (Betts and Chaney, 2004) showed that many members of women's NGOs were ready to engage in 'political activities'.[29] Whilst social reasons (that is, to meet and socialize with people) was the most-cited underlying motive for membership of the respective women's NGOs surveyed (one given by almost two-thirds of respondents), political motives were also to the fore. One in six of the women surveyed (16 per cent) said that they participated in the activities of their NGO mainly for 'political reasons'; over a half of respondents said their personal membership was based on 'a desire to make a difference to a social issue'; and over a quarter (27 per cent) said that they belonged because they wished to influence the views of politicians and decision-makers. Importantly, almost a half of women surveyed said that they participated voluntarily in the activities of organizations outside the home and the workplace in order to promote the rights of women (45 per cent). Moreover, just over a quarter of the women surveyed (26 per cent) said that their membership of respective women's NGOs was 'an opportunity to lobby the Welsh Assembly'.

PARTICIPATORY DEMOCRACY?

The emerging evidence of the first years of elected devolution shows that a significant shift has taken place in Welsh governance. Seldom in the past did the male-dominated Welsh Office consult women's NGOs on issues of policy and public administration (Edwards, 1995). The prevailing ethos of the period is encapsulated by the actions of William Hague, former Secretary of State for Wales, when, in 1998, he refused to meet the Equal Opportunities Commissioner for Wales, stating that 'there is nothing to talk about'.[30] In response, pro-devolutionists' concerns for 'inclusiveness' and 'participatory democracy' were incorporated in the design of the Assembly. Importantly, as a result of associated developments, such as the Voluntary Sector Partnership Council and the Assembly's Equality Committee, the participation of women (and other groups) in civil society has been institutionalized in the work of government (see Royles, 2004, 2007a, 2007b). Thus, via these – and other – entry points to the Assembly, women have been encouraged, and given state support and funding, to participate in the policy process and further women's substantive representation. As a result, there has been an increase in women's activism at a national level. Amongst members of the principal women's policy network, there is a general willingness to engage and use the new access to the policy process in order to attempt to influence the national political agenda. Many women's NGOs have already seized the opportunity to lobby and take part in policy consultations. Others say that they wish for greater training, knowledge and skills in order to enable their future participation. A broad range of issues have been the subject of the new interaction between the National Assembly and women in civil society. These include equal pay, women in public life, tackling domestic violence, and promoting gender equality in education. These are the types of gender equality issues that the previous decades of administrative devolution failed to address in an adequate manner; indeed, many were never on the policy agenda of those running the Welsh Office.

The new level of participation afforded by devolution has also presented a series of ongoing challenges and issues for women's NGOs. Starting from a 'low base', managers have often been on a steep learning-curve in developing lobbying and consultation skills in order to focus on the Assembly's policy-making structures. Limited organizational capacity and resources in women's NGOs have been a pressing issue during the first years of devolved governance, one that has created tensions between conducting extensive consultation with NGOs' entire grassroots membership and the expedient use of an 'executive' response by a limited number of managers on behalf of members. Whilst a welcome development, Assembly Government funding for women's policy networks nevertheless raises potential issues of organizational independence versus co-option. Other challenges include the need to increase the levels of engagement achieved thus far, and, in particular, to reach out and secure the political participation of individual women and women's NGOs that are not presently members of the policy networks working with the Assembly.

Overall, the advent of the Assembly has been accompanied by a reconfiguration of women's organizations as part of the ongoing development of a nascent women's lobby. In turn, this has involved increased inter-organizational links between elements of the women's movement, as well as, at an individual level, significant organizational restructuring, sometimes involving increased levels of autonomy (from British/UK management structures) for cross-border organizations.

A further aspect is the interconnectedness of women elected to the Assembly and women's organizations. This operates in two respects: first, the direct transfer of the managers of women's NGOs that occurred with the election in 1999 of individuals such as Jane Hutt (formerly with Chwarae Teg *and* Welsh Women's Aid), Val Feld and Helen Mary Jones (both formerly with the Equal Opportunities Commission in Wales), and second, it is sustained by the ongoing and active membership of women's NGOs by some women AMs.

In summary, the new women's lobby is characterized by its developing nature, a prevailing willingness to engage in policy-making, and its organizational complexity. Notwithstanding ongoing challenges facing women's NGOs, the evidence shows that, in the wake of elected devolution, women's growing participation in the policy process has lent greater democratic legitimacy to national decision-making. In the following chapter, we examine the way in which the Assembly Government has responded to this increased demand for gender equality to be addressed in public policy.

8

Gender Equality and Policy-making

> There is a definite wish to make equal opportunities the concern of the whole
> Assembly ... the executive will also need to take equality of opportunity factors into
> account in every policy decision. This mainstreaming approach is fundamental.[1]

This chapter presents a critical evaluation of devolved government's response to
the Assembly's statutory equality duty. In particular, we examine the aims and
characteristics of 'mainstreaming', the Assembly Government's chosen approach
to promoting equalities. This latter is an ambitious project concerned with: 'the
(re)organisation, improvement, development and evaluation of policy processes,
so that a gender equality perspective is incorporated in all policies at all levels
and at all stages, by the actors normally involved in policy-making' (Council of
Europe, 2003). We ask: how has the Assembly Government's approach to engendering policy worked out in practice? And what have been the achievements and
shortfalls of its mainstreaming strategy?

The origins of the Assembly Government's chosen method of promoting
equality can be traced back to the 1985 Third United Nations (UN) World
Conference on Women, in Nairobi. Here, mainstreaming first gained major attention. A decade later, it came to much wider notice, following the Fourth UN World
Conference on Women, held in Beijing. Focusing on 'institutional mechanisms for
the advancement of women', the ensuing Beijing Platform for Action called
upon governments to: 'create or strengthen national machineries and other
governmental bodies [in order to promote gender equality]; integrate gender
perspectives in legislation, public policies, programmes and projects; and
generate and disseminate gender-disaggregated data and information for planning and evaluation' (United Nations, 1995: 87). As result of such initiatives,
mainstreaming has become 'one of the most rapidly adopted, progressive, social
justice-oriented initiatives endorsed by the international community' (Chaney
and Rees, 2004: 174). Originally pertaining solely to gender equality, the concept
has broadened in its application and often relates to the general promotion of
equality. A key way in which the concept marks an advance over earlier
approaches to equality is its potential to address intersectionality, namely, the
development of a more nuanced approach to policy-making, with the capacity
to address the intersections between different dimensions of inequality associated

with 'multiple identities' (such as ethnicity and age, or gender and disability). By 2004, 165 member states of the United Nations reported some form of 'national machinery' for mainstreaming by government (IANWGE, 2005: 61).

We begin the present analysis of the Welsh mainstreaming 'project' with an outline of the social and economic backdrop to the new Assembly's work, one that reveals the daunting scale of the challenge faced by policy-makers. This is followed by an exploration of the Assembly Government's adoption of main-streaming, including the development of the institutional prerequisites necessary for this transformative approach to policy. Attention is then turned to selected examples of policy and law. These have been chosen because they provide early evidence of specific measures to promote gender – and other modes of – equality. They include: reform of the public appointments process, education policy and numerous examples of Wales-only legislation passed by the Assembly. In order to contextualize the Assembly's equality agenda we then turn to a comparative analysis of parallel measures undertaken by the Scottish Executive. This chapter concludes by drawing upon official evaluation reports published during the Assembly's first years, in order to assess the impact of constitutional reform on gender and policy. Based upon the emerging evidence we question whether we are currently witnessing 'decoupling' in respect of mainstreaming – in other words, a situation where the devolved government is managing a disjunction between its political vision for equalities, the formal rules and practices of the bureaucracy and actual policy outcomes. First, in order to contextualize the major shift that has taken place in government's approach to equality issues, we look back to the pre-existing situation and focus on social inequality and the policy process under the Welsh Office.

A NEW AGENDA?

Reference to the prevailing social and economic context into which the new Assembly was inserted reveals the extent of the challenge faced by policy-makers. By virtue of the equality clauses in the Assembly's founding statute, officials transferred from the Welsh Office suddenly found themselves tasked with addressing pronounced patterns of inequality and discrimination in Welsh society, as evidenced, for example, by a contemporary study of women's position in the labour market. This concluded that:

> [T]here is still a substantial pay gap between men and women, there are clear gender divisions in education, training and employment, and a lack of childcare facilities and uneven domestic division of labour has resulted in a female workforce in Wales whose skills, potential and qualifications are underused. There is clearly work to be done if women's life chances are not to be restricted by their gender and the Welsh economy is not to continue to be hampered by the under-utilization of women ... [Overall,] in

many sectors such as education and local government, the position of women appears to be worsening rather than improving. (Rees, 1999a: 86)

As noted in earlier chapters, throughout its thirty-five-year history the Welsh Office proved largely ineffective in addressing such inequality between the sexes (for a discussion of policy-making under the Welsh Office see Rowlands, 2004, and Rawlings, 1998, 2003), a situation not unrelated to the fact that, as an official report later revealed, the majority of its employees 'ha[d] received no training or awareness raising at all on equality matters' (NAW, 2001a: para. 3.1). This lack of knowledge was compounded by an absence of 'ownership' of equality matters. Prior to 1999 enquiries from individuals and NGOs about equality issues were repeatedly bounced back and forth between Whitehall departments and the Welsh Office, with each claiming that it was the other's responsibility (Williams and Chaney, 2001: 83). Reflecting the general malaise, Val Feld described women's inequality in Wales as 'com[ing] together in an underlying alienation of women from legislative institutions, in particular what can be perceived as male institutions, male agenda, male political methods' (Feld, 1992: 81).

In contrast, the equality mechanisms set into the legal and constitutional framework of Assembly (see chapter 3) effectively provided an 'enabling context' (Mackay and Bilton, 2000: 109) for addressing inequality and discrimination. Accordingly, in July 1999, at the first meeting of the Assembly's cross-party Equality Committee, a new basis for promoting equality was set out by Jane Hutt, the Assembly Government Equalities Minister. Her strategy paper detailed how politics and policy would be different under the new 'devolved' arrangements. It asserted that:

Assembly [ministers], as the executive, will need to: take equality of opportunity factors into account in every policy decision. This mainstreaming approach is fundamental and the Assembly has already endorsed it. (NAW, 1999b: unpaginated)

Importantly, the Assembly's statutory equality duty was cited as a driver for this new approach. The Equalities Minister's strategy document referred to the need to ensure that a 'proper framework is in place to support the delivery of the Assembly's duty on equal opportunities' (NAW, 1999b: unpaginated). It is worth dwelling on some of the details of Hutt's paper in order to appreciate the radical nature of the vision on offer and its implications for the substantive representation of women. 'Equality' was now to be the Assembly's 'consistent core message' (NAW, 1999b: unpaginated). The Assembly Equality Committee defined this as: 'treating people equally in status, rights and opportunities through a set of policies and actions, with the aim of securing equality of outcome for all' (NAW, 2004: 7). If the new emphasis on equalities was not evidence enough of a major shift in the position of government when compared to the Welsh Office era, the Assembly Government's subscription to *mainstreaming* equality left no room for doubt. Gender mainstreaming is a radical and proactive concept in public administration, a wholly transformative process whereby, as Jahan (1995: 13) points out; 'women not only become part of the mainstream, they also reorient the nature of the mainstream'. Within the present context this approach has been defined as:

> [T]he integration of respect for diversity and equality of opportunity principles, strategies and practices into the everyday work of [government . . .] and other public bodies. It means that equality issues should be included from the outset as an integral part of the policy-making and service delivery process and the achievement of equality should inform all aspects of the work of every individual within an organisation. The success of mainstreaming should be measured by evaluating whether inequalities have been reduced. (NAW, 2004: 6)

Whilst the Assembly Equality Committee's endorsement of mainstreaming principles was an ambitious step, in other respects it represented the continuing influence of key feminist activists. Five years earlier Jane Hutt, the minister sponsoring the new approach to equalities, was one of the women activists who secured the commitment to gender equality in the Parliament for Wales Campaign's Democracy Declaration (see chapter 2). According to Hutt's strategy paper, mainstreaming would be based upon: 'a clearly defined role for all parts of the Assembly in taking the agenda forward' (NAW, 1999b: unpaginated). The paper continued: 'we need to be clear about how each part of the Assembly will contribute, so that a definite dynamic is established' (NAW, 1999b: unpaginated). For this to be achieved there was an evident need to reform the bureaucracy inherited from the Welsh Office and put in place appropriate institutional mechanisms, or prerequisites, so that the new equalities work might develop apace. Building on the Assembly's internal law, or standing orders,[2] Hutt's strategy paper gave to the multi-party standing Equality Committee a central role in driving forward the equality agenda, whilst at the same time observing the primacy, and ultimate power of veto, of the executive.[3] The document stated that:

> The Equal Opportunities Committee will champion equal opportunities, provide leadership on the issue and be vigilant that it is being properly addressed across the board. However, it is equally important that the public and Assembly Members hear a consistent message on this subject from the First Minister and all Assembly [ministers]. I would also invite members of the Equal Opportunities Committee to endorse the themes of corporate and individual responsibility, increased awareness and genuine dialogue leading to clear priorities and targets for action. (NAW, 1999b: unpaginated)

In practical terms, and as part of 'a four-stage work programme', the ministerial paper set out the immediate need for a series of 'baseline audits' in order to assess the current position of the Assembly in relation to gender and other 'strands' of equality. Furthermore, it stated that:

> Assembly ministers will approve firm action plans for their area of responsibility; progress will be monitored against set targets; action will be needed in addressing

information gaps; a democratic, participative approach to mainstreaming will require the direct involvement of groups 'targeted' by equality reforms; and, the Committee on Equality of Opportunity will also need to consider the reports and the subsequent subject committee discussions [in respect to all areas of 'devolved' policy-making – from education and health to culture and economic development]. (NAW, 1999b: unpaginated)

Thus, this wholesale subscription to the mainstreaming principle was concerned with attempting to apply a transformative approach to policy by using the opportunities presented by the new, more inclusive structures of governance, a new political context that effectively provided a 'test-bed for initiatives in gender equality' (Rees, 2002a: 62). Yet, in order for mainstreaming to be applied in the manner set out in the strategy paper, it was clear that significant reform of the existing government administrative practices and procedures would be necessary.

DEVELOPING THE INSTITUTIONAL PREREQUISITES FOR MAINSTREAMING

The Civil Service transferred from the Welsh Office to the National Assembly in 1999 represented a powerful continuity with the earlier approach to public administration, one that had little to say on the topic of equality. Accordingly, it possessed none of the institutional prerequisites or 'building blocks' necessary for the application of gender mainstreaming (Mackay and Bilton, 2000; Rees, 2002b). Such prerequisites are wide-ranging and include: appropriate institutional arrangements, awareness-raising, training, expertise, appropriate staffing, reporting mechanisms, incentives to 'build ownership' of the promotion of equality, and securing adequate resources. The initial absence of these building blocks presented a major obstacle to realizing the goal of mainstreaming. Hall (1986: 19) offers a conceptual explanation for this. He states:

the organisation of policy making affects the degree of power that any one set of actors has over policy outcomes ... organisational position also influences an actor's definition of their own interests, by establishing their institutional responsibilities and relationships to other actors. In this way, organisational factors affect both the degree of pressure an actor can bring to bear on policy and the likely direction of that pressure.

In short, when applied to the case of the Assembly, this means that the descriptive representation of women as elected representatives would be more likely to translate into women's substantive representation (that is, policy outcomes) if accompanied by significant reform of the former Welsh Office bureaucracy. For this reason, and in order to evaluate the extent to which elected devolution has furthered government's capacity to advance sex equality, it is necessary to consider the progress made in securing the institutional prerequisites necessary for gender mainstreaming in public policy.

(i) Appropriate institutional arrangements

As noted in chapter 3, as a result of lobbying by gender equality activists, when the Assembly began its work in July 1999 a number of institutional arrangements necessary to a mainstreaming approach to equalities were enshrined in the Assembly's legal and procedural framework. At the forefront of these were the equality duties included in the Government of Wales Act (1998) (see chapter 3). According to Rees (2002a: 62), these 'seek to "lock" mainstreaming into the responsibilities of the Assembly'. Certainly, they gave legal backing for further institutional reform. Indeed, they *require* the Assembly to make such '*appropriate arrangements* with a view to securing that its functions [and its business] are exercised with due regard to the principle that there should be equality of opportunity for all people'.[4] Crucially, the Assembly's standing orders require that the cross-party Committee on Equality of Opportunity 'shall audit the Assembly's arrangements for promoting in the exercise of its functions and the conduct of its business the principle that there should be equality of opportunity for all people'.[5] From the outset, and in order to support the work of the Committee, a dedicated Equality Policy Unit (EPU) was created in the Assembly Government Civil Service (an administrative department with no parallel in the former Welsh Office). Other 'appropriate institutional arrangements' that have been put in place since 1999 include: formal limits on the institution's working hours, in order to promote work–life balance;[6] the requirement for gender-neutral official titles; and rules on the language permitted in political debate.[7] Interviewed in 1999, the late Val Feld AM summarized these developments by saying that:

> I think that we have succeeded in putting in place every structural measure that we could reasonably expect to try to create a new framework and ethos that means equality has a good chance of flourishing in the way that the Assembly carries out its business and in the way that it works internally and externally.

(ii) Reporting mechanisms

The Assembly's legal framework requires that reporting mechanisms measure progress in relation to the developing equalities agenda. Thus, again, the Assembly's standing orders oblige the Equality Committee to 'submit an annual report to the Assembly on ... arrangements [to promote equality] and their effectiveness'.[8] Crucially, this reporting mechanism extends beyond assessing the practices of the National Assembly to encompass the 'review [of] the Annual Reports submitted to the Assembly by public bodies'.[9] During the Assembly's first years, baseline equality surveys of the Assembly Civil Service were included in these reports. These aimed to establish: the extent to which gender (and race and disability) were taken into account in developing Assembly policies; the prevailing equal opportunities objectives and targets in the Civil Service; and the availability of data to monitor the outcomes of policies. A further example of the new reporting mechanisms is provided by ministerial remit letters. In a break from past practices, these require chief executives of Assembly-sponsored public bodies to report to the executive on measures that they have taken to promote equality.

(iii) Awareness-raising

The involvement of experts drawn from outside the Civil Service has fostered another dimension integral to a mainstreaming approach, namely, raising awareness of equality issues. This has been achieved through inter-agency and cross-party working as evidenced by the Assembly Government's successive 'Close the Pay Gap' campaigns to promote equal pay for women and men in respect of work of equal value. With a working group comprising AMs from all parties, the campaigns involved co-working between the Equal Opportunities Commission Wales, the Wales TUC and the Assembly Government. This approach to equalities was described by a senior participant as one that: 'adds considerable weight to campaigning and removes the sometimes adversarial party politics which can arise over issues' (quoted in Chaney, 2003b: 136).[10] Between March 2002 and April 2003, the campaign achieved extensive publicity. This included repeated coverage in the broadcast media, poster campaigns and a total of sixty-three articles in print, a mean frequency of over one press article per week (Chaney, 2003b: 71).

(iv) Resources

Although difficult to quantify (for equality has not generally been listed as a discrete heading in Assembly Government budget data), it is evident that, when compared to the 'zero base' of administration under the Welsh Office, there has been a major and significant increase in the resources allocated to the promotion of equality in areas such as policy-making, training and consultation. Nevertheless, it is still unclear as to how the Assembly Government's increased resource allocation to equalities work actually impacts on groups traditionally targeted by equalities policies. One technique that can increase understanding of the link between resource allocation and equality is gender budgeting (see Elson, 1998).[11] This technical equality tool is straightforward in its objectives: it examines, and makes adjustments in light of, the respective impact of public expenditure on females and males. Whilst the Assembly Government has recently undertaken to apply gender budgeting techniques to some aspects of its spending plans (Baumgardt, 2005), at present there is a general absence of gender-disaggregated statistics and a general declaratory approach to promoting equality in the allocation of the National Assembly's budget, a situation evidenced by the WAG document entitled *A Budget for the Future of Wales: The Assembly Government's Spending Plans 2005–06 to 2007–08*. This fails to set out detailed spending plans to promote equality. Instead, it offers the generality that, 'equality of opportunity underpins our budget provisions' (WAG, 2005: 2).

(v) Appropriate staffing arrangements

The academic literature emphasizes that 'difference is a political resource', meaning, in this context, that bureaucrats can draw directly upon a diversity of cultural values and life experiences in order to inform their professional work (for a discussion see Young, 1990; Broadnax, 2000; Frederickson, 2000). Devolution has resulted in a raft of initiatives to put in place staffing arrangements essential to the effective adoption of mainstreaming, in particular, the need to move towards a more diverse workforce in the Assembly when compared to the Welsh Office (see discussion in *Public appointments* below). During the Assembly's first years, there has been slow progress in increasing the diversity of Assembly Government civil servants. Indeed, the WAG bureaucracy is no exception to the vertical gender-segregation that characterizes the Welsh labour market as a whole (see Blackaby et al., 1999). Thus, women continue to face major inequalities. They constitute an overwhelming majority of those holding junior Civil Service grades (61.3 per cent of grades A, B and C, in 2003) yet a minority (28.1 per cent) of those in Senior Civil Service (SCS) posts. However, during the Assembly's first term there has been evidence of comparatively rapid change in the proportion of women holding middle-ranking official posts (between 2000 and 2003, a 13.9 percentage-point increase in the number of women in grades D and E). Yet other grades have seen an increase of only a few percentage points in the number of women holding posts in the bureaucracy.

(vi) Training

This is a key institutional prerequisite for mainstreaming and, given the low starting point of the former Welsh Office Civil Service, it is an area that has needed sustained consideration. In the words of one Assembly report it is: 'a vital part of ... work to promote equality ... [in order that] Assembly officials will have a more thorough understanding of the practical ways of mainstreaming equality effectively' (NAW, 2001a: 11). By 2003, mandatory equality awareness training had been delivered to 3,500 Assembly staff. Specialist training was also provided for management grades and personnel staff in the bureaucracy. The rationale for this extensive initiative was set out in the training strategy document. This highlighted the role of statute as the driver of equalities reform, stating that:

> [T]he National Assembly for Wales has a statutory duty to promote equality of opportunity in the discharge of its functions ... to assist the staff ... this Equality Training and Awareness Strategy has been developed to help staff at all levels operate an effective equal opportunities policy. (NAW, 2001b: para. 1.3)

Elsewhere, specific policy initiatives have also entailed an equality training component, such as the Assembly Government's Code of Practice for Ministerial Appointments to Public Bodies. In order to reach hitherto under-represented groups, this document sets out new requirements for those involved in interviewing for public appointments, and obliges them to undergo training in best practice in candidate selection (NAW, 2000c).

(vii) Expertise

The expertise necessary to drive and inform the new equalities agenda has mostly come from outside the former Welsh Office Civil Service. At a political level, the professional gender equality experience of several Assembly Members has been of key importance. For example, Jane Hutt, Helen Mary Jones and Val Feld had all held senior management positions in gender equality organizations before election to the Assembly. Thus, each had a strong record in developing organizations such as Welsh Women's Aid and Chwarae Teg. Academic expertise has also been forthcoming from a range of international mainstreaming experts and practitioners.[12] Furthermore, membership of the Assembly's Equality Committee has been expanded to include representatives from the Equal Opportunities Commission Wales, the Disability Rights Commission, the Commission for Racial Equality Wales, the Welsh Language Board, and the Lesbian, Gay and Bisexual (LGB) Forum Cymru (latterly Stonewall Cymru). In light of these developments, it is evident that there has been an attempt to combine 'expert-bureaucratic' and 'participative-democratic' approaches to mainstreaming (see Nott, 1999). Whereas the former method focuses primarily upon in-house expertise, the use of consultants and technical instruments, the latter emphasizes the expertise and involvement of civic actors and NGOs in the policy-making process. On balance, during the Assembly's first years there has been greater evidence of expert-bureaucratic inputs to further mainstreaming, a point highlighted in the Equality Committee's annual reports. One stated that:

> [I]n the past there has been less focus on equality issues in policy-making than in employment practice ... [there is a] need to promote equality in both policy-making and service delivery ... there is still a long way to go in involving and consulting under-represented groups and doing so at a much earlier stage of the process of policy development. (WAG, 2001a: 11)

(viii) Ownership

In order to achieve 'ownership', or clearly defined personal, professional responsibility for the Assembly Government's reforms, as noted earlier, equality concerns feature in the ministerial remit letters sent to chief executives of Assembly-sponsored public bodies. For example, writing to the chief executive of the schools inspectorate, ESTYN,[13] Jane Davidson, Minister for Education and Lifelong Learning, stated: 'I want to ... reinforce the message that ... the Inspectorate's work supports the vision and strategic direction set out by the Assembly ... to promote equality opportunity'.[14]

Overall, the foregoing developments show that a broad range of institutional prerequisites for mainstreaming equality into the work of government have begun to be put in place. This represents a major change in the potential capacity of national government in Wales to promote gender equality and facilitate the substantive representation of women. It marks the shift from the Welsh Office, a government department that did not generally regard equality as its responsibility, to the National Assembly, which has begun to build actively upon its legal obligations in this area in order to design institutional mechanisms and procedures broadly consistent with the mainstreaming ethos.

ENGENDERING POLICY AND LAW

Writing in the second year of devolved governance, Beveridge et al. (2000b: 403) questioned the impact on policy-making of the Assembly's institutional reforms. They state: 'there are strong, early indications that the new devolved governments are actively pursuing [a mainstreaming] agenda. However, it is at present too early to comment on whether or not they are likely to succeed in "engendering policy-making" in any comprehensive sense.' We now address this issue from the perspective offered by almost two terms of devolved government.

The Assembly Equality Committee's Fifth Annual Report outlines the work undertaken by the Assembly Government to promote equality of opportunity from 2003 to 2004. This summary document asserts that 'equality considerations have become increasingly embedded in the way we develop policies' (NAW, 2004, p. 32). Figure 8.1 details examples of the policy initiatives listed in the Report under the discrete heading 'gender'. These include: organizing 'workshop' events 'with a view to building women's confidence to encourage them to participate in a wide range of organisations in Wales'; funding for the second phase of the Equal Pay Campaign; initiatives to raise women's awareness of public appointments process; and improvements in the availability of gender-disaggregated statistics in education. Overall, the report concludes of WAG's equality initiatives: 'while this represents substantial progress and a considerable body of work, the Assembly Government recognises that more can be done to further improve the effectiveness of its work on equal opportunities and is committed to doing so' (NAW, 2004, p. 22). The following examples of policy and law provide further illustration of the work to promote gender equality undertaken during the Assembly's first years.

Public appointments
The public appointments process is a key area that has long perpetuated patterns of inequality by excluding and marginalizing a range of social groups from formal decision-making structures. Thus, according to Putnam (1976: 39), 'the pathway into the political elite is blocked by a series of gates, and [in determining access to this group] gatekeepers may consider candidates' social backgrounds'.

Assembly government department/unit	Action to promote gender equality
Social Justice and Regeneration Communities directorate	Home-working project • Funding was provided for the National Group on Home-working to scope the extent, nature and support for home-workers in Wales.
Equality Policy Unit	Wales Women's National Coalition Funding was provided to the Wales Women's National Coalition (WWNC), a consultative network established to promote gender equality in Wales. WWNC participated in and initiated a number of activities, including responding to the Home Office's 'Safety and Justice' consultation, and organizing a number of workshop events with a view to building women's confidence to encourage them to participate in a wide range of organizations in Wales. International Women's Day An International Women's Day event was hosted for minority ethnic women in March 2004. The event was organized by the Assembly in conjunction with a number of minority ethnic women's organizations, including: MEWN Cymru, BAWSO, Saheli, Valleys Women Ethnic Minority Support Group, Cardiff Somali Women and Youth, Women Connect First and Women in Action. • These organizations invited a selection of minority ethnic women from those most marginalized and disadvantaged within Welsh society. The overall aim of the event was to: promote greater awareness, understanding and collaboration between different groups of minority ethnic women; celebrate International Women's Day; provide an opportunity for minority ethnic women to discuss key issues relating to gender and race equality with Assembly officials and the Minister for Social Justice and Regeneration. Equal Pay Campaign • In November 2003, the Minister for Social Justice and Regeneration approved funding for the second phase of the Equal Pay Campaign. The total funding amounted to £60,253 and was broken down as follows: £45,253 of the funding was pledged to the Wales TUC to employ two dedicated secondees to assist union officials and employers to begin pay reviews; £10,000 of the funding was pledged to the Equal Opportunities Commission to: commission research into equal pay in relation to minority ethnic men and women, and raise awareness of the Equal Pay Review Kit with small and medium enterprises; £5,000 of the funding has been earmarked for the evaluation of the second phase of the Equal Pay Campaign.
Public administration division	Welsh Women's National Coalition • Public Appointments Unit attended an event organized by WWNC to raise awareness of public appointments.
Statistical directorate	Examination and assessment achievement: gender analysis (statistical bulletin) • Published annual statistical bulletin comparing the attainment of males and females at Key Stage assessments and external examinations.

Figure 8.1 WAG gender equality reforms 2003–4 (NAW, 2004).

Such exclusive practices have a highly gendered dimension, one based upon 'a hierarchy of authority underpinned by strongly masculine norms of sociability resulting in women predominating in subordinate positions and supporting male power' (Connell, 1987: 151). In Wales, this has a particular resonance. Traditionally men have been vastly over-represented amongst those holding public appointments. At the outset of elected devolution women constituted just 31 per cent of those holding public appointments and 30 per cent of all applicants for such posts (NAW, 2000b: 5). An initial report commissioned by the Assembly government summarized the situation by stating that:

> representation of women at the highest levels in public bodies, just as it is in employ-ment, is low; women tend towards the lower-profile jobs, are paid less or are not paid at all. There seems to be a pecking order, with wide-ranging payments and for no obvious reason. (NAW, 2000c: 24)

Edwina Hart, then Equalities Minister, referred to the daunting challenge that lay ahead:

> the task is difficult, because it involves not only changing processes, but challenging perceptions and re-educating everyone to the point where it is taken for granted that public appointments are open to all and representative of the society in which we live. That is a tall order.[15]

In response to the long-standing discrimination against women, as noted, a new Code of Practice for Ministerial Appointments to Public Bodies was imple-mented (NAW, 2002a). This asserted that:

> The principles of equal opportunity and diversity are not only socially just, but will benefit any [public appointments] board to which they are applied. Individuals from all sections of society may have much to offer a public body by virtue of their diverse experience and background. Therefore: the principles of equal opportunity and diversity must be inherent within the appointments process. Care must be taken, at every stage, not to discriminate on the grounds of gender. (NAW, 2002a: 12)

The code of practice included a raft of measures that were consistent with these aims. They included: information-dissemination strategies to reach women's NGOs; targeted advertising of posts; training in best practice in candidate selec-tion for those involved in interviewing for public appointments; and involving independent assessors who are fully trained in equality issues at a much earlier stage in the appointment process than was the case before elected devolution. Perhaps the most radical step in this area was the decision, taken at the end of 2000, to dismiss all the existing independent assessors involved in making public appointments. As a result of this 'equality coup d'état', fifty-five new assessors were appointed, thereby signalling a clear break with past practices and putting in place assessors with greater equality competencies. Importantly, 56 per cent of the new assessors were women (NAW, 2003). The code of practice also set out how management procedures would be changed to promote gender equality. It stated: the 'Public Appointments Unit [of the Assembly government] will have discretion to look for the next man or woman on the list [of available assessors] in order to ensure gender balance on a[n appointments] panel' (WAG, 2004a: 61). A further move designed to increase the representation of women was the requirement that, 'for all posts there should be provision for reimbursement of receipted childcare or carer costs' (NAW, 2002b: 8).

Notwithstanding the evident determination to promote reform on this issue, reference to the composition of chairs and members of Assembly-sponsored public bodies and NHS Wales bodies as at 1 April 2003 showed that to date these reforms had had only a modest impact in terms of outcomes. Just 34 per cent were women (NAW, 2003).

Education policy

From the outset of devolved government, promoting gender and other modes of equality was identified as a core aim in the provision of state education. This can be seen in four areas: strategic leadership, curriculum planning, training, and inspection arrangements. These developments form part of a new approach whereby:

> democratic devolution has created the circumstances in which education policies in Wales have become increasingly distinct from those in England; and in some instances real innovations have been brought about ... it is extremely unlikely that things would have developed this way if the old Welsh Office regime had continued. (Rees, 2004: 28)

Accordingly, equality is a central theme in the Assembly government's 2001–10 education strategy. This document was prefaced by the statement that, 'the Government of Wales Act lays a distinct and special responsibility upon the National Assembly over the pursuit of equal opportunities' (WAG, 2001b: 40). Amongst the strategy's detailed aims was: 'the need to focus the attention of governing bodies for schools, colleges and universities, upon tackl[ing] gender imbalances within their governing bodies and staff teams' (WAG, 2001b: 38).

Similarly, in its strategy for higher education the Assembly Government again highlighted the need for promoting gender equality. It asserted:

> It is important that the [Welsh higher education] sector be seen to have a high regard for the principles of equal opportunity ... To back these aspects of modernisation for the sector we shall be prepared to consider providing additional funds to ... conduct equal pay audits, and help HEIs respond to the conclusions [of equal pay audits]. (WAG, 2002: 11, para. 36)

In addition, the Welsh executive's first programme for government referred to the need to 'ensure that the [schools] curriculum reflects the diversity of our communities, [by] tackling sex ... stereotyping' (NAW, 2000b: 27). Introduced in September 2000, the first Wales-specific National Curriculum was developed, with 'explicit attention to the Assembly's key policy priorit[y] of promoting equality of opportunity' (NAW, 2001b: 25, para. 47). Accordingly, a range of initiatives have been introduced to end gender-segregation and promote equality in the school curriculum. One example was the inclusion of personal and social education (PSE) and work-related education (WRE) as statutory elements within the basic Welsh curriculum for children and young people aged five to nineteen (see, for example, ACCAC, 2000, 2001a, 2001b, 2002; Careers Wales, 2002) (Figure 8.2.). These new aspects of the curriculum prescribe 'attitudes, values, and skills' to promote gender equality. Thus, the Framework for Careers Education and Guidance for eleven- to nineteen-year-olds highlights the need for pupils and students to 'challenge stereotypes and broaden their career horizons'. Similarly, the Schools' PSE Framework for Key Stages 1 to 4 sets out the requirement for 'equality of opportunity and acceptance of others ... regardless of ... gender (e.g. in education, training and work)' (ACCAC, 2000: 9). In addition, the Framework for WRE for fourteen- to nineteen-year-olds sets out the requirement for 'using personal and social skills well and having respect for themselves and others in working situations (across gender, race and disability)' (ACCAC, 2002: 4).

Education policy has also focused on tackling gender stereotyping in the choice of subjects studied at school and in individuals' choices of career (see Figure 8.3). One framework document set out the Assembly Government's approach:

> The Assembly's vision is that of a progressive society in which the needs of all groups are effectively addressed. This includes a commitment to prevent discrimination against individuals or groups because of gender ... girls continue to leave school with low career aspirations. Girls and boys make stereotypical choices of options and subjects at all stages and this difference is more marked in Wales than in other parts of Britain. There is still a long way to go in respect of education and equality issues. Girls and boys are no longer expected to conform to a conventional stereotype and children should be encouraged to challenge traditional views of career options. (ACCAC, 2001a: 3–7)

In order to tackle gender stereotyping, the official framework for careers education and guidance (CEG) for eleven- to nineteen-year-olds states that: 'the CEG learning outcomes represent a common minimum entitlement. They provide challenging, but realistic, goals that the majority of young people can achieve. They have been designed so that they can ... challenge stereotypes based on gender' (ACCAC, 2001a: 8, para. 4.2). Amongst official examples of how young people might develop such skills, subsequent CEG guidance includes 'project work designed to: use national reports/surveys to explore in detail the social, economic and moral issue of gender stereotyping in work' (ACCAC, 2002: 53).

In respect of regulatory practices, the inspection framework of the Welsh Schools inspectorate, ESTYN, asserts: 'throughout the inspection ... inspectors

Published policy initiatives have identified the challenges schools face in a diverse developing society and changing democratic framework. The National Assembly for Wales recognises the role of PSE in empowering pupils to be active, informed and responsible citizens aware of their rights and committed to the practices of participative democracy and the challenges of being a citizen of Wales and the world. In particular, PSE will help schools to promote: progress toward concern and action for equal opportunities, social justice and sustainable development at local to global scales.

Key Components of the PSE Framework; Attitudes and Values:
Pupils' attitudes to the knowledge they have acquired and the issues they are discussing often determine the way they behave. Our attitudes derive from personal values and PSE can either promote or enable pupils to clarify those attitudes and values. Some examples of attitudes and values incorporated in the framework are listed below ... equality of opportunity and acceptance of others regardless of race, religion, gender, sexuality, age or disability

KEY STAGE 1 Learning Outcomes; Attitudes and Values:

PSE provision should enable pupils to:

- Recognise and value cultural differences and diversity.

KEY STAGE 2 Learning Outcomes; Attitudes and Values:

PSE provision should enable pupils to:

- Respect others and their property, value their achievements and their uniqueness and recognise the importance of equality of opportunity.
- Value and celebrate cultural difference and diversity.

KEY STAGE 3 Learning Outcomes; Knowledge and Understanding:

Pupils should:

- Value cultural diversity and equal opportunity and respect the dignity of all.
- Know that each person is different but understand that all are equal in value.
- Understand that people have different preferences, views and beliefs.
- Understand the nature of local, national and international communities with reference to cultural diversity, justice, law and order and interdependence.

KEY STAGE 4 Learning Outcomes; Attitudes and Values:

PSE provision should enable pupils to:

- Value cultural diversity and equal opportunity and respect the dignity of all.
- Know how to form supportive and respectful same-sex and opposite-sex relationships.
- Recognise and know how to challenge expressions of prejudice and stereotyping.

Figure 8.2 Promoting equality in the school curriculum: the mandatory Personal and Social Education (PSE) component (ACCAC, 2000).

Why is promoting equal opportunities an important part of the curriculum and the work of schools?

The Assembly's vision is that of a progressive society in which the needs of all groups are effectively addressed. **This includes a commitment to prevent discrimination against individuals or groups because of gender.** (p. 3)

Girls continue to leave school with low career aspirations. Girls and boys make stereotypical choices of options and subjects at all stages and this difference is more marked in Wales than in other parts of Britain. There is still a long way to go in respect of education and equality issues. Girls and boys are no longer expected to conform to a conventional stereotype and children should be encouraged to challenge traditional views of career options. In this context, schools can help significantly ... work with ACCAC, Estyn and the NAfW supports the aim of challenging sex stereotyping strategically across Wales. We have a unique opportunity to impact on the curriculum, the inspection programme and the education sector as a whole through our partnership and advisory role with these bodies. However, the key role in gender equality in schools rests with the governors, teachers, managers and local authorities. These are the people who create the atmosphere and culture of our schools on a day-to-day basis. We try, therefore, wherever possible to work with schools in whatever way we can to promote the issues and ethos which will change gender stereotyping in Wales. During the last 18 months, with the support of LEAs, we have been actively promoting our publication *Different but Equal* which provides guidance for schools on achieving gender equality. The EOC has also, in conjunction with the Association of Directors of Education in Wales, invited schools to celebrate the 25th anniversary of the Sex Discrimination Act. These events have demonstrated the wealth of commitment, information and good practice we have in relation to equality in schools around Wales. Where schools adopt a 'whole school' approach to equality issues this gives the best results. This approach covers all aspects of school life, including all the subjects of the curriculum, extra-curricular activities, organisation, staffing and management. It would be easy to overstate the impact schools can make in influencing and shaping values and attitudes that can challenge stereotyping, but they can and do make a significant contribution. (pp. 6–7)

Figure 8.3 Tackling gender stereotyping in state education (ACCAC, 2001).

must ensure that the full range of age, gender, ability, special educational need, and ethnic and linguistic background are taken into account' (ESTYN, 2002a: 5). Accordingly, the framework sets out a range of points to be considered by inspectors (see Figure 8.4). Thus, the official guidance prompts schools inspectors to ask: 'does the school promote gender equality and challenge stereotypes in pupils' choices and expectations? You should evaluate: whether policies and practices actively promote gender equality; and how effective the school is in challenging stereotypes in pupils' choices and expectations' (ESTYN, 2004: 23).

New measures have also been implemented to ensure that equality of opportunity is addressed in assessing teacher training. Recent guidance to tutors states:

> Does the training promote equality of opportunity and actively address issues of gender …? In judging how well the training promotes equal opportunities, you will need to evaluate the extent to which trainees are stimulated to think critically about tackling social disadvantage, extending entitlement and related issues. You should judge the quality of the training by the extent to which trainees can apply their knowledge and understanding of these issues in their planning and teaching. You should pay particular attention to how trainees are prepared to teach particular groups of pupils. (ESTYN, 2002a: 28)

Overall, the Assembly's first years have seen the start of a series of unprecedented measures to engender state education policy in order promote equality, from compulsory-age schooling and lifelong learning to careers advice, as well as in respect of the breadth of education functions, from teaching and education management to training and inspection.

Welsh legislation

The experience of the first years of elected devolution reveals the conclusions of some early analyses of the impact of constitutional reform to be largely unfounded. For example, one account asserted that the 'foremost limitation on the devolved UK administrations' future scope for action would be the fact that equality is a reserved power of the UK parliament. As a result the new legislatures in Wales and Scotland are unable to initiate primary equality legislation' (Livingstone, 2001: 5). In contrast, legal instruments passed by the Assembly – and the Scottish Parliament – have had the effect of broadening the scope of equality law in the devolved nations, leading to increasing divergence from legal equality requirements applying in England. Thus, examination of the hundreds of pieces of distinct Wales-only legislation passed by the National Assembly each year[16] shows that a significant number are concerned with the promotion of gender equality.

Full details of the new Welsh legal instruments that promote gender equality are given in Table 8.1. Their purpose is to effect change in a broad range of areas. They include:

- requiring greater consideration of maternity leave and ordinary adoption leave in respect of the induction arrangements for schoolteachers;
- measures to enable persons to undertake courses of further or higher education by providing financial assistance towards meeting the cost of childcare incurred in consequence of their attending such courses;
- schools' governing bodies and head teachers being required to exercise their respective functions with due regard to the need to eliminate unlawful discrimination on grounds of sex and to promote equal opportunities and good relations between males and females;

STANDARDS
Key question. 1: How well do learners achieve? In making their judgements, inspectors should consider, where applicable, the extent to which learners: 1.15 demonstrate an awareness of equal opportunities issues and a respect for diversity within society. You should evaluate and report on the standards achieved by pupils including: the extent to which pupils: 1.15.1 recognise, understand and respect the diversity of beliefs, attitudes and social and cultural traditions.

THE QUALITY OF EDUCATION AND TRAINING
Inspectors should evaluate and report on: 2.6 Do teachers promote equality of opportunity and actively address issues of gender, race and disability equality? You should evaluate how well teachers: 2.6.1 promote equal opportunities and challenge stereotypical images and views; and 2.6.2 treat all pupils equally, irrespective of their race, gender or disability.

Key question 4: How well are learners cared for, guided and supported? Inspectors should evaluate and report on: the quality of provision for equal opportunities. In making their judgements, inspectors should consider, where applicable, the extent to which providers:

4.13 support and guide learners appropriately, taking account of their social, educational, ethnic or linguistic background;

4.14 promote gender equality and challenge stereotypes in learners' choices and expectations;

4.15 promote good race relations across all areas of activity;

4.16 have effective measures to eliminate oppressive behaviour, including racial discrimination, bullying and all forms of harassment;

4.17 secure equal treatment of disabled learners and make reasonable adjustments to avoid putting them at substantial disadvantage; and

4.18 recognise and respect diversity.

You will evaluate and report on: The quality of provision for equal opportunities: 4.13 Does the school support and guide pupils appropriately taking account of their social, educational, ethnic or linguistic background? You should evaluate: 4.13.1 the extent to which the school recognises the diversity of pupils' backgrounds; and 4.13.2 whether the school acts appropriately and effectively on this information.

4.14 Does the school promote gender equality and challenge stereotypes in pupils' choices and expectations? You should evaluate: 4.14.1 whether policies and practices actively promote gender equality; and 4.14.2 how effective the school is in challenging stereotypes in pupils' choices and expectations. (Further guidance: The Sex Discrimination Act 1975 places a duty on all schools to treat girls and boys equally. It has produced major changes in the practices of schools, in particular in providing equal access to the main curriculum, curriculum options and extra-curricular activities. Despite this progress, there are still issues in the equal opportunities and relative performance of boys and girls. Boys as a group underachieve compared with girls. Girls tend to leave school with low career aspirations. Girls and boys often make stereotypical choices of options and subjects at all stages.)

Figure 8.4 Promoting equality: extracts from *Guidance on the Inspection of Secondary Schools* (ESTYN, September 2004).

Table 8.1 The promotion of gender equality in selected examples of Welsh secondary legislation.

Policy area	Scope of new legal equality requirements	Details of Welsh legislation
Education	Provision of grants to teachers of personal and social education to fulfil curriculum requirements relating to education on equal opportunities.	Approval of the Special Educational Needs and Disability Tribunal (General Provisions and Disability Claims Procedure) Regulations (2002), 18 July 2002.
	A new requirement that equal opportunities information must be included in the school prospectuses.	Welsh Statutory Instrument 2001 No. 1111 (W. 55), The Education (School Information) (Wales) (Amendment) Regulations 2001.
	Greater consideration of maternity leave and ordinary adoption leave (as well as parental leave or paternity leave) in respect of the induction arrangements for school teachers.	Welsh Statutory Instrument 2004 No. 872 (W. 87), The Education (Induction Arrangements for School Teachers) (Amendment) (Wales) Regulations 2004.
	Imposition of duties on the National Council for Education and Training for Wales to have due regard to the promotion of equality of opportunity.	Statutory Instrument 2000 No. 3230 (W. 213) (C. 103), The Learning and Skills Act 2000 (Commencement No. 2) (Wales) Order 2000.
	'To enable persons to undertake courses of further or higher education designated for the purposes of that Scheme, by providing financial assistance in or towards meeting the cost of books, equipment, travel or childcare incurred in consequence of their attending such a course.'	2002 No. 2814 (W. 271), The Education (Assembly Learning Grant Scheme) (Wales) (Amendment) Regulations 2002.
	Places legal duties on governing bodies and head teachers to exercise their respective functions with due regard to the need – (a) to eliminate unlawful discrimination on grounds of race or sex; and (b) to promote equal opportunities and good relations – (i) between persons of different racial groups, and (ii) between males and females.	School Government (Terms of Reference) (Wales) Regulations (2000), 9 November 2000.
Health	Provision of comprehensive cervical screening by contractors to NHS Wales.	Welsh Statutory Instrument 2004 No. 478 (W. 48), The National Health Service (General Medical Services Contracts) (Wales) Regulations 2004.
	Greater regulatory protection for women having an abortion.	Abortion (Amendment) (Wales) Regulations (2002), 19 November 2002.

		Welsh Statutory Instrument 2002 No. 325 (W. 38), Private and Voluntary Health Care (Wales) Regulations 2002.
Local govt./ public sector	Enhanced disability premiums in means tests for determining the amount of housing-renovation grant and disabled facilities grant.	Welsh Statutory Instrument 2001 No. 2073 (W. 145), The Housing Renewal Grants (Amendment) (Wales) Regulations 2001.
	A new ethical framework for local government and public authorities in Wales – employees of relevant authorities must comply with policies relating to equality issues.	Welsh Statutory Instrument 2001 No. 2280 (W. 170), The Code of Conduct (Qualifying Local Government Employees) (Wales) Order 2001.
	Incorporating equality as a public-sector performance indicator.	Welsh Statutory Instrument 2001 No. 1337 (W. 83), The Local Government (Best Value Performance Indicators) (Wales) Order 2001.
	The number of domestic violence refuge places per 10,000 population which are provided or supported by the best-value authority.	Welsh Statutory Instrument 2001 No. 1337 (W. 83), The Local Government (Best Value Performance Indicators) (Wales) Order 2001.
Housing	*Inter alia*, adds to those persons with priority need for accommodation: 'a person fleeing domestic violence or threatened domestic violence – a person without dependent children who has been subject to domestic violence or is at risk of such violence, or if he or she returns home is at risk of domestic violence'.	Homeless Persons (Priority Need) Wales Order (2001), 16 April 2002.
Childcare	'Payment to a member of the authority who is a councillor of an allowance ("care allowance") in respect of such expenses of arranging for the care of children or dependants as are necessarily incurred in the carrying out of that member's duties as a member.'	Local Authorities (Allowances for Members of County and County Borough Councils and National Park Authorities) (Wales) Regulations (2002), 18 July 2002.
	Duty on local authorities to broaden nursery education and prepare and submit childcare plans to the National Assembly for approval.	2003 No. 893 (W. 113), Education, Wales, The Education (Nursery Education and Early Years Development and Childcare Plans) (Wales) Regulations 2003.

- provision of comprehensive cervical screening by NHS Wales;
- greater regulatory protection for women having an abortion;
- the inclusion of the number of domestic violence refuge places per 10,000 population amongst the best-value indicators of local authorities;
- adding to those persons with priority need for emergency local authority accommodation: 'a person fleeing domestic violence or threatened domestic violence';
- placing a duty on local authorities to broaden nursery education and requiring them to prepare and submit childcare plans to the Assembly Government for approval;
- requiring that local authorities make payments to councillors in respect of the care of children or dependants that is necessarily incurred in the carrying out of the councillor's duties.

A TRANSFORMATIVE APPROACH TO POLICY?

In addition to the foregoing institutional developments and policy examples, the findings of two recent evaluation reports (one commissioned by three of the statutory equality commissions in Wales, and the other forming part of the National Assembly's cross-party Equality Committee Mainstreaming Review) further enable an interim assessment to be made as to whether devolution is delivering the transformative approach to policy anticipated in the gender-mainstreaming literature (see Beveridge et al., 2000b; Donaghy, 2004).

The first evaluation report (Chaney and Fevre, 2002a; see also Chaney, 2004a) found that, between 1999 and 2002, the new legislature's equality duties had led directly to a reprioritization of equality in the process of government, such that equality of opportunity was beginning to be addressed systematically at an all-Wales level of government, for the first time. The report continued:

> The level of political will and expertise that key politicians and officials have invested in promoting equality in the process of government is unprecedented. The initial actions of the Welsh executive and opposition parties suggest a clear intention to be proactive in some areas, go beyond the equality measures thus far seen at Westminster. (Chaney and Fevre, 2002a: 86)

Notwithstanding the positive effect of the new legal equalities framework, the 2002 review also highlighted a number of key failings in the post-devolution equality agenda; in short, these centred on a failure to implement a mainstreamed approach to equalities fully. Amongst the shortcomings identified by the report were:

- That the National Assembly's policy-scrutinizing subject committees were generally failing to mainstream equality into their policy-making;

- Policy consultations were under-resourced, lacking in transparency, and often last-minute;
- The majority of policies exhibited a 'declaratory' approach to equalities – meaning that they declared the need for change, but were frequently vague on the means to achieve reform;
- In the bulk of cases, policies lacked specific and measurable equality targets linked to a prescribed time-frame;
- Policies failed to specify the individuals/organizations responsible for implementing reforms;
- And, financial and human resource implications were ignored or not addressed comprehensively. (Chaney and Fevre, 2002a: 78)

In January 2003, a senior official presented the Civil Service's responses to these points to the Equality Committee. These were generally vague and non-committal in nature, and lent credence to the observation made by a leading opposition Assembly Member when, presciently, she referred to: 'the way that cultures within organizations can unconsciously protect themselves against change ... and this has got "unconscious resistance" written through it like a stick of Brighton rock' (cited in Chaney and Fevre, 2002a: 21). The upshot was that few, if any, of the measures, tellingly listed under the title '*Possible* Method[s] of Implementation' (NAW, 2003, italics added) were executed.

Competing pressures on the bureaucracy, not least in developing the new legislature, as well as general politicking, meant that it was not until the beginning of the Assembly's second term that the Equality Committee returned to an overall, comprehensive consideration of 'how equality can be mainstreamed into the work of the Assembly and the Assembly Government' (NAW, 2004: 5). Within a UK government context, this marked a pioneering step, for it saw the commencement of a systematic, cross-party review of equality mainstreaming in government. The 2003-4 *Mainstreaming Review* was organized around four key themes: strategy and leadership; people; practical action, levers, guidance and advice; and monitoring and evaluation. In respect of 'strategy and leadership', the review's conclusion was an indictment of the incumbent Equalities Minister and senior WAG policy officials. Using stark language, it concluded that: 'currently the Assembly does not have an overall equality strategy, and in our view there is no doubt that this is hampering the Assembly's efforts in relation to mainstreaming equality'. It continued, 'there is a lot of positive activity is going on but with *little strategic direction* ... there [is] a high level of variation across the organisation' (NAW, 2004: 31–2). In response, it recommended that all Assembly Government ministers should ensure that action was taken within their portfolios to ensure that equality was mainstreamed in all the policy areas for which they were responsible.

The review also focused on the need for an ongoing programme of equality training, one that moved beyond the initial equality-awareness training given to all Assembly staff. The importance of central institutional equality units in driving forward reform was also highlighted, as was the need for clarity about the role of the Equality Policy Unit (EPU) in the Assembly Government Civil Service. The latter has been an ongoing area of critical concern during the Assembly's first years because of the way in which the EPU suffered consistently high staff turnover rates, staffing shortages and claims of ministerial interference in staffing issues. According to at least one press report, official Assembly documents released under the Data Protection Act 'indicated that [the WAG Equalities Minister] Mrs Hart had [allegedly] put pressure on senior civil servants to remove [the head of the EPU] from his job and replace him with an individual of her nomination'.[17]

Away from such controversy, the *Mainstreaming Review* also called for improvements in order to address existing shortcomings in the Assembly Civil Service's capacity to offer advice and guidance, both to internal Assembly Government Civil Service divisions and to external public bodies. Furthermore, the recommendation was made that: 'the Assembly's [policy] consultation guidance is reviewed to ensure that it is firmly based on equality of opportunity principles and addresses the need to engage the diversity of the public in Wales' (NAW, 2004: 64). Calls were also made for the future use of gender needs assessments and gender budgeting to assess the level of equity in financial allocations. In respect of the monitoring and evaluation of equality initiatives, the review criticized the existing Annual Equality Reports and Equality Audits as being: 'process focused; [and not able to] report on a coherent set of objectives; [moreover, they] contained great variation between different parts of the Assembly and provided little sense of development year on year' (NAW, 2003: 73). In response, the review recommended that independent equality audits be undertaken of the Assembly by an external body. Lastly, and again echoing the earlier 2002 report (see Chaney and Fevre, 2002a: 92), the 2004 *Mainstreaming Review* recommended that the Equality of Opportunity Committee have a strategic and monitoring role over other Assembly committees' work programmes to ensure that they complied with the Assembly's statutory equality duty. At the time of writing, following a commitment from the WAG Equalities Minister to 'developing and implementing a Mainstreaming Equalities Strategy' (NAW, 2005: 1), discussions were underway between officials and equality practitioners in order to begin to address the recommendations of the *Mainstreaming Review*. Notwithstanding the latter developments, the failure to implement the recommendations of the 2002 evaluation report (Chaney and Fevre, 2002: 89), and the fact that, five years after the Assembly Government's mainstreaming vision was presented to the Assembly Equality Committee, the *Mainstreaming Review* concluded that 'currently the Assembly does not have an overall equality strategy' (NAW, 2004: 73), suggest continuing institutional resistance to reforms designed to mainstream equality in public policy.

MAINSTREAMING: A COMPARATIVE WELSH–SCOTTISH PERSPECTIVE

The issues highlighted in the aforementioned evaluation reports are not unique to the post-devolution experience in Wales. Rather, reference to developments in Scotland (Mackay, 2001c, 2004c; Chaney and Mackay, 2003; Breitenbach, 2006) reveals that similar concerns also relate to the Scottish Executive's attempts to apply mainstreaming to its policy work. (The principal points of the following discussion are summarized in Table 8.2.)

In both Wales and Scotland there remain substantial shortfalls in capacity, expertise and resources for mainstreaming. This relates both to internal actors, such as civil servants, and to civil society groups. As noted in earlier chapters, the new devolved bodies provide multiple points of access and there are enhanced opportunities to be consulted about policy development. Yet, there is little evidence to suggest that mainstreaming has become embedded in the everyday work of the devolved institutions. This failure to achieve 'joined-up' government is a key weakness in both administrations. Beyond declaratory statements of commitment to equality, the treatment of equality issues in key policy documents remains very uneven and the setting of measurable targets remains the exception, rather than the rule. Furthermore, institutional resistance to mainstreaming should not be underestimated. It is also clear that a broad equality-mainstreaming agenda is being pursued in both Wales and Scotland in a manner that moves beyond a sole focus on gender and embraces, for example, race, disability, sexual orientation, age and language. This has led to concerns that a hierarchy of equalities has emerged and that gender has slipped down the list of competing priorities. Linked to this, there is a disappointing lack of evidence of intersectionality, namely, the development of a more nuanced approach to policy-making with the potential to address the intersections between different dimensions of inequality associated with 'multiple identities' (that is, simultaneously addressing two or more equality strands, such as the needs of, for example, BME elders or Welsh-speaking disabled people). Instead, the more prevalent approach seems to be one of treating equalities as a 'menu', rather than an interconnected 'package'. In both countries, the scale of task is becoming apparent: this relates to generic problems of effecting cultural change, and in trying to promote an integrated and cross-cutting approach to strategy and policy-making, and to specific issues about promoting equality goals. In particular, there have been considerable difficulties in coordinating policy across departments within devolved government, both 'vertically' between different levels of government (for example, Cardiff/Edinburgh and Westminster), and horizontally (for example, agencies, partnerships, networks, public bodies). In both countries, work on equalities takes place in a complex legal and structural landscape with piecemeal legislation, and differentially located and funded statutory equality bodies. Successive reviews and studies of the promotion of equality in Wales and Scotland have further

Table 8.2 Post-1999 progress towards establishing mainstreaming prerequisites in the Welsh and Scottish national government bodies.[18]

Institutional mainstreaming prerequisites	*Indicative Welsh developments*	*Indicative Scottish developments*
Appropriate institutional arrangements	Statutory equality duty; National Assembly for Wales (NAW) Equality Committee; role of Assembly Administration Ombudsman in compliance with equality duties; Equality Policy Unit in the Assembly Government (EPU); equality duty compliance pro forma for policy-makers; annual equality audits; creation and funding of women's consultative policy network, Wales Women's National Coalition (WWNC); Cabinet Minister with responsibility for equalities issues; limits on Assembly working hours in order to promote a work–life balance; gender-neutral official titles; and rules on the language permitted in political debate.	Equality provisions in Scotland Act, including power to impose duties; Scottish Parliament (SP) Equal Opportunities Committee; Equality Unit in Scottish Executive (SE); strengthened Equal Opportunities Unit in SE (human resources); equality strategy (2000) (but no gender equality strategy); equal opportunities impact statement as part of policy memoranda to accompany Executive Bills; Equality Proofing Budgets and Policy Advisory Group (EPBPAG) set up within SE with input from the Scottish Women's Budget Group; Women in Scotland Consultative Forum (first set up in 1998); creation of Scottish Women's Convention (2003); Cabinet Minister with responsibility for equalities issues; limits on Assembly working hours in order to promote a work–life balance; crèche for visitors' children in SP; gender-neutral official titles; and rules on the language permitted in political debate.
Resources	Steady increase in staffing and resources for EPU and for consultative channels, e.g. sponsorship of WWNC and Stonewall Cymru; funded equalities research; funding for extensive staff equality training.	Steady increase in staffing and resources for equality policy units, including setting-up of equality mainstreaming team, and for consultative channels, e.g. designated equality budget for first time in 2003–4 (£5m); support for Scottish Women's Convention; Scottish Women's Budget group; funded equalities research.
Training	Mandatory equality training for 3,500 Assembly Government civil servants; ongoing mandatory equality-awareness raising; Equality Committee recommendation of equality training for Assembly Members.	Training as part of general diversity training for civil servants; training for Parliamentary Bill teams; module on equality mainstreaming as part of Better Policy-making training; SP EO committee has recommended EO training for MSPs.

Expertise	Gender-equality experience of key AMs who held senior management positions in gender equality organizations; engagement with academic expertise; commissioning equalities research (review of the statutory equality duty, 2002; *Mainstreaming Review*, 2004); involvement of experts from statutory equality commissions as standing advisers to Equality Committee.	Explicit aim in equality strategy to improve consultation and dialogue with equality experts and equality groups, strengthen research in policy areas (e.g. women and transport) and about different strands of equality (e.g. ground-breaking work on LGBT), and achieve improvements in gender-disaggregated statistics; research by SE and SP on mainstreaming tools and techniques; involvement of gender budget experts in SE gender budgeting pilots; SP EO Committee research on mainstreaming and equality proofing legislation.
Reporting mechanisms	Annual Equalities reports from Equality Committee; annual plenary debate (and vote) on annual Equalities reports; development of dedicated equality units in NHS Wales, and the Welsh Local Government Association; new monitoring mechanisms in the public sector (e.g. pupil-level annual school census (PLASC) introduced in August 2003).	Annual reports from SE Equality Unit, reporting on progress made on equality strategy; periodic 'taking stock' exercises conducted by SP EO Committee; equality statements made in draft Budget documents.
Incentives to 'build ownership'	Cabinet Minister with responsibility for equalities; 'equality' part of personal performance review of division managers in Civil Service; annual ministerial remit letters to chief executives of Welsh public sector bodies.	Cabinet Minister with responsibility for equalities.
Awareness-raising	Successive 'Close the Pay Gap' campaigns; promotion of the Equality Standard for Welsh unitary authorities.	'Close the Gap' equal pay campaigns; domestic abuse public-awareness campaigns; promotion of anti-racist and anti-sectarian values; surveys of social attitudes to discrimination.

indicated the difficulty of maintaining momentum over the long term. Whilst some of these challenges are country-specific, such as the unwieldy law-making arrangements covering Wales, and sectarianism in Scotland, many of the afore-mentioned problems are consistent with the international literature (see, for example, True, 2003; Rubery et al., 2004; IANWGE, 2005). In short, the foregoing factors have led to 'decoupling' in both devolved assemblies. This is the means by which organizations manage a disjunction between formal rules, informal practices and actual activities (Meyer and Rowan, 1991; Chaney, 2006e). In other words, it is the situation whereby an organization espouses one thing but prac-tises another. Nevertheless, despite the present slippage between the political vision for equalities and the realities of the policy process, the fact that, in both devolved nations, a mainstreaming approach has been integral to the institutional design, practices and procedures of government augurs well. Furthermore, whilst not understating the scale of the challenge fully to realize gender main-streaming in devolved government, it is clear that significant progress has been made in both countries, following devolution, to develop the institutional pre-requisites for mainstreaming equality.

CONCLUSION: GENDER EQUALITY AND POLICY-MAKING

As a result of the parallel trends in the promotion of gender equality by strategic women in Wales and elsewhere in the UK, as well as EU and UN developments, extensive policy machinery and mainstreaming policies have *begun* to be put in place in the Assembly as a means to enhance the substantive representation of women. The Assembly's first years show that elected devolution has resulted in both achievements and shortcomings. On the positive side, as noted, there has been a significant and far-reaching conceptual shift in the approach to gender equality and the substantive representation of women. This has been re-priori-tized as a core political aim of government in Wales. It is a development that is contingent upon a number of factors including women's role in (re)shaping the institutional framework of the Assembly and the increased presence of women as elected politicians. The examples of emerging gender-equality policies and law discussed in this chapter show that, on a selective basis at least, there is evidence of a determination to further the substantive representation of women and produce policy that addresses the needs of girls and women in Welsh society.

However, this shift in the approach to equalities has been far from straight-forward. Rather, the evidence of the Assembly's first years show it to be a period of contestation, as new values bed down or are discarded. This is consistent with the wider international experience of mainstreaming, as government attempts to move beyond an initial declaratory embracing of the concept and put principles into practice (IANWGE, 2005: 61). Accordingly, in the Assembly, the greatest emphasis has thus far been on the process of policy-making, rather than on policy outcomes. Attention has centred on putting in place a raft of institutional prerequisites in order to develop the future capacity to engender policy. Yet, this has not been trouble-free. A range of factors, such as inadequate staffing, limited resources and institutional resistance to reform, has meant that operationalizing mainstreaming principles in the Assembly has been far from a straightforward case of applying a new set of principles to the devolved policy-making machinery. Rather, it has been characterized by gradual progress, checked by faltering momentum, drift and setbacks. Partly as a function of the low starting-point in respect of equalities inherited from the Welsh Office, as well as the relatively underdeveloped nature of 'equalities' groups in civil (and civic) society, and notwithstanding the development of WWNC and other networks (see chapter 7), Assembly officials have privileged the use of expertise, as opposed to the active engagement in policy-making of the wide range of women and women's organizations predicted in the earlier rhetoric of creating a 'participatory democracy' (see for example, Hain, 1999: 14). This failure to embrace the participatory dimension of mainstreaming fully has been compounded by further problems, which include: limitations in ministerial leadership (see p. 178); the absence of an adequate enforcement mechanism in respect of the Assembly's statutory equality duty (for a discussion see O'Cinneide, 2003); and the lack of an external monitoring and compliance body to oversee the Assembly Government's conformity to its legal equality obligations (see Chaney, 2004b).

Overall, the experience of the Assembly's first years presents something of a paradox in respect of gender and policy. On the one hand there is the seeming institutionalization of mainstreaming, as witnessed by the measures taken to put in place the building blocks or institutional prerequisites, a development that has been accompanied by high-profile political will. Yet, on the other hand, as the foregoing discussion suggests, whilst there are individual examples of policy to promote gender equality, these are not part of a routinized, joined-up approach to policy that has been, and is, consistently delivering concrete policy outcomes. Instead, civil servants and politicians have tended to regard mainstreaming as a discrete policy area in its own right, rather than embracing it as a transformative approach to policy. In turn, this reflects the powerful continuities that are present between elected devolution and the former mode of administrative devolution, not least with officials' continuing emphasis on bureaucratic process, rather than on achieving gender equality outcomes. In short, the experience of the Assembly's first years suggests a process of 'decoupling' whereby the devolved government is currently managing a disjunction between its political vision for equalities, the formal rules and practices of the bureaucracy, and actual policy outcomes. Whilst not condoning the uneven development of mainstreaming in the Assembly, as noted above, arguably, the ambitious nature of the concept, particularly when applied to a challenging political and social context, was always likely to be problematic.

A key issue for the future trajectory of gender mainstreaming in the Assembly will be the resilience of the new equalities framework in the face of ongoing resistance from civil servants unwilling to modify their working practices (as evidenced by the failure of officials to implement the recommendations of the 2002 policy review of the Assembly's statutory equality duty (Chaney and Fevre, 2002b: 121) and the conclusion of the 2004 *Mainstreaming Review* that 'currently the Assembly does not have an overall equality strategy'). Notwithstanding such obstacles, there is some scope for cautious and qualified optimism. Gender equality policies in Wales are now underpinned by EC, UK and Welsh law, supported by an increasing range of institutional mechanisms and procedures in government, and monitored by a new and extensive state regulatory framework that includes: the Commission for Equality and Human Rights (CEHR) Wales Committee, the Wales Audit Office, the Welsh Public Services Ombudsman, the Care Standards Inspectorate for Wales and the Welsh Schools Inspectorate (ESTYN), as well as the offices of the Welsh Commissioners for Children and Older People. Nevertheless, the present evidence shows that significant challenges remain before the Assembly government achieves its stated goal of a fully mainstreamed approach to engendering policy.

9

In Their Own Words: The Views of Women Candidates and Assembly Members

We now have the opportunity to achieve genuine equality. We are through stage one. We are now 'in there', on the agenda and part of the game. What matters now is what we do with this chance.[1]

The preceding chapters have traced a journey that identified the long-standing marginalization of women in Welsh politics, typified by the fact that they were sidelined in the political parties to such an extent that gender equality claims were initially absent in the momentum of post-1987 devolution campaigns. We have chronicled women's expanding role in the devolution campaigns, the institutionalizing of gender equality in the design and operation of the National Assembly, and positive action in candidate selection for elections to the new legislature. In seemingly unpropitious circumstances, and somewhat unexpectedly to most observers, numerical gender parity was ultimately achieved in the 2003 Assembly elections (see chapter 4), a development of international significance. Thus, devolution can be said to have had a major impact on the position of women, both in national politics and within three of the four main parties. Yet, the status of women in both legislature and party remains far from secure. Throughout the period covered by this book, the role of women in politics has been – and continues to be – open to resistance and challenge from those more comfortable with earlier modes of male-dominated politics.

In order to deepen our understanding of the major effect that constitutional change has had on the role of women and politics, this chapter adopts a singular approach. It differs from the preceding analysis by presenting the first-hand accounts of women candidates and Assembly Members (a comparative dimension is also provided by selective reference to the experience of male politicians). This material was gathered during a series of approximately 200 research interviews undertaken between 1998 and 2005.[2] In respect of women and politics, these recollections provide clear evidence of the extent of the change associated with constitutional reform and the hard-won nature of the advances made to date. By allowing women's voices to be heard in this way, the following accounts provide unique insights, impossible to gain through a traditional narrative approach and academic analysis. In terms of the structure of this volume, the following discussion is also designed to summarize for the reader the progress, challenges and achievements in a journey that has, thus far, taken a little over a decade. Our purpose then, is to gain an understanding of what it was like to participate in the events analysed in earlier chapters, and thus be better placed to re-address this book's key themes in the following, concluding chapter. Accordingly, we now turn to women's accounts of the struggle to be selected for – and elected to – the National Assembly. We then explore women AMs' own views of the qualitative shift away from the earlier phase of male-dominated politics that has accompanied constitutional reform.

POSITIVE ACTION: NEGATIVE REACTION

For many women active in the political parties, recollection of the period following the 1997 General Election involves contrasting feelings and experiences. While several have positive memories of the cross-party pro-devolution campaign (see chapter 2), others remember competing for the right to stand as party candidate as a difficult, often unpleasant undertaking. A Labour woman AM's account is typical of the many positive recollections of the 1990s devolution campaign. She said:

> I felt that there was a *real* excitement that we were having this establishment [the Assembly]. It was something that many of us, cross-party, had campaigned hard for. And I remember that we did have a campaign in Cardiff, and I remember women marched to the steps of the Welsh Office – *cross-party* – to encourage women to stand, and to make sure that this new institution that represented so much hope for us, that we could move forward with that 51 per cent of the population being represented.

Away from such collaboration, discussions at a party level were often much less consensual. Male domination in all the main parties reflected the strongly embedded cultural and political values about sex and gender then, and now, pervading Welsh society. Androcentric power-structures and patterns of organizing at party level underpinned the dissatisfaction expressed by many woman candidates. For example, one activist in Plaid Cymru was critical of the way that local branch meetings were convened at times that excluded those with childcare responsibilities. Recalling one selection meeting she stated:

> At the first meeting I went to I wasn't intimidated as such because I was ready for it. But you know it's not nice sitting there on your own. The [male party members] are discussing something and you think, *hang on!* You need to talk about this [that is, with women party members as well]. And they kind of do this without even thinking. I don't think that it is a malicious thing. I just think that, you know, they have been conditioned into ignoring you, ignoring that single voice. The maximum number of women that have been in a meeting with me is two other women, which is quite pathetic.

In the face of such inequalities, candidates' comments reveal how the parties attempted to circumvent rather than fully address deep-set male domination of their organizations. Speaking after the first elections, a Plaid woman AM summarized the approach that the party had taken in order to achieve more equitable patterns of representation:

> We wanted to have gender balance not in the candidates but in the people that actually got in. We could see that Labour were tearing themselves apart [over twinning] so there was no point in going down the same road as that! We have got a membership that is sort of fifty-fifty but you still find that it is the men that make it in the long run. So what was agreed by the national party was that we would leave the constituencies to continue to decide as to how they select their candidates themselves. When a constituency committee meets to select a candidate, you cannot expect them to take into consideration the gender of the other candidates that have already been selected. We did think that was going to create problems that would be difficult to get over. So we decided that we were going to put a female at the top of every [regional candidate] list. And we won more seats than we expected so we didn't get gender balance. If, we had any idea that we were going to win first-past-the-post seats with women, then we probably would have taken that into account in the template of the composition of the lists. But we are dealing with hindsight here – which is a marvellous thing!

Interviewees' recollections also reveal tensions between reformers' predisposition for greater levels of equality and the need to 'toe the party line'. For example, interviewed in late 1999, a male Welsh Conservative AM expressed regret at his party's failure to have any women AMs. He also reflected the position of many Tories on positive action:

> One of the concerns I have as a Conservative member of the Assembly is that we don't have any women members representing the Conservative group here. I'm very reluctant to introduce legalistic ways in which we can address that. I'm rather hoping that we will finish up having an equal balance of men and women representing the Conservative Party but it being the choice of the Conservative membership. I think the way things worked out this time is that we had quite a lot of female candidates but they weren't in seats that eventually secured a place in the Assembly which is very disappointing to me. But whether we can change that at the next election? *I hope we can.* I'm certainly very pleased we're trying to take some steps to make certain that the Conservative Party isn't thought of as being a bastion of chauvinism which I think some people have accused us of being because we didn't have any female members. I think that's unfair. I hope we will be able to address this problem simply through straightforward democratic processes. I'm certain we're going to have to discuss this in some detail. I'm not ready to commit myself to any new mechanism yet. I will be disappointed if we have to go down that road. But I certainly think we do have to find some way of being represented in various bodies with a decent share of women. To my mind it's a weakness of our party that we're in the Assembly without any women members. I think it damages the party.

Others spoke of the difficulties in encouraging women party members to challenge established organizational practices at party level by standing for election. As one Welsh Liberal Democrat woman AM reflected:

we tried very hard to get, to encourage women to put their names forward. We didn't have any fixed solutions like the Labour Party did, but we have actually ended up with a balanced group, three men and three women. But you know, I was very aware that a lot of women saw the whole thing as a white middle-class male game and didn't want to get involved.

The challenges and opposition facing women activists during this period were particularly evident within the Welsh Labour Party. One candidate recalled:

It got quite nasty when we had the twinning debate in Swansea. That would have been 1998, the Welsh Labour Party conference. It was *very* bitter and *very* nasty. They were extremely threatening, sort of 'in your face'. And these were your macho males and they were physically trying to intimidate women – or any male – (and I would perhaps guess that it was slightly worse for the males that were standing with us). It was quite frightening. I witnessed *a lot*. I mean, I won't be intimidated. I've been around a long time fighting for these issues. But there were clearly women who were very, very upset. These men were sticking their heads and their chests forward saying 'who do you think you are?' And you would even hear: 'this isn't your place. *We've* been here a long time, *we* know what people want, *we* know how it works.' And yet they couldn't see that outside [the party] people weren't voting for them. They couldn't put the two together.

Women trade unionists who stood as Assembly candidates for the different parties spoke of the way in which deeply embedded patterns of sex discrimination replicated those that they were used to facing in their daily work. One former Welsh Labour candidate noted:

Very often for these women the same sorts of barriers hit them in the trade union movement as well. Because, whilst women do quite well at lay [trade union] rep level, and to a certain extent paid officers, they tend not to be right at the very top level. There are *very few* female general secretaries of trade unions in Wales … so women in the trade unions are used to all of these barriers and issues and they were keen to see that any new political scene was different and reflected much better the make-up of society in terms of gender.

Similarly, another Labour candidate reported her experiences:

When I went to the [south Wales] valleys, then I had my eyes opened! Then I truly understood the bullying that went on. And y'know, we're talking about sections having *power*. You had unions with power and their membership was predominantly male. Men were taking all the positions except for the unpaid or low-status posts. You'd find lots of female secretaries. But after all, *that* was considered a female role. Women were to be seen but definitely not to be heard.

Many woman candidates had their own personal tales of the extent of cultural resistance to gender equality in the respective parties. One Welsh Labour Party (WLP) AM referred to the case of a colleague:

a woman in the Labour Party who was selected to be a candidate – but in the particular constituency where she was selected there was *a lot* of hostility. She was going around the branches to introduce herself as the candidate and she was told by the chair of one branch: 'well, come along to the meeting but could you play down the fact that you are actually the candidate now, could you come and just talk about anything – but don't really promote the fact that you are the candidate'!

The bitterness and infighting that accompanied Welsh Labour's use of twinning has left deep scars and, as the 2005 General Election result in Blaenau Gwent revealed, remains a hugely contentious issue for sections of the party.[3] One Labour woman AM recalled the passion associated with the struggles at WLP conferences to overcome this enduring resistance to change and secure positive action:

> I have got some colleagues here today that went through the twinning battle and I can say that in terms of the hostility and the bad feeling that was generated in the Labour Party it was a *very* hostile period. And a lot of people who had, prior to this, been very good friends actually stopped speaking to one another. Because it said more about you as an individual, it wasn't just disagreeing about certain policies, it clearly went to the *core of you as a person* and whether you believed in fair play and equality. And, the split wasn't a man–woman split: you have two mixed gender campaigns. You had the pro-twinners and the anti-twinners. And, at the 1998 Welsh Labour Party conference in Swansea we scraped a victory for the twinning campaign by approximately one per cent. I remember at the time sitting by Val Feld, who was a good friend, and many other women there, we were holding our breath because we realized that this could really change the course of history in Welsh politics. And when that result came through, I cannot begin to tell you the feeling; the whole place just erupted! – It was quite, quite magnificent.

The comments of candidates also reveal the incongruity that positive action measures were viewed by significant numbers of male party members as being anti-democratic. One asserted:

> There was an awful lot of hostility around the twinning. I've got personal experience of that, it was quite hostile ... this is the silly thing about it, you don't get this sort of hostility whipped up by the general public, it's actually within the party itself! Again, I'm not particularly blaming the Labour Party because I'm sure this happens in other parties and other male-dominated organizations. But my own experience is that there was *a lot* of hostility as far as the twinning issue and as far as myself as a candidate went. And I know this is the experience of some of the other women members. The irony of it is, although twinning gives equal rights to *men* and women it was only the women who seemed to have these problems, it was never an issue for the men.

Women interviewees emphasized the attitude of the local party officials as an important factor in the promotion of gender equality. The words of one WLP candidate reveal officials' power to aid or subvert women's selection:

> It depended very much on whether, as a woman, you were seeking nomination in a constituency that was comfortable with the twinning process, or uncomfortable, or opposed to the twinning process – and that affected women more than men. There were some [electoral] wards in some constituencies where the atmosphere was

nothing short of hostile. Especially, if you were a both a woman *and* someone who didn't live in the constituency. One of the reasons I kept going with it was I believed that it was going to be a good opportunity for the [Welsh Labour] Party to be able break some moulds in selecting people who weren't perhaps the 'obvious' candidates but might be in a position to really take Wales forward – and that had to be one of the things that kept you going. Some of the conversations that went on between the prospective candidates, they were superb and supportive of each other – unless you had someone who really thought they were in with a chance, then they were a little suspicious of everyone else. In terms of talking to the wards, it varied enormously depending on how they viewed the process: whether they were happy/unhappy with the process made a tremendous difference.

Several women identified power structures within the parties as a key factor that enabled gatekeepers and power-brokers to resist change. When asked whether the intra-party divisions over twinning had been resolved after the first Assembly election, one women WLP AM representing a local party that was opposed to twinning (so much so that, as in a number of cases, the national party had to move in to administer the candidate-selection procedures) said:

It's a lot better. I've worked on it. When I say people are against me, you are still talking about a very small number. They're the people who sometimes wield all the power. But I'm working very hard to get to know everybody. I still think I was the right person for the job. But it's not seen like that. I think, really, unless we get a system like this [twinning] you're never going to change anything because I, under the old [candidate selection] system, I could have more or less said well I knew who would be selected as the candidate [that is, before the selection procedure commenced].

A paradox referred to by several WLP candidates was that twinning was felt to increase the competition between women in order to advance gender equality. One said: 'it was tortuous for the people looking to be selected and for the ordinary party members because they had *so many* people all trying to achieve selection in so many areas, because it was a whole new [form of] organization. It became *very* competitive.' One black woman candidate highlighted the way in which, in her opinion, this competition compounded the existing prejudice and ignorance that she faced. She stated:

I think it was quite difficult to get nominations because we were all trying at the same time. That is the other difficulty, that you had all these women who were very able, all trying for seats at the same time. I still believe that the [twinning] system actually would favour white women, and of course it did. And again I became on the periphery.

She continued:

People are always sceptical; you get questions like 'could you represent everyone?' As if you can only represent black people and you can't possibly represent anyone else! So in some people's minds they can probably see black people in a certain role, in a fixed, certain role and they don't come out of those roles.

Despite the extensive divisions over gender and candidate-selection procedures that affected all parties, the run-up to the second Assembly election quickly revealed that few lessons had been learned and that divisions remained.

THE 2003 ELECTIONS

Prior to the second Assembly elections, Plaid Cymru's chair Elin Jones stated:

> Plaid is keen to maintain and increase women representation in the National Assembly and to build on our party's achievements in the 1999 elections ... it is important that we do not slide back in relation to the number of female candidates and potential members that we have in the Assembly.[4]

Once again, reflecting the way in which gender equality was far from the settled state of affairs in the party, as in 1999, the chosen approach was a pragmatic one aimed at outcomes. Thus, Plaid's response was reactive, one based on compensating for the over-representation of male candidates challenging for the first-past-the-post seats. The party chairwoman described the party's strategy, stating: 'if we find there is an under-representation of women from the constituencies I believe we should retain our policy of positive discrimination in favour of women for the lists. On each list a woman should come first and a man second.'[5]

Welsh Labour women candidates' comments made during this period throw light on the continuing controversy, strife and uncertainties associated with the use of twinning. A woman WAG minister said:

> There's going to be problems with the selections for women in my opinion, I think some of them are going to have an horrendous time. You can see it starting already. I have great concerns about a couple of women Labour AMs who are very good, what is going to happen at the next reselection process for them? I think the party is *duty bound* to protect them centrally, because there's no doubt in my mind the Llew Smiths[6] of this world are yesterday's politicians.

The comments of a woman AM when referring to the experience of a colleague at a local constituency meeting confirm the validity of the minister's concerns. They also show an understanding or belief on the part of anti-reform male party members that twinning was just a temporary mechanism, one that did not address underlying discriminatory attitudes at a grassroots party level. She said: 'some chap had come up to her and said "well look, enjoy your four years because at the end of it *you* will be *dead meat*"'. Another woman candidate recalled the heated WLP conference debates on twinning in the following terms:

> I was at the conference, the year before last, when they were talking about the all-women shortlists for selection for the Assembly election and this younger-than-myself male asked me how long I'd been in the Party. I told him ten years. And he quite clearly said to me, 'it is people like you who make me sick, because you are going to

support this, you've only been in the Party ten years. I've been a member all my life.' And he was going for selection in a constituency where there would be an all-women shortlist. So, it was all *my* fault, *all women's fault* . . . There *is* an arrogance. He made it clear that he felt that he had a *right* to that seat and he wasn't going to stand aside.

Given this troubled history, a woman former Assembly candidate expressed concern that twinning was a short-term 'fix', rather than a long-term strategy to address discrimination. She said:

It [gender equality in the WLP] *hasn't* become *mainstreamed*. Twinning was seen as a specific mechanism for a specific purpose at a specific time rather than being seen as a mechanism to begin to change the whole concept of selection procedures into the future. *This opportunity needs to be grasped and needs to be taken.*[7]

As one woman candidate observed, the turmoil associated with Labour's adoption of twinning was not restricted to internal party debate, but surfaced in campaigning for the National Assembly elections. Interestingly, she highlighted cultural barriers to gender equality, not from men, but from women opposed to twinning. She said:

When I went around campaigning, some males would say to me 'I'm not voting for the Labour Party because they just want to push women.' [She adds ironically] – You know, as if males – we're a threatened species: [parodying someone adopting such a position:] 'I'm a white middle-class male and I'm a threatened species by the Labour Party'! But you'd have *women* as some of the fiercest opponents to this [that is, twinning]. I found that a little worrying to say the least! Their argument would be different though. It would be: 'but we don't want tokenism', 'we want merit and we don't want women being pushed through, we want the best person for the job, whoever that might be'. What they couldn't understand was because they weren't involved in putting *themselves* forward unless [they felt that] the environment was right – then taking that line you're *never* going to put yourself forward, you are going to be there with the hostility. If you're at a [candidate] selection meeting – and I've been to a few – there are women clearly being intimidated by males. You know: *you need another female*, just to help you through. *You need that critical mass.*

'GWAWR NEWYDD?'[8] THE VIEWS OF WOMEN ASSEMBLY MEMBERS

We now focus attention on the experiences of women who succeeded in the candidate-selection procedures and who were subsequently elected to the National Assembly in 1999 and/or 2003. Specifically, the rest of this chapter draws upon women AMs' own accounts of post-devolution politicking between 1999 and 2005. Thus, the following discussion is based upon interviews with women elected to the new legislature and supplemented with quotations from the Assembly's Official Record. First we turn to women Assembly Members' expectations of devolved national politics, as expressed in a series of interviews undertaken during the first year of the new Assembly.[9] Subsequent attention is then placed upon a range of key issues, with women Assembly Members' views on: the effects of women's 'critical mass' in the Assembly; the existence of a 'feminized' style of politics; and putative notions of a cross-party sisterhood amongst AMs.

Beginnings

There was a frisson of excitement, and not a little nervousness, as the Assembly began business in May 1999. The newly elected women AMs were optimistic about the prospects for transforming politics and seizing the opportunity to achieve greater gender equality. Their confidence was based on both the presence of twenty-five women[10] in the Assembly and the way in which equal opportunities had been successfully enshrined into its structure and operation. This positive outlook was reinforced by the link between feminism and activism, specifically the fact that, as noted in chapter 7, several 'strategic' women elected to the Assembly had considerable professional experience in the promotion of equal opportunities. One female AM identified the National Assembly's core task as one of 'working towards a more equal society'. Yet, she conceded a lot would depend on 'the political will to make it happen'. Nevertheless, she was hopeful of achieving progress, stating: 'looking around the chamber, there are a lot of people there who you would expect to have that political will'. Overall, there was a general consensus on the immediate effect of the virtual gender-parity that had been achieved. According to one AM, women Assembly Members were more 'upfront' and challenging, because of their critical mass. Some referred to a unity or 'sisterhood', something that transcended party allegiances. There was often a perceived common concern to promote a 'women's agenda'. Hindsight reveals the contrast between these statements, made during the Assembly's first months, and the fierce inter-party rivalry seen during subsequent years. Thus, speaking in 1999, one opposition AM said of women in the Assembly Government Cabinet: 'those women know they have the good wishes of all the other women in the chamber with them, not just the women from their own party ... I feel there is a sort of sisterhood thing definitely.' Other women AMs had clear views on the way that they would influence the style of political debate during the legislature's first term. One observed,

> I think the Assembly ... is going to operate in a way which probably looks so much more low-key than Parliament – in that there will be a *distinctive* influence of women because there are so many of us here ... when you get all women debating – or a majority of women debating – the tone of the debate changes.

Another woman AM felt that, 'there was a determination to break down tribal, confrontational politics' and to 'relate better to ordinary voters who don't like all this shouting and banging and all the rest of it'. According to another, there would be a further qualitative change in Welsh politics:

I'm hoping that because the Assembly is going to be able to address issues in very much more depth than [they have] ever been addressed in public before, you know, decisions have previously been made very much by three [Welsh Office] Ministers for the whole of Wales and they've done it in private. Well now these things are going to be addressed and debated and discussed in public and I'm very much hoping that we'll identify problems and solutions in a much more efficient manner than has been done in the past.

Major variations were evident in the views of male AMs on the way that gender issues would be addressed by the new Assembly. The comments of some reveal that they felt equality matters to be of a lesser order, or, as one put it, 'largely a matter for the cross-cutting [equality] committee'. However, for others gender equality was a mainstream issue. One said of the Equality Committee, it is 'not just an "add-on" committee but we recognize it as being very, very important'. As part of an emerging consensus most male AMs reflected the view that, as one stated, 'women's concerns are absolutely fundamental to the work of the whole Assembly'.

For the majority of women AMs there was a clear determination to bring about change and to mainstream equality. Yet many recognized the major challenges that lay ahead, not least in developing the participatory democracy set out in the 1997 devolution White Paper. As one woman AM put it, she and her colleagues had 'an obligation to get "out there" and get involved and to get the organizations ... to come and see our committees'. For another, this was about 'being inclusive. [This] means allowing people easy access to the political system and making sure that what we're doing is done well and is providing a full service, particularly public services to people out there.' Co-working with voluntary organizations was at the heart of this proposed new engagement with civil society. It was something highlighted by a significant number of women AMs. As one noted, 'I've actually made an effort to go out to visit as many voluntary organizations as possible and say "look, I *want* to get involved with you and I *want* you to influence me in the Assembly, I *want* us to work together".' Others raised concerns about engaging women's NGOs that lacked personal connections to the new women AMs. One said: 'we're supposed to be accessible; it just appears to me that some groups are going to be off the starting blocks a little quicker than others.' As another put it, the challenge was: 'to get to that mass of people "out there" who are not very well skilled in accessing the political process'. To further civic engagement, a women AM cited the need to: 'deconstruct the world of politics ... to make it as down to earth as possible ... to make it accessible'. Generally, women AMs were realistic about the pace with which the 'inclusiveness' advocated by pro-devolution campaigners could be realized. As one women AM asserted: it was not 'something we've achieved all of a sudden because we've set up an Assembly'. Many women AMs were in no doubt about the difficult task that they faced in promoting equality. One noted that:

I have no illusions, it's not going to work perfectly and I will undoubtedly be disappointed in certain ways, but there's one thing you cannot change, you *cannot* change the sex of those there and *that's really going to have an impact*, I'm sure of that.

Val Feld summarized the prevailing view of most women AMs during the Assembly's first months: 'we now have the opportunity to achieve genuine equality. We are through stage one. We are now "in there", on the agenda and part of the game. What matters now is what we do with this chance.'

Strength in numbers: critical mass

As the Assembly's first term progressed, women AMs identified a range of effects that they perceived to stem from having a significant number, or 'critical mass', of women in the National Assembly. Not least, several highlighted the link between women's newly achieved descriptive representation in national Welsh politics and the substantive representation of women, in other words, ensuring that women's needs and priorities were embedded in public policy. One stated:

The significance of the number of women that we have in the Assembly? ... What's clear is that the number of women there is influencing the agenda and it is making a significant change. The discussions now are very much people-centred. They are about the need to develop strategies and the ability for people to manage work and family and the need for carers. The kind of issues that we have talked about for many, many years are the issues now which get a serious consideration in a way which they have not had before ... and I think we are starting to get that integration across in all the [Assembly's] measures.[11]

A female Welsh Liberal Democrat AM also highlighted the way in which the substantive representation is based not only on the physical presence of women as elected politicians but also on the need for the adoption of a specific, conscious gender identity. She said:

If women politicians are to make a difference here in this Assembly, or indeed in any other institution, it does rely very heavily on them identifying themselves as *female* politicians and having a critical mass of female politicians around them to help them to pursue that particular agenda. I think that it is true to say that the issues that the National Assembly has spent a great deal of time looking at have been because of the proportion of women here at the National Assembly for Wales ... now we are seeing a shift in emphasis in the agenda.

A woman minister in the Assembly Government highlighted the link between critical mass and the enhanced ability to ensure that gender equality was near the top of the agenda in the face of numerous competing political priorities. She stated that:

I think if there hadn't been so many women, we wouldn't have moved this equality agenda so fast. Because I think there is a definite willingness to move the gender issues forward ... And so the greatest compliment, probably, is that when organizations come to see us from elsewhere, they can't get over the fact, the way that we are moving equality issues forward.

Others cited the impact of women's descriptive representation in the Assembly on the political culture of political parties and the future engagement of women in national Welsh politics. A female Welsh Conservative AM said:

> The devolution we've seen in place for the last four years has, in its way, in my own party, prompted a kind of natural evolution rather than a revolution. I think that people are now – it's starting to occur to them that we need more women and we've been very slow to address that in the past. We need better training opportunities; [and] we need fifty-fifty splits on interview [candidate selection] panels.

A Plaid Cymru woman AM thought that the critical mass of women would encourage others to stand for office. She said:

> I am hoping that it will give them a bit of confidence when they see that the Assembly is open to women to get elected. I am hoping that they will put themselves forward for election and, if not for the election then maybe taking a post in public life. As we are just, and I don't know about other women here, but I will admit openly to being 'very ordinary'. So I hope that women in Wales are getting that impression, that if they really wanted to go for this then they could ... I would like women to think that 'if she can do that, and she is ordinary – then I can do it'.

This view was echoed by a woman Labour AM who said:

> I would certainly hope that women would see us as role models and especially for younger women, girls that are coming through school. Just that difference of 'Oh my God, women can do these jobs too', women *can* get there'. So I think that is a first positive step or difference the Assembly will make.

Another Labour woman AM highlighted the challenges in engaging women in the new politics. She started:

> As far as women are concerned, I do think a lot of women do feel that politics is not for them and really what I'm trying to get over is that it's really what they make of it, and it should be about how it affects their lives. So one of my missions really is just to try and get this message across. The issues that we are dealing with in the Assembly are education, jobs and health, I mean those are very relevant to our lives. It's not far removed is it? And that's what I'm trying to get this message across to [women] to try to get them involved really, because I think a lot see politics as something that happens elsewhere, and that's not what it's about, is it?

When asked about the impact of having a majority of women in the Assembly Government's Cabinet, a woman minister highlighted the way in which party political and institutional contexts shaped both gender dynamics and the promotion of equality. She said:

> I find that quite odd because I think it's hard to answer because there is a dynamic in terms of having a coalition government[12] that sometimes overtakes all other dynamics. It's certainly true to say that inside the Cabinet – and Cabinet minutes will show a reference to one of us wanting to increase an equality perspective in some policy or other ... and of course we have actively had equality training as a Cabinet. I think it [the Assembly's equality duty] has influenced us in that we all want to make it work.

One woman Plaid Cymru AM was disappointed with the impact of women Cabinet members. She said:

> I would say though, generally, that I can't see how having a majority of women there in the Cabinet has made that much of a difference in terms of policy – because you could argue that in some of the decisions that have been made, the women politicians have acted traditionally as male politicians. That was one of the criticisms of Thatcher, wasn't it? She was a woman but she conducted her politics very much like a man and I think that, I get the feeling anyway, that there hasn't been as much of an impact as I would have liked. I think things like discussion of the [second Gulf] War. Now it just seems that it's a lot of men talking about the War with other men, you know? We don't hear women's voices there at all. And where are the women in the Assembly [Government] Cabinet speaking out against the War as women have traditionally done in the peace movement? And lots of women who are there [in the WLP] now have come from the peace movement. I think possibly because of collective responsibility within the Cabinet, it's meant that they haven't been able to speak out – and that confirms everything about the way we know men do politics, really.

A Labour woman AM was clear on the impact that the increased representation of women in the Assembly had on informing policy debates, by enabling women to draw directly on their own gendered life-experiences. She stated:

> The changes that we have made [in terms of women's representation] are of enormous importance ... what matters is what we, as women, do with the positions that we have. Having women involved in decision-making makes a difference in terms of the opportunities to make policies to change things for women ... The extent to which we can shift the culture of policy-making and decision-making and the extent to which we can bring in a wider range of experience and understanding and a broader sense of priorities will make the difference to whether the needs of women will be met ... there is no question that the life experience of women is different to that of men. That has been my belief for years, which has been reinforced by my experience [of being an AM] during the last nine months. It is not that women do not have many issues about which we feel equally passionate, but that we have *different* priorities, *different* expectations and *different* aspirations. Policy and decision-making is not effective unless it takes account of *all* of those considerations.[13]

'NEW' POLITICS? WOMEN'S IMPACT ON THE STYLE OF POLITICS

The comments of women AMs reveal how institutional factors have impacted upon and shaped the style of post-devolution politics. Thus, for example, many of the women AMs were cautiously positive about the influence of the Assembly's statutory equality duty. Speaking in 2000, Val Feld observed:

> I think that culture is shifting and it is changing. The work that we have done has been of enormous significance in preparing the ground but clearly we have got to now take it a stage further ... We've got to keep 'pushing on the doors' to make sure equality is still firmly 'in there'. I was struck yesterday at realizing that even though the

Assembly has the statutory [equality] duty in [respect of] everything it does and the
requirement to set up an equal opportunities scheme ... it's still the Cinderella down
there [in the Assembly] and we still have to keep hammering away, no doubt about
that. I think as we enter the second stage, we should, all of us, feel that we don't have
to feel at all embarrassed or sidelined about raising the [equality] issues and continually hammering away at these issues, because what is clear is that the work that we
have done is absolutely central to the regeneration of the Welsh economy, we are not
on a 'lunatic fringe': we were right about addressing these kind of issues.[14]

Underlining the key link between feminism, the Assembly's statutory equality
duty and the substantive representation of women, another woman AM said that
having an appropriate legal framework was only part of the reason for the
emerging post-devolution equality agenda. According to this view, another key
reason was having 'strategic women', or those with equalities expertise and
convictions. For her, this was a matter of ensuring that: 'there were individuals
in the right place at the right time that were able to make sure that those issues
were mainstreamed from the very beginning'. Despite the equality laws and
procedural mechanisms set out in the Assembly's institutional framework, some
women AMs expressed concern at the lack of embeddedness of the equality
agenda and that further work was needed to mainstream these throughout the
work of the entire legislature. For example, one woman minister referred to the
impact of the Assembly equality duty, saying:

I feel really proud of this. I mean, this is the only place where this is a statutory duty
in this way and I think that commitment [applying to us] has meant we have particularly good structural relations with the equality lobbies in Wales. We can't always
deliver in what everybody wants – but I think we have those structural relationships,
such as the fact that we have a separate [Equality] Committee and the fact we have
an annual [Equality] Report to the Assembly ... I'm not sure it's mainstreamed well
enough through [Assembly subject] committees yet. I think now in our second term
we've got to think about ways we ensure what happens.

Away from institutional factors, women AMs were divided on the way that their
increased representation had impacted on the style of politics during the
Assembly's first years. One female minister said:

I think it *has* made a difference, but I also think that some women when they get into
politics – and this applies to some now – and I wouldn't name them, take on male
values and you can see them doing it now. And I don't think that that's good because
you shouldn't change the way you operate just because you are somewhere and the
pressure is on for you to change ... But [overall,] I think we have made a difference
in terms of the way we discuss issues.

Another woman AM observed:

If you look at the various [National Assembly] committees that have been successful
in generating cross-party work, with issue-based work, the gender of the minister and
the gender of the [committee] chair makes *a lot* of difference ... And this touches on
several things. It touches on cooperation, it also touches on a willingness to be open

and to bring in influences and resources and to bring in ideas and views from outside the Assembly. And again, I find that my experience is that, on the whole, the women ministers are much more ready to do that than a lot of the men are.

A number of women AMs perceived it to be the case that women were less egotistical than men. Referring to the creation of the regulatory office of the Children's Commissioner for Wales, one said:

> Now, we had a minister [Jane Hutt] there who was prepared to tear up her proposal – who was absolutely prepared to tear all that up and write it all again in face of the evidence. Now, I think, my experience is, that it's been much easier here for women politicians to be ready to do that than it is for the men. I don't know whether that's to do with ego or what it is – but my practical experience is that they [women AMs] have found that easier to do.

A woman Welsh Liberal Democrat AM highlighted, and deprecated, the style of politics promulgated by the male-only group of Welsh Conservative AMs during the Assembly's first term. She stated that:

> I think it is interesting that the group with no women is the group that's been standing out, by interrupting things, taking a totally negative line, refusing to come to the [Business] committee. I mean it is a different culture. And you can see they're already trying, beginning to play it as a boys' game. I think if they'd had maybe three or four women in their group they'd have been told not to be so bloody stupid and to get on with it, and stop making a fuss and also to follow the procedures ... I think they *might* learn, but at the moment they're trying to play it like a parliamentary thing.

According to another female AM, women's presence had determined 'the nature and tone of discourse'. She continued:

> The simple fact that we have Standing Orders that forbid sexist, racist and other discriminatory language ... [changes] the whole tone and nature of the discourse. And I want to give one controversial example of where I think that the number of women [AMs] has made a difference and that was in an early stage in the history of the National Assembly when the whole Assembly decided to sack the First Minister. Now, can you imagine the scene at Westminster where the Prime Minister is being sacked? [Imagine] the shouting, the banging on the table, the stamping of the feet? Now we – as opposition parties – felt that we had good reason to do that. *But it was done in silence. It was done in silence,* and there was a real sense from all of us, even those of us that felt that we were doing the right thing, of that being a person there [that is, Alun Michael] and of that being a person in pain. And we felt that we had to do it and we felt that it had to be done – but there was none of that baying for blood, none of that howling. I was very proud of that.

Another woman AM reflected on the balance between a new style of politicking and continuing resistance to it from some quarters in the Assembly. She stated:

> I have been struck in the Assembly by the change in style of debate and the emphasis on family issues which has occurred. I believe it has happened because of the large number of women here to influence it. At least, I *was* struck by the change in style of debate until Alun Cairns [Tory AM] spoke yesterday [in advancing an amendment

in a plenary debate] in what must be regarded as a last-ditch attempt to turn the clock back to the good old days of [House of] Commons knockabout.[15]

In a discussion on the debating protocol in the Assembly chamber Jenny Randerson, Welsh Liberal Democrat AM, reflected upon this traditional male style of politicking, promulgated by several of the Welsh Tory AMs. She said:

> I welcome this document wholeheartedly. It states that racist and sexist language should always be considered to be out of order ... It is well known that the Conservative group campaigned against devolution and that they are disappointed at not being in the House of Commons. I regret that they seem to be intent on establishing principles of behaviour in this Chamber that are akin to those of the House of Commons. I call this behaviour that of the Tory boys ... The phrase 'yah yah' has always amazed me.[16]

Women AMs' opposition to male attempts to promote a Westminster style of conducting debate (see examples in Figure 6.2, chapter 6) has been a consistent feature of the Assembly's first years. Strikingly, women AMs have used the Assembly's legal framework in order to legitimize and strengthen their claims. Thus, they have repeatedly used points of order and other interventions in Assembly debates to prompt rulings from the Presiding Officer or his Deputy that uphold gender equality in the face of traditional male politicking.

Such criticism of the Assembly's 'new politics' by male politicians aspiring to Westminster ways of politicking was not restricted to plenary debates of the whole Assembly, but extended to committee work. One woman AM told of how she had ultimately capitulated in the face of such macho politicking:

> I have also looked at the way that some male AMs conduct themselves to some female committee chairs and I haven't liked it. I have actually asked to be taken off the [Assembly] Economic Development Committee because I've had enough of the posturing and macho 'arm-wrestling'. I was bored with it. I wanted to go away and do something useful instead. And it is interesting that it's [that is, the Economic Development Committee] a[n Assembly] Committee where the work of opposition members has made no difference at all on policy; *none*. Because you had male members who didn't want to listen and, in fairness, you had male spokespeople for the opposition who were happy to operate in a confrontational manner and I think that *that's very telling*.

A Labour woman AM highlighted the way some women emulated male colleagues. She put this down to the fact that, traditionally, 'politics in Wales is a very sort of masculine activity and if you're a successful woman politician, sometimes you have to be like men to get there'. Another Labour woman AM asserted that women AMs should resist such pressure to conform to male patterns of working. She cited the need to:

> tackle some of the issues about the macho, knockabout culture of politics. If we are to achieve a genuine equality, women should not – and must not – have to operate like men in order to succeed and get to the top. We must achieve a way of ensuring

genuine fairness and inclusiveness by valuing and cherishing the differences and diversity between women and men and the people in our communities and yet building firmly on the principle of equality.[17]

In addition to attempting to 'Westminsterize' Assembly debates, resistance to a 'new' style of post-devolution politics also manifested itself in attacks on the new family-friendly working practices. One woman AM observed:

> We mustn't be complacent. I mean, we had the day before yesterday, *yet again,* a motion brought forward to this Assembly to suggest that we should extend our working hours to seven o'clock at night. We have been very clear from the beginning that this is a proper workplace where people go to in the morning and in the evening they go home – Assembly Members don't of course stop work at five thirty at night that's not what we do – but at least there's an option. I can go home to my little girl at half past six and then pick up my committee papers at half past nine if I chose to do so. And this was the second time that this motion to extend hours had been brought before us – but a coalition of women across parties defeated it ... we won again, but the point is that there were powerful figures within this institution – men – with a Westminster background who had brought that back when we'd already kicked it out once. So I think that we need to be proud of what having a critical mass of women in this Assembly has achieved.

Other woman AMs pointed to a generational difference in AMs' approach to equalities. One noted that:

> There'll always be some in their sixties who you'll never change. And I learnt a long time ago, right, and I don't particularly like people calling me 'dear', right? Of all the people in the Welsh Labour Party in their sixties who speak to you like that, I don't take offence when they say comments that I don't really like. I don't take offence. They are a different generation to me. I don't worry now about people that don't say the right things if they are over fifty. What I worry about is the ones that are *under* fifty when they say the wrong things. And I think we are gradually whittling that number down in the Assembly.

Sisters united?

As noted, women AMs' expectations of a new mode of post-devolution politics often included notions of a 'cross-party sisterhood'. The Assembly's Official Record of Proceedings reveals numerous examples of speakers putting gender equality over party-political considerations. For some, 'cross-party sisterhood' was an enduring aspect of Assembly politics. One highlighted the importance of social networks and co-working between women AMs of different parties that pre-dated the National Assembly, stating:

> Some of it also comes down to the fact that many of the women who work in this institution on different sides of the political divide have a tradition of working together on other issues before we got here. Jane Hutt [AM] the Health Minister was the first ever national coordinator of Welsh Women's Aid, the body that campaigns to counter domestic violence. I was one of its first national chairs – now you don't bring that shared experience of twenty years working on women's issues together into an

institution and then instantly drop it as soon as one of us is elected with a green rosette and one of us is elected with a red one. And I just use Jane and I as an example, there are lots and lots of examples of that. There are photographs of Sue Essex, the Environment Minister, standing at the fence at Greenham Common fifteen years ago with the Shadow Environment Minister Janet Davies. So those shared experiences, those *are* important. It is interesting that a lot of the men have known each other for as long and it does not seem to lead to the same levels of cooperation cross-party I have to say.

Another woman AM observed:

We all need to maintain the cross-party cooperation without being sentimental, without being soppy about our differences – because we sit here with different political colours on, because we believe some very fundamentally different things about some very important things, *but* there are things as women, across parties that we *do* have in common. I think we do have to be very sure that we don't allow the male hierarchies to co-opt us.

When asked whether the 'sisterhood' had endured into the Assembly's second term, another woman AM replied in the negative, and highlighted both the death of Val Feld and tensions between party politics and 'gender solidarity'. She referred to the specific impact of one event: a no-confidence motion in the Agriculture Minister, Christine Gwyther. She stated:

Sadly, I don't think it has, not least because we lost our chief sister [Val Feld]. When we all got together initially [in 1999] we used to have cross-party dialogue about being strong women and I thought that was very healthy. We referred to people who were either supporters of sisterhood or not. We lost that fairly quickly and I think we lost it over Christine Gwyther because that – I have never seen such an appalling action as the vote of no confidence for Chris[tine] Gwyther. She was doing a perfectly reasonable job and the farmers wanted her to go because she was a woman and the opposition just wanted her to go to score a point over Labour. They were not prepared to think about the consequences of what happened when you took somebody who was doing their job well to the best of her ability with absolute integrity. I think that's the point when it [the sisterhood] went. When the women in other parties did not support Chris. It was too much. I remember Val [Feld] described one woman in another party as a woman who would always wear her principles on her sleeve but would drop them for political expediency – and we saw that then.

Such events in the Assembly's first years neatly illustrate the acute tensions that can develop in day-to-day politics between personal feminist conviction and party loyalty, a point evidenced by the comments of a woman AM in the Gwyther no-confidence debate. She said: 'I acknowledge that the issues that your party has raised today are serious ones. However, as your party's equal opportunities spokesperson, do you have concerns about the way that this weapon is used against women Ministers but not men?'[18]

Overall, amongst women AMs, opinions differed on the issue of whether, in the wake of devolution, equality was in anyway becoming 'normalized'. One woman minister said:

We have got a few [Assembly Members] who will *never* change because they don't *want* to change – and they don't understand the issues. On the other hand, to understand the issues of politics and equality, it's very difficult for some people. It's a very difficult concept because they have never had to fight and they have never known what it is like. That's why I always think that it's very easy sometimes for women to understand what discrimination is because they were – and are – a discriminated-against group, therefore they have empathy with other discriminated groups. And it's not something that men are generally seeing, the irony is now, women are getting on, men are now saying to us, 'what about equality of treatment for us'!

Another stated:

I think that it is very important not to be complacent. Not to think that the fact that we got it right to begin with [that is, the effects of 'twinning', and the institutional blueprint of the Assembly] means that we don't need to be vigilant. We need to be vigilant within parties to ensure that women get selected and then, when women are Assembly Members, that they get prominent jobs to do, not just 'girly stuff'. I mean I was very glad when my party selected – we had a reshuffle and we now have a woman Economic Development [Shadow] Minister – we needed to do that. We needed to have some of the girls doing some of the [supposed] 'boys' stuff'.

Another woman AM was angry at the continuing essentialist attitude[19] of some male colleagues. She stated:

Women are interested in issues *across the board*. What I find offensive is that when some issues are of crucial importance such as childcare, care for the elderly, working hours, equal pay, sometimes these are represented as 'soft' issues, women's issues; when these issues are *fundamental* to the economy and our society – and to call them soft is to devalue them and not to put them higher on the agenda where they should be.

Other women AMs warned that they needed to be watchful against a 'drawbridge' mentality, whereby women act as gatekeepers with the power to limit the progression of other women in politics. As one explained, this is the tendency of 'women across the board who have been guilty of [taking the attitude] "I've got here and damn it! I'm not letting any one come up here."' She continued,

there are issues around that for women who have got into positions of responsibility, whether they will use that position of responsibility positively on behalf of others ... I think that's incumbent upon us that we don't draw that ladder up [rather] we keep on going, we use the power that we've achieved to make sure that other people have the opportunities. Otherwise it's worth *nothing*. Me being here [as a woman Assembly Member] is *worth nothing otherwise*.

CONCLUSIONS

These women's words reinforce the analysis of earlier chapters and lend support for the main theoretical arguments for the equal representation of women in contemporary politics. Broadly stated, these assert that the presence of women enhances legitimacy and changes both the nature of politicking and the policy priorities of elected representatives. The personal testimonies serve to illustrate the challenges linked to women's struggle for equality and legitimacy at both party and national level. In attempting to understand the interaction between reformers and those resisting change, the comments of participants show that a straightforward split between the sexes is oversimplistic. Rather, at both party and national level, gender alliances were apparent, with women and men combining to advocate moves towards greater gender equality. Participants' comments also provide ample evidence of the (sometimes intense) bitterness and hostility associated with the adoption of positive action measures in the main political parties. Power structures and other systemic factors were identified by women interviewees as reinforcing androcentric practices at a party level. These accounts also suggest that gender equality is far from being 'normalized' in the parties represented in the Assembly, and that much further work is necessary in order to break down enduring discriminatory attitudes towards greater equality in candidate-selection procedures, as well as amongst sections of the electorate.

During the first years of the Assembly, women AMs asserted the case for a different, feminized, less confrontational style of politics. Notwithstanding the opposition and resistance of a minority of male AMs, participants' accounts also provide clear evidence of an emerging consensus between the sexes over the move to a new, gender-equal mode of politics. Furthermore, women AMs are clear that having a critical mass of women is an important factor, for it not only impacts on the style of politics, but, crucially, also translates into more effective substantive representation, because women AMs are able to set and influence the political agenda.

The comments of women AMs show that several were also quick to allude to their hopes for a role-model effect, such that women in the electorate were sufficiently encouraged by their example to stand for office, or to lobby and engage with the National Assembly. Women AMs' words also highlight the role of the institutional and legal context of the Assembly as an aid in stating their case for legitimacy and equality. Furthermore, a number of accounts refer to the way in which women AMs have been able to draw directly upon their own life-experiences in order to inform political debate. Overall, the words of women AMs and candidates provide further evidence of the way in which, during the Assembly's first years, they have begun to effect a transformation in the nature of politicking and the political agenda. This is an important beginning towards gender-equal national politics. Nevertheless, their comments also point to the need for continuing work to overcome prevailing discrimination and inequality operating in Welsh politics and society.

10

Conclusions: Dal Dy Dir / *Stand Your Ground*

Women's contributions to both 'traditional' party and electoral politics, and to Welsh politics in a much wider sense, have historically been largely ignored or marginalized. This book is the first comprehensive attempt to rectify this by offering a critical narrative of women's distinctive inputs to, and impact upon, contemporary politics in Wales leading up to, and since, the establishment of the National Assembly in 1999. It builds upon crucial pioneering work that explored different contributions by women to Welsh life (John, 1991; Davies, 1994; Aaron et al., 1994; Beddoe, 2000; Aaron, 2001), as well as on the limited work undertaken on women in the political parties, both generally and in Wales specifically (Lovenduski and Norris, 1993; Brown, 1996, 1999, 2002; Bradbury et al., 2000; McAllister, 2001b; Russell et al., 2002). It supplements and complements earlier assessments of the Assembly's impact (Chaney et al., 2001b; Hazell, 2003; Chaney et al., 2004), as well as research on women politicians in other institutions, at UK and devolved level (Brown, 1996, 1999; Brown et al., 1998; Brown et al., 2002; Breitenbach and Mackay (eds), 2001; Childs, 2004a; Mackay, 2004b; Childs et al., 2005).

Unsurprisingly, we begin our concluding remarks by reiterating that women in politics remains an under-researched and poorly understood area. As a consequence, the extent of women's specific contributions is severely underplayed. This applies virtually everywhere, and especially to Wales. The fact that women have so visible a presence in Wales post-devolution has made this lacuna even more noticeable and incongruous.

The book has drawn upon research carried out by the authors during the period since 1997 that used an array of different approaches and methodologies. Perhaps its uniqueness lies in the collection and structuring of a range of previously unpublished research – including a comprehensive set of formal interviews and informal communications with women themselves, together with empirical analysis of gender-related debates at the Assembly – to inform both the book's content and our analysis and findings. Wherever possible, our discussion has tried to adopt a women's perspective, allowing women to speak for themselves. We felt this direct input was long overdue and critical in assessing the value of specific gender-based contributions to the shaping of a new politics in Wales.

The campaigns since 1979 for more autonomy at a Welsh level that led to the establishment of the National Assembly in 1999 featured distinctive contributions by individual women and from the wider women's movement. This recognition formed the starting point and the critical backdrop for our study. Our analysis synthesizes women's contributions across many spheres, incorporating party and non-party, formal and informal, individual and collective, political interventions. Immeasurable opportunities came from 'being in at the start' of a new institution. In an unprecedented manner, devolution established a more accessible stage for women to participate. It rapidly brought together civic, civil, social and political actors in a new democratic arena, giving unique opportunities for women to participate, represent and be represented. Our book has documented the various different ways (albeit less formalized and publicized than in Scotland) in which women contributed to the campaigns for devolution via the formal structures of pressure and campaigning groups, as well as within the political parties. Additionally, we assess women's input to the wider movements directly or indirectly connected with the constitutional agenda.

Devolution heralded a new dawn for women, initially via the broad campaigns for constitutional change and then with the establishment and operation of the National Assembly itself. The planning and structuring of the new institution absorbed *some* of the important dynamics that had characterized women's political and civil participation. However, this came from sustained and hard-fought pressure and, in some important respects, gender equality remained limited in scope in the eventual design and operation of the institution. Thus, whilst the incorporation of equality 'within the bricks' of the new institution was a major achievement, it by no means brought the guarantees that some had expected or hoped for. Given the perpetually precarious nature of equality gains, it is important not to lose sight of the single-mindedness of many (mainly women) actors who have propelled us to where we currently are. Their contribution has been seriously underplayed in existing accounts of devolution. That said, we fully acknowledge that there is a considerable distance to travel. Until now, women have acted as the principal agents of change, particularly with regard to pressure for substantive political representation; clearly, this cannot be relied upon indefinitely. Notions of substantive representation, which link it to descriptive representation, assume female politicians will 'act for' other women. There is also an argument suggesting that as levels of women's descriptive representation grow, there will be increased gender mainstreaming across the board. Thus, women politicians might have less direct involvement with promoting a new generation of female politicians. We have already seen the signs of this in a gender-balanced Assembly. As Val Feld recognized:

> as we enter the second stage, we should all of us feel that we don't have to feel at all embarrassed or sidelined about raising the issues and continually hammering away at the issues, because what is clear is that the work that we have done is absolutely

central to the regeneration of the Welsh economy, we are not on a 'lunatic fringe', we were right about addressing these kind of issues.

We have used the critical 'politics of presence' literature to challenge the traditional assumption that there is a straightforward and linear relationship between descriptive and substantive representation. Some point to the 'probabilistic' (rather than 'deterministic') nature of substantive representation (Beckwith, 2000). We agree, and validate this with examples of the contingent nature of women's participation in Wales, alongside the powerful influence of systemic factors, such as a new legislative and policy-making environment, a more proportional electoral system, and changing dynamics of party organization and competition. Without rehearsing the arguments about the dynamics of 'critical mass' and its impact (see, for example, Norris and Lovenduski, 2001), one of our principal findings is the contingent and complex character of the politics of presence in the National Assembly. Equal numbers of men and women politicians cannot alone explain the relatively different political exchanges operating there. Our book explores the links between critical mass and gender mainstreaming, whilst unpacking some of the wider stimuli for the embryonic 'new' politics in Wales.

The representation of women was central to devolution's new lexicon of participatory, inclusive politics. Whilst inherently flimsy and underdeveloped, this did at least offer some unique opportunities for improving women's position in the new Assembly. Yet only some of these were successfully taken up. Gaining fair representation was a particularly difficult battle within the political parties and candidate selection, in particular, provoked considerable controversy and ongoing tensions. Despite this, at one level at least, we have seen major improvements in descriptive representation for women (although these have been party-specific and almost exclusively at the Assembly, rather than at other elected levels). In terms of democracy and the state, the latter development represents a major advance for national-level politics in Wales, for it has achieved no less an outcome than boosting the legitimacy of government. This follows because theories of representative democracy assert that legitimacy is derived from the people. Thus, for a purportedly democratic institution to be truly representative, it must secure the participation of all groups in society – as citizens, employees and as elected representatives. Enhanced democratic legitimacy over the earlier mode of administrative devolution has therefore been secured, by virtue of the fact that women are no longer marginalized and excluded but, in the Assembly at least, have secured an equal role as elected representatives. As a result, women now have a core role in making political decisions, national budgetary allocations and framing legislation.

In exploring women in contemporary politics, we have located (again, for the first time) this study of post-devolution Wales within the wider literature on political representation and equality. Where relevant, we have also adopted a comparative perspective, focusing especially on the other devolved institutions in the UK. This is important, for there are clear inter and intra dynamics at play, especially in the position of women in post-devolution Scotland. Ours is an attempt to locate equality progress in Wales within the context of wider developments in women's political participation and representation. There are various conceptual frameworks within which to understand wider trends in women's political involvement, many of which have been utilized during the course of our study. Specifically, we explored the systemic and structural factors devolution provided; these constitute the basic opportunities for change. We also analysed the ways in which the political parties, individual women and equality bodies responded to these opportunities. The relative receptiveness of political parties as 'carrying agents' for gender equality has been particularly important in Wales and is reflected in some of the gender-balanced party groups in the Assembly. We explored the notion of 'contagion', as well as examining different forms of representation and the 'politics of presence' literature – all through a distinctive Welsh lens.

A noticeable feature in Wales is the way in which key women activists successfully carried across their long-standing contributions to civil society (in its broadest sense) as elected politicians in the new devolved arena. Many women elected to the new body were long-standing feminists, particularly in the Labour and Plaid Cymru groups. Their involvement with the new institution from the outset was highly significant and helped establish some important 'ground rules'. It also reinforces the close connection between feminism, political and constitutional activism, and wider gender campaigns.

Our book has pointed to a number of measurable benefits from increased women's representation: the gradual emergence of a more gender-balanced policy-making driving the incremental re-gendering of politics, the normalization of women politicians in the public and media mind, a new and less macho political rhetoric, even the seeds of a more cooperative approach to policy-making, although this is uneven. The Assembly's own output underlines some of the new opportunities it has itself ushered in, both for promoting women politicians and for heralding a different policy agenda. We discussed the statutory duties in relation to equality of opportunity set out in the Government of Wales Act (1998) and the manner in which they have underpinned the Welsh Assembly Government's self-stated, ambitious aim of mainstreaming equality in public policy. Yet, our analysis has also shown that the experience of the Assembly's early years presents something of a paradox in respect of gender and policy. On the one hand, there is the seeming institutionalization of mainstreaming, as witnessed by the measures taken to establish equality building-blocks or institutional prerequisites – a development accompanied by high-profile political will. On the other hand, there are individual examples of policy to promote gender equality. However, these are not part of a routinized, joined-up approach to overall policy that can consistently deliver concrete policy outcomes. This, in turn, reflects the powerful continuities that are present between elected devolution and the former mode of administrative devolution, not least with officials' continuing preoccupation with bureaucratic process, rather than equality outcomes. In short, we conclude that the experience of the Assembly's first years suggests a 'decoupling', whereby the devolved government espouses one thing, whilst practising another.

As elsewhere (see Breitenbach, 1990; Lovenduski and Randall, 1993), the women's movement in Wales has been structurally loose, diverse in character and, at times, lacking organizational coherence. Yet, it has a number of distinctive characteristics that have shaped the extent of its impact and influence. A key one is an overwhelmingly 'top-down' feel to the movement at points of greatest influence. By this, we mean that many of the most significant gains have been achieved by a few strategic leaders within a loosely organized and, at times, disparate women's movement. This has both reflected and internalized wider gaps and weaknesses in civil and civic society in Wales, and in the depth and maturity of the devolution debate. We have shown, for example, how the Scottish Constitutional Convention provided a forum for the developments of specific, better-argued rationales for equal representation or, as Breitenbach and Mackay suggest, 'the mobilisation of a broad-based and pluralist movement of women activists ... to put gender on the agenda – and to keep it there through the various twists and turns of the broader campaign for constitutional change in Scotland' (2001: 15). The Convention, the 50:50 campaign and the Women's Co-ordination Group internalized an equal representation agenda through incorporating many of the principal Scottish civic institutions in their campaigning and preparation for a Scottish parliament. In the absence of a broad-based, cross-party organization in Wales, there needed to be effective channels within traditional party structures and in the eventual internal architecture of the Assembly to ensure women took more prominent roles.

In respect of women in civil and civic society and the earlier hopes that elected devolution would deliver a 'participatory democracy', our findings show that the advent of the Assembly has been accompanied by a reconfiguration of women's organizations as part of the ongoing development of a nascent women's lobby. Overall, this new women's lobby is characterized by its developing nature, a prevailing willingness to engage in policy-making, and its organizational complexity. Notwithstanding ongoing challenges facing women's NGOs, the evidence shows that, in the wake of elected devolution, the growing participation of women in the policy process has had the important effect of lending greater democratic legitimacy to national decision-making. This is in sharp contrast to the pre-existing, exclusivist practices of the male-dominated Welsh Office.

The statutory integration of the equality agenda – in all its various guises – within the new institution has been a major factor in this new climate. This was designed for all poorly represented groups and has begun to create a broader and more participatory environment than had existed previously, and continues to exist elsewhere. In addition, and against the backdrop of the pro-devolution arguments about increased levels of democratic engagement and accountability, our analysis of election study data points to the emergence of a new electoral politics, characterized by subtle differences between the political behaviour of the sexes. This, we suggest, arises from gendered responses to political factors, such as party ideology, leadership style and public policy priorities.

Our analysis of the gender dynamics of the Assembly's first term shows that the substantive representation of women involved both the actions in political debate of a substantial portion of female AMs and the interventions of key women 'equality champions', defined by their feminist conviction, professional experience, and gender-equality knowledge. The evidence of the Assembly's early years shows that, through these processes, descriptive representation has begun to translate into the substantive representation of women. Strikingly, the data reveal that women AMs have a greater propensity than their male colleagues to both engage in, and initiate, political debate on 'women's issues' in order to further the substantive representation of women. It is also evident that women AMs draw directly upon gendered life-experiences in order to inform debate. Furthermore, they have acted to promote women's interests across a broader range of policy areas than have their male counterparts. These findings underline the extent of the transformation in politics brought about by elected devolution. However, as in the other areas of politics explored in this volume, there is evidence of fragility in some of the new practices. In terms of the gender dynamics of Assembly political debate, this is illustrated by women AMs' disproportionately high use and invocation of the National Assembly's statutory equality duties, a fact that probably reflects a lack of embeddedness of the equality agenda.

Clearly, we are not suggesting that all is rosy, or that equality campaigners can retire with their work complete! This book has shown how issues connected with party politics, internal power-structures, scarce resources, competition and the powerful continuity of sexist cultures have hindered the selection of women candidates, the development of a consensual operational culture in Cardiff Bay and, ultimately, a more gender-balanced approach to policy-making. Whilst there have been major victories at some levels, we suggest here that such progress is also inherently vulnerable, since it lacks a broader supporting base and relies upon a fragile political consensus. In the absence of 'bottom-up' political campaigns, women (and, in some cases, men) have been forced to construct temporary organizational infrastructures – both separate and within other bodies – to achieve their objectives. This is illustrated by the impact of 'strategic' women in various organizations, such as the Campaign for a Welsh Assembly, the 'Yes for Wales' campaign, the NAAG and, within the political parties, in the debates over promoting and mainstreaming gender. This is not a criticism of the women's movement in Wales as such; rather, we suggest it has focused historically on other civic and international affairs, rather than constitutional change. It is a case of rather late in the day that the movement has taken political shape and form, and this has contributed to the fragile and unstable equality terrain in Wales.

We have emphasized the enormous strides taken towards greater equality in the face of much opposition, especially from the political 'elites'. Women have massively influenced the shape of the much-vaunted inclusive politics that was meant to accompany devolution. It simultaneously offered them opportunities to assume greater prominence on the Welsh political stage. Taking a women's perspective on devolution has helped us better understand some of the unique dynamics behind the wider moves for a new and different system of governance. The achievement of equal numbers of women and men in the second Assembly is a magnificent success for descriptive representation and brings with it the potential for further substantive gains. That said, there remain concerns with the process by which women have achieved political status. That many of them have been inspired from above and have relied on a fairly underdeveloped civic and civil society, within which the women's movement – in all its guises – has been loosely organized and patchy in influence, means one must be guarded in praise at this stage. Neither can we attribute to elected politicians (of both sexes) the full responsibility for effecting what represents a vast and unprecedented cultural change. Cultural and political values about sex and gender are strongly embedded, and it would be facile to suggest that thirty elected AMs might change these overnight.

This book has shown that the long-established women's movement in Wales has won some notable and unprecedented successes, including improving women's formal political representation, some major concessions in a range of policy areas and more subtle changes in political operational styles. In this way, women have gradually but importantly contributed to the reconfiguring of politics in Wales. Further tensions surely lie ahead within the ongoing debate on mechanisms for promoting women, for the simple reason that as women politicians begin to achieve critical mass, the base of the movement is likely to widen, and new and diverse voices must be heard and incorporated (as highlighted by current AMs in this volume's foreword).

This work represents a starting point in a massively underdeveloped debate. There is vast scope for developing research on women in contemporary Welsh politics. In particular, we highlight the need for further consideration of: women electors' changing attitudes to a gender-balanced Assembly; the impact of gender parity on political operational styles; qualitative work on women's participation in the work of the Assembly, and the associated challenges of this; the way in which the Civil Service is responding to the move to gender-equal politics/engendered policy; girls' and young women's attitudes and political/electoral behaviour in post-devolution Wales; communication and awareness between women and government in civil society; and a specific audit of gender and public policy outcomes. Work is already under way that might provide further answers, such as Charles, Aull Davies and James's ESRC project on gender and political processes after devolution (Universities of Warwick and Swansea).

Finally, whilst applauding the major progress towards gender equality within the context of Welsh devolution, we have flagged up some of its inherent vulnerabilities and instabilities. We are mindful that these are early days for the National Assembly and that the wider dynamics of devolution are far from settled. Nevertheless, despite some significant improvements in women's representation and a concomitant rise in the gender profile of Welsh politicians, together with major steps forward in promoting gender equality in decision and policy-making, there remains substantial work to be done – for example, in the adoption of gender-budgeting techniques to spending plans of the Welsh Assembly Government – drawing perhaps on experiences from elsewhere, including Australia, the Philippines and South Africa; the development of a more nuanced approach to gender equality in public policy that recognizes women are not a single or homogeneous group, and so addresses simultaneous, multiple identities founded on gender as well as age, sexual orientation, language or socio-economic status, for example; fostering extensive, mature, well-informed media coverage of post-devolution politics that, in particular, engages girls and younger women; and increasing the numbers of women – and women's NGOs – in civil society, able and willing to engage in, and shape, the devolved policy process. We predict that progress will not be linear or straightforward; rather, evidence suggests the trajectory is likely to be faltering, with gains counterbalanced by a slowing momentum, drift or setback. Until the structures and opportunities for equality are fully entrenched and mainstreamed, questions as to their security and stability will remain. As such, there is a need for women politicians and activists – and their allies – to maintain momentum and stay vigilant in their struggle for a voice and a place in Welsh politics. Mary Lloyd Jones's artistic declaration that graces the front cover of this book serves as both current advice and a forewarning – *Dal Dy Dir:* Stand Your Ground.

Notes

1. Introduction

1 Sally Weale, 'At last! The new Welsh Assembly is the first legislative body in the world made up of equal numbers of men and women', *Guardian*, 9 May 2003.

2 Baroness Anita Gale, quoted by Nicola Porter, 'Baroness attacks Welsh men', *Daily Mirror*, 29 June 2001.

3 It should be acknowledged that there are differences between 'national' and sub-state devolved legislatures, and that therefore an exact international comparison cannot be drawn. It is also the case that the National Assembly for Wales is relatively weak in terms of formal powers, even compared to other sub-state entities, such as the Scottish Parliament and the Northern Ireland Assembly. Nevertheless, the achievement of gender parity in a national political forum with a substantial budget is ground-breaking.

4 The world average stands at 15.9 per cent, according to the Inter Parliamentary Union (IPU) figures, 2005.

5 See later discussion.

6 Authors' note: we have endeavoured to use the appropriate designation of the Wales/Welsh Labour Party based upon the date of the reference, but there is widespread overlap in the use of the term by those interviewed during the preparation of this book and in a range of cited sources/publications. Accordingly, readers are advised to cross-refer to both the Welsh and Wales Labour Party in the bibliography.

7 See IDEA/University of Stockholm global database of quotas for women for further information on party quotas and other sorts of quota systems; *www. quota project.org/*.

8 *Who Runs Wales?* (EOC/WWNC, 2004), *http://www.eoc.org.uk/cseng/abouteoc/who%20runs%20wales.pdf*.

9 Eight women MPs were elected in the May 2005 General Election: Madeleine Moon (Bridgend), Jenny Willot (Cardiff Central), Julie Morgan (Cardiff North), Betty Williams (Conwy), Ann Clwyd (Cynon Valley), Nia Griffith (Llanelli), Jessica Morden (Newport East), Siân James (Swansea East).

10 Indeed, one of the legacies of feminism and feminist politics has been to challenge traditional definitions of what counts as politics. Conventional definitions tend to neglect aspects of political activism, such as capacity-building, consciousness-raising and other sorts of community activism, which may lack a 'public' dimension (Sudbury, 1998; Lister, 2003).

11 The authors are engaged in work to develop a systematic three-jurisdiction analysis of the gendered aspects of devolution in the UK.

12 The project was led by Fiona Mackay (University of Edinburgh). Team

members were Paul Chaney and Hâf Elgar (covering Wales, University of Cardiff, and University of Edinburgh, respectively), Elizabeth Meehan and Tahyna Barnett Donaghy (Northern Ireland, Queen's University Belfast), and Alice Brown and Ann Henderson (Scotland, University of Edinburgh). See the Gender and Constitutional Change website at: *http://www.pol.ed.ac.uk/gcc.*

[13] The project was led by Professor Ralph Fevre (Cardiff University), with Paul Chaney (Cardiff University), Charlotte Williams, John Borland and Sandra Betts (University of Wales Bangor).

[14] The project was led by Professor Ralph Fevre (Cardiff University), with Paul Chaney (Cardiff University), Charlotte Williams and Sandra Betts (University of Wales Bangor).

[15] Carried out as part of a wider programme of research by Laura McAllister in the period 1999–2003.

[16] Source for elected women MEPs *http://www.qub.ac.uk/cawp/UKhtmls/ UKMEP1.htm*; Source for women candidates *http://www.europarl.org.uk/guide/candidates99/wales.html*; for women candidates/MEPS 2004 *http://www. europarl.org.uk/guide/Gelectionsmain. html.*

2. Feminist Movements, 'Strategic Women' and Feminist Ideas; En-gendering the 1990s Devolution Campaign?

[1] Woman activist referring to the 'Women Say Yes for Wales' rally in Whitland, 30 August 1997.

[2] On Good Friday 1998, all the main political parties in Northern Ireland – with the exception of the Democratic Unionist Party – announced agreement on a power-sharing devolved government that would be formed with ministerial posts distributed according to party strength.

[3] The Northern Ireland Human Rights Commission (NIHRC) was given the task under the Belfast (Good Friday) Agreement and the Northern Ireland Act 1998 of consulting and reporting on the scope for defining rights in a Bill of Rights for Northern Ireland (see NIHRC, 2004).

[4] There is strong evidence to suggest that the process of devolution and the associated increase in awareness about women's representation led to a record number of women being elected from Northern Ireland to Westminster in 2001. See Donaghy (2004).

[5] Consultation with women's groups undertaken by the Scottish Women's Co-ordination Group in the run-up to the UN Women's Conference in Beijing identified three core issues for women: violence against women; representation in political and public life; and women's poverty.

[6] *www.lse.ac.uk/collections/CCS/introduction.htm.* Accessed 20 December 2005.

[7] The power to legislate to prohibit discrimination and to regulate equal opportunities is reserved to the UK Parliament. However, lobbying by statutory equality agencies, equality groups and women activists resulted in the insertion of 'exceptions' to the reservation in the Scotland Act 1998 in these two respects. See Scotland Act, Schedule 5 Section L.2.

[8] We draw upon the small literature on women in Wales (see Introduction), including substantial reviews of women's movements by Reeves (1988), Rees (1999a, 1999b),

Beddoe (2000) and Rolph (2003), sources from contemporary women's movement journals and newsletters (Masson and Rolph, 1997), and interviews with activists. We are indebted to Hâf Elgar, researcher on the Gender and Constitutional Change project Welsh team in the summer of 2001, upon whose literature review much of this following section draws.

[9] Initially developed as a UK manufactory of naval missile propellants, Caerwent became a US depository of armaments in Wales (without consultation with Welsh people).

[10] Quoted in B. Jones, 'Blaenau Ffestiniog and the miners', *Radical Wales* (autumn 1984), 14–15.

[11] J. Evans, C. Hudson and P. Smith (1985) 'Women and the miners: it's a whole way of life', *Radical Wales*, 8 (spring 1985), 14–15.

[12] Ibid.

[13] Welsh. Translation: 'Fair Play'.

[14] Welsh. Translation: 'The Welsh Language Society'.

[15] Under this scheme, constituencies are matched as far as possible in terms of a variety of indicators, including winnability. Both men and women could stand for selection for a pair of constituencies. Under twinning, the woman applicant with the highest number of votes was selected as the Labour candidate for one of the twinned seats, at the same time as the man with the highest number of votes was selected for the other.

[16] Julie Morgan MP, Hansard, Debate on the Government of Wales Bill (1997), 9 December 1997, col. 857.

[17] For example, Wales Labour Action, a pressure group within the Labour Party lobbying for an Assembly with far-reaching legislative and tax-raising powers, also lobbied for gender balance. Members included Gareth Hughes, David Morris MEP and Sue Essex, a leading feminist politician and activist (Andrews, 1999: 63).

[18] I.e. to involve citizens without party affiliation or membership, as well as co-working with non-governmental organizations.

[19] Occasionally known by the longer formulation: 'Women Say Yes for Wales'.

[20] Source: National Library of Wales, 'Yes for Wales 1997 Referendum Campaign Records', Box ref. G12/1/7, 'Speaking Notes for Press Conference 23.06.97'.

[21] Source: National Library of Wales, 'Yes for Wales 1997 Referendum Campaign Records', Box ref. G12/1/6.

[22] Source: National Library of Wales, 'Yes for Wales 1997 Referendum Campaign Records', Box ref. G12/1/11.

[23] Quotations from: *Women Say Yes* (1997) Whitland Rally publicity flyer, National Library of Wales Archive and Manuscript Collection, Aberystwyth, 'Yes For Wales Referendum Campaign Records', Box 6/G12/1/4.

[24] Quotations from: *Women Say Yes* (1997) Whitland Rally publicity flyer, National Library of Wales Archive and Manuscript Collection, Aberystwyth, 'Yes For Wales Referendum Campaign Records', Box 6/G12/1/4.

[25] Source: Interview by Jill Evans published in *Radical Wales*, 1 (winter 1983), 4–6.

[26] See, for example, *http://www.bbc.co.uk*, Wednesday, 21 April 1999, 'Welsh language demands grow'.

[27] Source: National Library of Wales, 'Yes for Wales 1997 Referendum Campaign Records', Box ref. G12/1/6.

3. Gender and Politics: A Blueprint for Change

[1]   Val Feld, unpublished speech to Chwarae Teg's annual conference, Llandrindod Wells, 1999.

[2]   National Library of Wales, Yes for Wales 1997 Referendum Campaign Records, Box G12/1/6.

[3]   Forerunner of the Wales Women's National Coalition, WWNC, a network of women's NGOs, such as the National Federation of Women's Institutes Wales and the Minority Ethnic Women's Network Cymru.

[4]   Cf. WLP, *Preparing for a New Wales: A Report on the Structure and Workings of the Welsh Assembly,* Welsh Labour Party Conference 10 and 11 May 1996 (Cardiff: WLP), p. 4, para. 3.7.

[5]   Unpublished minutes of WWNC meeting 5 September 1997.

[6]   Interviewed 6 November 2002, original emphasis.

[7]   Val Feld, Official Record, 12 July 2000.

[8]   Papers of WWNC 18 July 1998.

[9]   Unpublished minutes of WWC meeting 19 December 1997.

[10] Julie Morgan MP, Hansard, Debate on the Government of Wales Bill (1997), 9 December 1997, Column 857.

[11] The members of the National Assembly Advisory Group were: John Elfed Jones, Nick Bourne, Ioan Bowen Rees, Marjorie Dykins, Ken Hopkins, Mari James, Helen Mary Jones, Howard Marshall, Eluned Morgan, Joyce Redfern, Viscount St Davids, Ray Singh, Ian Spratling and Kirsty Williams.

[12] Unpublished minutes of WWNC meeting 19 December 1997.

[13] Unpublished minutes of WWNC meeting 17 February 1998.

[14] Unpublished minutes of WWNC meeting 29 July 1998.

[15] These recommendations are strikingly similar to those being developed in Scotland by the Consultative Steering Group on the Scottish Parliament (CSG 1998).

[16] See also the CSG key principles, adopted by the Scottish Parliament.

[17] Standing orders can be amended only by a two-thirds majority in a vote by the whole Assembly.

[18] Transcript of unpublished speech to Chwarae Teg's annual conference, Llandrindod Wells, 1999.

4. Women and the Political Parties in Wales: Victories and Vulnerabilities

[1]   Scarce power-resources (specifically, access to and use of political patronage) is a principal obstacle to women's advancement in the case of the smaller parties.

[2]   See the tables in ch. 1.

[3]   Originally, there were fifteen women and thirteen men, but Labour's Delyth Evans replaced former First Secretary Alun Michael following his resignation as AM in early 2000, bringing the number of Labour women AMs to sixteen.

[4]   These were Edwina Hart (Finance), Jane Davidson (Education), Jane Hutt (Health) and Sue Essex (Environment).

[5]   These women covered Finance (Edwina Hart, Labour), Education (Jane Davidson, Labour) Culture and Sport (Jenny Randerson, Liberal Democrat), Health (Jane

Hutt, Labour) and Environment (Sue Essex, Labour). However, men dominated the second level of senior politicians, holding four of the five deputy minister posts.

[6] 'Zipping' refers to the positioning of candidates on the party lists in proportional systems like AMS. Women and men alternate in the zigzag form of a zip.

[7] It should be noted that, whilst substantial proportions of female activists, particularly feminists, in the Labour Party were in favour of twinning, women were by no means united. Indeed, the 'Members Against Twinning' group was chaired by a woman.

[8] The Conservatives returned no MPs (male or female) from Wales between 1997 and 2005.

[9] Source: *http://www.parliament.uk/directories/hciolists/gender.cfm.*

[10] Source: *http://news.bbc.co.uk/1/hi/uk_politics.*

[11] More recently, the Conservative Party has begun to consider positive action mechanisms. The 'Women2Win' campaign was launched in October 2005, arguing for positive action, such as creating an 'A-list' of the top 100 candidates, of whom 50 will be men and 50 women, to stand in the top 100 Conservative target seats. Theresa May added her support to this campaign and, in December 2005, the party's newly elected leader, David Cameron, indicated his support for measures that would help improve the number of Conservative women MPs.

[12] See J. Edwards and C. Chapman, 'Women's political representation in Wales: waving or drowning?', *Contemporary Politics,* vol. 6, 4 (2000).

[13] Source: *http://www.wld.org.uk.*

[14] *Western Mail,* 25 March 2002.

[15] *Western Mail,* 13 May 2002 (original emphasis).

[16] *Western Mail,* 11 May 2002.

[17] *Western Mail,* 7 August 2002.

[18] Interestingly, and perhaps symptomatic of the persistence of institutional sexism in the political parties, there has been little evidence in Scotland of 'contagion' between levels. So, for example, there have not been increases in levels of women's representation at local or Westminster level, nor much appetite by any of the parties, including Labour, to use the enabling legislation to apply quota-type measures. The Labour victor who fought the safe seat of Livingston in a by-election in 2005, caused by the death of Robin Cook MP, was drawn from an all-men shortlist.

[19] This was shown in Blaenau Gwent during the 2005 General Election, although it is difficult to disentangle the issue of all-women shortlists there from wider concerns about centre interference in local constituency matters.

[*] All unattributed quotes which appear in this chapter are drawn from interviews conducted by the authors on a range of different research projects between 1997 and 2005.

5. Women and the Ballot Box

[1] Analysed using SPSS software. Prior to all analyses data-sets were weighted to take account of differing selection probabilities.

[2] A study jointly conducted by the Institute for Welsh Politics, University of Wales Aberystwyth, and Crest Centre For Research into Elections and Social Trends, an

ESRC Research Centre at the National Centre for Social Research and Department of Sociology, University of Oxford.

[3] The Wales Life and Times Study 2003, conducted by Dr Richard Wyn Jones, University of Wales Aberystwyth, Professor Anthony Heath of the Department of Sociology, University of Oxford, and the National Centre for Social Research (NatCen). It was funded by the Economic and Social Research Council under the Devolution and Constitutional Change Programme (grant number L219 25 2042).

[4] *Passim*; the present discussion refers to the 2003 data unless otherwise stated.

[5] Pearson Chi-squared test, value 23.339, df = 6, sig. 0.001. N = 998.

[6] Pearson Chi-squared test, value 133.549, df = 70, sig. 0.00. N = 978.

[7] Not statistically significant, Pearson Chi-squared test, value 3.341, df = 3, sig. 0.188. N = 516. Face-to-face interviews only in order to eliminate mode effects.

[8] Not statistically significant, Pearson Chi-squared test, value 0.46, df = 1, sig. 0.831. N = 989.

[9] Pearson Chi-squared test, value 123.841, df = 14, sig. 0.000. N = 989.

[10] Pearson Chi-squared test, value, df = 19, sig. 0.008. N = 364.

[11] Pearson Chi-squared test, value 37.048, df = 19, sig. 0.008. N = 364.

[12] Pearson Chi-squared test, value 27.7, df = 17, sig. 0.049. N = 504.

[13] Pearson Chi-squared test, value 3.882 df = 11, sig. 0.973. N = 988.

[14] Pearson Chi-squared test, value 8.485, df = 5, sig. 0.131. N = 989.

[15] Pearson Chi-squared test, value 38.993, df = 20, sig. 0.07. N = 488.

[16] Although not statistically significant. Pearson Chi-squared test, value 1.235, df = 6, sig. 0.975. N = 990.

[17] Compared to 48.6 per cent of men.

[18] Compared to 10.8 per cent of men.

[19] Compared to 33.5 per cent of men.

[20] 2.9 per cent of women and 2.8 per cent of men voted on 'world issues/the Gulf War'; 1.6 and 1.8 per cent respectively 'other'; and 0.5 and 0.2 per cent respectively, 'don't know'.

[21] Not statistically significant. Pearson Chi-squared test, value 7.594, df = 5, sig. 0.180 N = 785.

[22] Pearson Chi-squared test, value 26.520, df = 5, sig. 0.00. N = 989.

[23] Pearson Chi-squared test, value 11.332, df = 4, sig. 0.023. N = 988. 'Reduce taxation and spending': women 4.1 per cent, men 4.6 per cent; 'none of the other options': men 5.6 per cent, women 5.2 per cent, 'don't know': men 0.2 per cent, women 2.2 per cent.

[24] Follows Wales Election Study Cooling.

[25] Pearson Chi-squared test, value 13.432, df = 3, sig. 0.04. N = 987.

[26] Pearson Chi-squared test, value 8.125, df = 3, sig. 0.044. N = 987.

[27] 3 per cent compared to 5.8 per cent.

[28] Pearson Chi-squared test, value 12.290, df = 6, sig. 0.056. N = 987.

[29] Pearson Chi-squared test, value 17.507, df = 6, sig. 0.008. N = 989.

[30] Respectively, 16.5 compared to 20.6 per cent, and 12.9 compared to 17.6 per cent.

[31] No statistically significant difference between sexes. Chi-squared test, value 3.451, df = 6, sig. 0.751. N = 989.

[32] No statistically significant difference between sexes. Chi-squared test, value 11.676, df = 6, sig. 0.070. N = 989.

33 Overall, reflecting broader survey trends, in respect of the Election Study Data it should be noted that women were more likely to say 'don't know'.

34 Pearson Chi-squared test, value 17.461, df = 4, sig. 0.002. N = 988. 50.3 per cent and 38.6 per cent of men and women respectively said that Plaid would be less able than the other parties.

35 19.9 compared to 13.7 per cent.

36 61.4 compared to 59.3 per cent, Pearson Chi-squared test, value 19.994, df = 11, sig. 0.045. N = 988.

37 32.9 compared to 29.3 per cent of men Pearson Chi-squared test, value 33.534, df = 12, sig. 0.001. N = 987.

38 Pearson Chi-squared test, value 20.041, df = 6 sig. 0.003. N = 988. 4.7 per cent of women and 5.1 per cent of men said it had made it a little worse; 1.6 per cent of women and 5.8 per cent of men said that it had made it a lot worse; 1.8 per cent of women and 1.9 per cent of men said that it was 'too early to tell'; and 5 per cent of women and 2.1 per cent of men said that they did not know.

39 Pearson Chi-squared test, value 8.432, df = 84 sig. 0.000.

40 Pearson Chi-squared test, value 7.955, df = 1 sig. 0.005. N = 209.

41 Pearson Chi-squared test, value 10.415, df = 4, sig. 0.034. N = 989.

42 Pearson Chi-squared test, value 6.130, df = 2, sig 0.047. N = 500.

43 The Register General's Classification of Occupational Class: I = professional etc. occupations; II = managerial and technical occupations; III = skilled occupations; III (N) = non-manual; III (M) = manual; IV = partly skilled occupations; V = unskilled occupations.

44 Pearson Chi-squared test, value 3.960, df = 1, sig. 0.047. N = 355.

45 Pearson Chi-squared test, value 15.430, df = 4, sig. 0.004. N = 987.

46 Pearson Chi-squared test, value 72.216, df = 56, sig. 0.011. N = 986.

47 Pearson Chi-squared test for category 'National Assembly', value 77.636, df = 8, sig. 0.0. N = 414. Pearson Chi-squared test for category 'UK government', value 57.167, df = 8, sig. 0.0. N = 367. Pearson Chi-squared test for category 'unitary authorities', value 14.573, df = 9, sig. 0.042. N = 37. Pearson Chi-squared test for category 'European Union', value 17.343, df = 7, sig. 0.015. N = 91.

48 Constitutional preferences columns for each sex do not total 100 because the following categories are omitted from the summary table: 'skip, ask partner', 'skip, never had a job', 'armed forces' and 'insufficient info'.

49 No statistically significant difference between sexes. Chi-squared test, value 10.158, df = 7, sig. 0.180. N = 61.

50 Pearson Chi-squared test, value 24.550, df = 7, sig. 0.001. N = 72.

51 Pearson Chi-squared test, value 48.545, df = 8, sig. 0.000. N = 354.

52 Pearson Chi-squared test, value 44.736, df = 7, sig. 0.000. N = 251.

53 Pearson Chi-squared test, value 16.770, df = 7, sig. 0.019. N = 51.

54 Pearson Chi-squared test, value 24.430, df = 4, sig. 0.00. N = 989.

55 Columns for males and females do not total 100 because the categories 'skip, ask partner', 'skip, never had a job', 'armed forces' and 'insufficient info' are not included in this summary table.

56 An area-based community regeneration strategy.

6. The Gender Dynamics of the National Assembly

1   Val Feld, Official Record, 14 September 2000.
2   Adobe Acrobat Reader 6.0.
3   A non-discrete approach to coding was adopted in this methodology. This means that parliamentarians' speeches and interventions containing more than one of the different key terms explored in this paper severally comprise part of the sub-analysis of each – and all – respective key terms referred to by the speaker. Thus, for example, a single debating point that refers to both to 'domestic violence' and 'equal pay' will be logged and simultaneously form part of the respective analysis of each term, i.e. the same speech or interventions will appear in the statistics for both 'domestic violence' and 'equal pay'. This approach was undertaken to provide a holistic insight into the debate around key terms, and to avoid the creation of a hierarchy of gender-equality terms explored in the present analysis. Repeated references to the same term by a single speaker in a speech or intervention were recorded but once.
4   This coding was undertaken by one of the authors, Paul Chaney. In order to increase accuracy and consistency this process was repeated by a research assistant. In a small minority of instances (five cases) different codes were allocated – these were re-examined and consensus reached over the final coding designation.
5   For coding methodology see Reingold, 2002: 138, 166–7.
6   'Women's issues are issues that mainly affect women, either for biological reasons (for example, breast cancer screening, reproductive rights) or for social reasons (for example, sex equality or childcare policy)', Lovenduski and Karam (2002: 5). See discussion in Introduction.
7   The search term 'women' was used to identify debate on 'women's issues', i.e. public policy with a gendered dimension relating to the needs and wants of women. For the purposes of the present analysis, instances falling outside of this definition were disregarded – i.e. general usages of 'women', unrelated to the gendered construction of public policy in political debate.
8   Pearson Chi-squared test, $P = 0.001$, $df = 4$, $X^2 = 30.966$.
9   Edwina Hart, Official Record, Statement on Diversity in Public Appointments, 17 July 2001.
10   Although not statistically significant, $df = 4$, $X^2 = 5.881$.
11   Record of Cabinet meeting, 8 October 2001.
12   Record of Cabinet meeting, 26 June 2001.
13   Record of Cabinet meeting, 15 January 2001.
14   Record of Cabinet meeting, 25 November 2002.
15   Pearson Chi-squared test, $P = 0.001$, $df = 4$, $X^2 = 22.770$.
16   Not statistically significant.
17   Not statistically significant.
18   When First Minister Alun Michael resigned in February 2000, he was replaced by Delyth Evans, raising the number of women Assembly Members to twenty-five (42 per cent) out of a total of sixty. Calculations are based upon this latter figure.
19   These were instances in debate when speakers responded to – and referred directly to – earlier interventions by a speaker from another party stating their support for the measure under discussion.
20   Jane Hutt and Helen Mary Jones, Official Record, 12 December 2000.

21   Helen Mary Jones, Official Record, 29 October 2002.

22   Helen Mary Jones, Official Record, 1 March 2001.

23   Janet Ryder and Edwina Hart, Official Record, 18 June 2002.

24   Edwina Hart, Official Record, 1 March 2000.

25   Jane Hutt, Official Record, 7 November 2000.

26   Gwenda Thomas, Official Record, 1 March 2000.

27   Helen Mary Jones, Official Record, 6 July 1999.

28   It should be noted that major revisions in the operation of the Assembly and a move away from a 'body-corporate' to a parliamentary mode of working (see Rawlings, 2003, for a discussion) has reduced the earlier consensual nature of earlier committee work.

29   Pearson Chi-squared test, $P = 0.001$, df = 4, $X^2 = 31.042$.

30   i.e. reporting on or acknowledging the existence of such issues without giving – or implying – a value judgment about whether they should be supported.

31   See interventions in plenary debate by the following members of the Welsh Conservative Party: 29 October 2002, Davies, D.; 8 March 2000, Davies, D.; 5 July 2001, Davies, D.; 30 November 1999, Davies, G.; 15 May 2001, Cairns, A.; 2 July 2002; Morgan, J.

32   David Davies and Val Feld, Official Record, 'The Inappropriate Slide towards Political Correctness in the Assembly', Short Debate, 14 September 2000.

33   Alun Cairns, Official Record, 5 July 2001.

34   David Davies, Official Record, 14 May 2002.

35   David Davies, Official Record, 14 May 2002.

36   Nick Bourne, Official Record, 14 February 2002.

37   Delyth Evans and David Davies, Official Record, 14 February 2002.

38   Delyth Evans, Official Record, 14 February 2002.

39   Alun Cairns, Official Record, 15 May 2001.

40   Alison Halford, Official Record, 5 July 2001.

41   Jane Hutt, Official Record, 18 April 2002.

42   Elin Jones, Official Record, 14 December 1999.

43   Delyth Evans, Official Record, 14 February 2002 and Helen Mary Jones, Official Record, 11 March 2003.

44   Kirsty Williams, Official Record, 23 October 2002.

45   Helen Mary Jones, Official Record, 11 March 2003.

46   'Equal opportunity issues cover a range of views. I will mention my experience in the Fire Brigades Union, which is traditionally a male-dominated trade union'; Ann Jones, Official Record, 12 July 2000.

47   See Christine Chapman, Official Record, 9 November 2000.

48   Jenny Randerson, Official Record, Debate to Mark International Women's Day, 8 March 2000.

49   Jane Hutt, Official Record, Debate on Childcare, 6 July 1999.

50   Christine Chapman, Official Record, Debate on Social Exclusion, 29 June 1999.

51   Edwina Hart, Official Record, Debate on Economic Development, 17 July 2001.

52   Christine Chapman, Official Record, Debate on School Governing Bodies, 9 November 2000.

53   Val Feld, Official Record, Debate on Social Exclusion, 29 June 1999.

54   Jane Hutt, Official Record, 21 November 2000.

55 Val Feld, Official Record, 30 September 1999.
56 Helen Mary Jones, Official Record, 30 September 1999.
57 Alun Cairns, Official Record, 13 October 1999.
58 Val Feld, Official Record, 5 December 2000.
59 156 debates out of a total 327, or 47.7 per cent.
60 174 debates out of a total 327, or 53.2 per cent.

7. A Participatory Democracy? Women's Engagement in Post-devolution Politics

1   National Assembly Advisory Group, *Recommendations* (1998), p. 7.
2   Assembly-sponsored public body (ASPB) that aims to support women's enterprise and increase women's participation in the labour market.
3   WWNC unpublished minutes and Annual Report 2001.
4   Source: WWNC Funding Application to the Assembly Government's 'Promoting equality in Wales project development fund', April 2001.
5   WWNC Memorandum of Association (2001), p. 1, section 3, 'Objects and Powers'.
6   Source: *http://www.mewn-cymru.org.uk,* accessed April 2005.
7   MEWN Link, 'MEWN Cymru – Culture Capital & BME' (May 2003), p. 10.
8   Source: *http://www.welshwomensaid.org.*
9   Source: *http://www.welshwomensaid.org.*
10 Source: *http://www.merchedywawr.com,* 'Mae Merched y Wawr yn ymgyrchu dros hawliau'r iaith Gymraeg a hawliau merched', accessed April 2005.
11 Source: *http://www.WCVA.org.uk.*
12 MEWN Cymru, Annual Report (2003), p. 6.
13 MEWN Cymru Newsletter (July 2003), p. 6.
14 MEWN Cymru Newsletter (May 2003), p. 3.
15 MEWN Cymru Newsletter (September 2002), p. 4.
16 MEWN Cymru Newsletter (September 2002), p. 5.
17 Papers of VSPC Meeting, 18 October 2002.
18 Papers of VSPC Meeting, 18 October 2002.
19 Papers of VSPC Meeting, 27 May 2004.
20 Papers of VSPC Meeting, 14 February 2003.
21 Papers of VSPC Meeting, 10 May 2001.
22 National Federation of Women's Institutes Wales response to Assembly government consultation on the initiative, 'A Sustainable Wales – Learning to Live Differently', dated 20 April 2000.
23 Xy-Zero Project, Welsh Women's Aid, see *http://www.accac.org.uk.*
24 Welsh Assembly Government press release, 'Minister launches national strategy for tackling domestic abuse', 30 March 2005.
25 NAW Equality Committee, Report on Welsh Assembly Government Work to Promote Equality 2003–2004 (Cardiff, 2005).
26 Welsh Assembly Government, Sex and Relationships Education in Schools, National Assembly for Wales Circular No. 11/02 (Cardiff, 2002).
27 Welsh Assembly Government Response to the Recommendations of 'Counted Out – The Findings from the 2002–2003 Stonewall Cymru Survey of Lesbian, Gay And Bisexual People in Wales', Papers of the National Assembly Equality of Opportunity Committee, 1 April 2004.

28 Source: *http://www.mewn-cymru.org.uk*, accessed April 2005.
29 Survey of 800 members of the affiliate organizations of WWNC.
30 Interview with Professor Teresa Rees, 2004.

8. Gender Equality and Policy-making

1 'The Approach to Equal Opportunities: A Paper by the Chair of the Committee on Equality of Opportunity' [Jane Hutt], July 1999.
2 Cf. Standing Order 14.
3 Welsh Labour – and later Labour and Welsh Liberal Democrat coalition. 'The *executive*, will also need: to take equality of opportunity factors into account in every policy decision' ... 'Subject committees will also wish to contribute to debate and discussion of equal opportunities examine the extent to which *the executive* is taking equal opportunities into account.'
4 Government of Wales Act (1998) s.48 and s.120.
5 Standing Order 14.1.
6 See National Assembly Standing Orders 5.2 (2002): 'Motions under paragraph 5.1 shall be tabled having regard to any advice offered by the Business Committee under paragraph 13.1(i). Wherever possible, motions shall be framed having regard to the family and constituency or electoral region responsibilities of Members, and their likely travel arrangements; and in any event shall seek to avoid programming business before 9 a.m. or after 5.30 p.m. on any working day.'
7 Office of the Presiding Officer of the National Assembly for Wales (1999), Protocol on Conduct in the Chamber/Presiding Officer's Protocol on Conduct in Chamber/Rules of Debate, Key Principles.
8 Standing Order 14.2.
9 Standing Order 14.2.
10 Interview with Felicity Williams, General Secretary, Wales TUC.
11 The Council of Europe Informal Group of experts on gender budgeting has defined gender budgeting as: 'an application of gender mainstreaming in the budgetary process. It means a gender-based assessment of budgets, incorporating a gender perspective at all levels of the budgetary process and restructuring revenues and expenditures in order to promote gender equality' (Council of Europe Informal Group of experts on gender budgeting, 2002).
12 E.g. the 'Mainstreaming Equality in Public Appointments' action plan, which was drafted in 2002 under the supervision of Professor Teresa Rees.
13 Her Majesty's Inspectorate of Education and Training in Wales.
14 Jane Davidson AM, Minister for Education and Lifelong Learning, 'The Remit for the Chief Inspector of Education and Training in Wales for the Financial Year 2002–3', unpaginated.
15 Official Record, 17 July 2001.
16 See *http://www.wales-legislation.hmso.gov.uk/legislation/wales/wales_legislation.htm*.
17 Martin Shipton, 'AMs to investigate if Hart broke the rules', *Western Mail*, 22 January 2004.
18 Adapted from P. Chaney and F. Mackay, 2003.

9. In their own Words: The Views of Women Candidates and Assembly Members

[1] Val Feld AM.
[2] Selected use is also made of published accounts. Italics are used in quotations from research interviews in order to reflect the original inflection of the speakers as captured on audio recordings and evident during the transcription process.
[3] Former Welsh Labour Assembly Member the late Peter Law stood as an independent candidate (partially in protest at the WLP's imposition of an all-women shortlist of candidates) in this UK parliamentary constituency and secured a resounding victory, with a majority of 9,121 votes.
[4] Quoted in N. Speed, 'Women could top the lists', *Western Mail*, 11 May 2002.
[5] Quoted in C. Betts, 'Plaid urged to vote for women first', *Western Mail*, 9 March 2002.
[6] Former MP for Blaenau Gwent and firm opponent of twinning who was at the forefront of threatened legal challenges to the Labour Party on its use of positive action.
[7] See discussion on 'add-on' and 'built-in' in chapter 4.
[8] Welsh. Translation 'new dawn'.
[9] Selected quotations here are taken from Betts, Borland and Chaney, 2001.
[10] When First Secretary Alun Michael resigned in February 2000, he was replaced by the next Labour candidate on the regional list, Delyth Evans, raising the number of women AMs to twenty-five (42 per cent).
[11] Speech to Chwarae Teg Annual Conference 2000.
[12] Welsh Labour and the Welsh Liberal Democrats were in a coalition government for the majority of the Assembly's first term, 1999–2003.
[13] Val Feld, Official Record, 8 March 2000.
[14] Val Feld, speech to Chwarae Teg Annual Conference 2000.
[15] Jenny Randerson, Official Record, 8 March 2000.
[16] Jenny Randerson, Approval of Revised Protocol on Conduct in the Chamber, Official Record, 12 April 2000.
[17] Val Feld, Official Record, 8 March 2000.
[18] Helen Mary Jones, Official Record, 1 May 2000.
[19] Essentialism suggests that there are any shared characteristics common to all women that underpin distinct types of political and social activities and viewpoints. A. Stone (2004) summarizes four different senses of 'essentialism',

> all regularly criticised within feminist discussion: (1) metaphysical essentialism, the belief in real essences (of the sexes) which exist independently of social construction; (2) biological essentialism, the belief in real essences which are biological in character; (3) linguistic essentialism, the belief that the term 'woman' has a fixed and invariant meaning; and (4) methodological essentialism, which encompasses approaches to studying women's (or men's) lives which presuppose the applicability of gender as a general category of social analysis.

Bibliography

Aaron, J. (1994). 'Finding a voice in two tongues: gender and colonization', in J. Aaron, T. Rees, S. Betts and M. Vincentelli, M. (eds), *Our Sisters' Land: The Changing Identities of Women in Wales*, Cardiff, University of Wales Press, ch. 10.

—— (2001). 'A review of the contribution of women to Welsh life', *Transactions of the Honourable Society of Cymmrodorion*, new series, 8, 188–204.

——, Rees, T., Betts, S. and Vincentelli, M. (eds) (1994). *Our Sisters' Land: The Changing Identities of Women in Wales*, Cardiff, University of Wales Press.

—— and Williams, C. (eds) (2005). *Postcolonial Wales*, Cardiff, University of Wales Press.

Adamson, D. and Johnston, E. (2003). 'Communities First', in J. Osmond and J. B. Jones (eds), *The Birth of Welsh Democracy: The First Term of the National Assembly for Wales*, Cardiff, IWA, ch. 10.

Adler, D. (1989). 'Struggling on', *Planet – The Welsh Internationalist*, 77, 45–50.

Albertyn, C. (2003). 'Towards substantive representation: women and politics in South Africa', in A. Dobrowolsky and V. Hart (eds), *Women Making Constitutions*, Basingstoke, Palgrave, pp. 99–118.

Andrews, L. (1999). *Wales Says Yes: The Inside Story of the Yes for Wales Referendum Campaign*, Bridgend, Seren.

Ashton, S. (1994). 'Farm women and Wales', in J. Aaron, T. Rees, S. Betts, and M. Vincentelli (eds), *Our Sisters' Land: The Changing Identities of Women in Wales*, Cardiff, University of Wales Press, ch. 7, pp. 123–45.

Awdurdod Cymwysterau, Cwricwlwm ac Asesu Cymru (ACCAC) (2000). *A Framework for Work-Related Education for 14- to 19-Year-Olds in Wales*, Ref. AC/GM/0027, Cardiff, ACCAC.

—— (2001a). *A Framework for Careers Education and Guidance For 11- to 19-Year-Olds in Wales*, Ref. AC/GM/0225, Cardiff, ACCAC.

—— (2001b). *Equal Opportunities in the School Curriculum in Wales, Consultation Draft May 2001*, Cardiff, ACCAC, *http://www.accac.org.uk*.

—— (2001c). *Equal opportunities and diversity in the school curriculum in Wales*, Cardiff, ACCAC.

—— (2002). *Careers Education and Guidance – Supplementary Guidance*, Ref. AC/GM/0288, Cardiff, ACCAC.

—— (2003). *Links between PSE, CEG and WRE in Secondary Education Guidance for Curriculum Managers*, Ref. AC/GM/0326, Cardiff, ACCAC.

Balsom, D. (ed.) (2000). *Wales Yearbook*, Cardiff, HTV.

—— (ed.) (2005). *Wales Yearbook*, Cardiff, HTV.

Banaszak, L. A., Beckwith, K. and Rucht, D. (eds) (2003). *Women's Movements Facing the Reconfigured State*, Cambridge, Cambridge University Press.

Barnes, M., Stoker, G. and Whiteley, P. (2003). 'Delivering civic renewal: some lessons from research', *Economic and Social Research Council Seminar Papers; Mapping the Public Policy Domain*, Swindon, ESRC.

Bashevkin, S. (1998). *Women on the Defensive: Living Through Conservative Times*, Chicago, University of Chicago Press.

Baumgardt, A. (2005). 'A critical evaluation of the application of gender budgeting by a government agency: the case of the Sports Council for Wales, unpublished M.Sc. dissertation, Cardiff University.

Beckwith, K. (2000). 'Beyond compare? Women's movements in comparative perspective', *European Journal of Political Research*, 37, 431–68.

—— (2002). 'The substantive representation of women: newness, numbers and models of representation', paper presented at the annual meeting of the American Political Science Association, Boston, 29 August–1 September.

—— (2003). 'The gendering ways of states: women's representation and state reconfiguration in France, Great Britain and the United States', in L. A. Banaszak et al. (eds), *Women's Movements Facing the Reconfigured State*, Cambridge, Cambridge University Press, pp. 169–202.

Beddoe, D. (1986). 'Images of Welsh women', in T. Curtis (ed.), *Wales the Imagined Nation*, Bridgend, The Poetry Press, pp. 227–38.

—— (2000). *Out of the Shadows: A History of Women in Twentieth Century Wales*, Cardiff, University of Wales Press.

—— (2004). 'Women and politics in twentieth-century Wales', Welsh Political Archive annual lecture, 5 November 2004, National Library of Wales, Aberystwyth.

Betts, S. (1994). 'The changing family in Wales', in J. Aaron, T. Rees, S. Betts and M. Vincentelli (eds), *Our Sisters' Land: The Changing Identities of Women in Wales*, Cardiff, University of Wales Press, pp. 62–82.

——, Borland, J. and Chaney, P. (2001). 'Inclusive government for excluded groups: women and disabled people', in P. Chaney, T. Hall and A. Pithouse (eds), *New Governance – New Democracy?* Cardiff, University of Wales Press, ch. 3, pp. 48–78.

—— and Chaney, P. (2004). 'Inclusive and participatory governance? The view from the grass roots of women's organisations in Wales', *Wales Journal of Law and Policy / Cylchgrawn Cyfraith a Pholisi Cymru*, 3, 173–88.

Beveridge, F., Nott, S., and Stephen, K. (2000a). 'Mainstreaming and the engendering of policy-making: a means to an end?' *Journal of European Public Policy*, 7, 3, 385–405.

—— —— (eds) (2000b). *Making Women Count*, London, Ashgate.

Blackaby, D. (1999). *Women in Senior Management in Wales / Menywod mewn Swyddi Uwch Reoli yng Nghymru*, Manchester, Equal Opportunities Commission.

——, Moore, N., Murphy, P. and O'Leary, N. (2001). *The Gender Pay Gap in Wales*, Cardiff, Equal Opportunities Commission Wales.

Blair, T. (1996). *Speech by the Rt. Hon. Tony Blair MP, Leader of the Labour Party to the Wales Labour Party Conference*, Brangwyn Hall, Swansea, 10 May 1996.

—— (1998). *The Third Way: New Politics for the New Century*, Fabian Pamphlet 588, London, Fabian Society.

Bochel, C. and Briggs, J. (2000). 'Do women make a difference?' in *Politics*, 20, 2, 63–8.

Bogdanor, V. (1999). *Devolution in the United Kingdom*, Oxford, Oxford University Press.

Bradbury, J., Bennie, L., Denver, D. and Mitchell, J. (2000). 'Devolution, parties and the new politics: candidate selection for the 1999 National Assembly Elections', *Contemporary Wales*, 13, 159–81.

Breitenbach, E. (1989). 'The impact of Thatcherism on women in Scotland', in A. Brown and D. McCrone (eds), *The Scottish Government Yearbook 1989*, Edinburgh, Unit for the Study of Government in Scotland, University of Edinburgh.

—— (1990). 'Sisters are doing it for themselves': the women's movement in Scotland', in A. Brown and R. Parry (eds), *The Scottish Government Yearbook 1990*, Edinburgh, Unit for the Study of Government in Scotland, University of Edinburgh, pp. 66–75.

—— (1996). 'The women's movement in Scotland in the 1990s', University of Edinburgh New Waverley Papers; repr. in E. Breitenbach and F. Mackay (eds), *Women and Contemporary Scottish Politics: An Anthology*, Edinburgh, Polygon at Edinburgh, pp. 77–89.

—— (2006). 'Development in gender-equality policies in Scotland since devolution', *Scottish Affairs*, 56, 10–22.

——, Brown, A., Mackay, F. and Webb, J. (1999). *Equal Opportunities in Local Government in Scotland and Wales*, Edinburgh, Unit for the Study of Government in Scotland, University of Edinburgh.

——, —— and Myers. F. (1998). 'Understanding women in Scotland', *Feminist Review*, 58, 92–121.

——, Brown, A., Mackay, F. and Webb, J. (2002). *The Changing Politics of Gender Equality in Britain*, Basingstoke, Palgrave.

—— and Mackay, F. (eds) (2001). *Women and Contemporary Scottish Politics: An Anthology*, Edinburgh, Polygon at Edinburgh.

Brennan, K. (no date). 'Twinning a better balance', *Welsh Democracy Review*, 3, 5–6.

Briskin, L. (1999). 'Mapping women's organizing in Sweden and Canada: some thematic considerations', in L. Briskin and M. Eliasson (eds), *Women's Organizing and Public Policy in Canada and Sweden*, Montreal and London, McGill–Queen's University Press, pp. 245–72.

Britton, H. (2002). 'Coalition building, election rules and party politics', *Africa Today*, 49, 4, 33–67.

Broadnax, W. D. (2000). *Diversity and Affirmative Action in Public Services*, Boulder, CO, Westview Press.

Brown, A. (1991). 'Thatcher's legacy for women in Scotland', in *Radical Scotland*, April–May, 32–5.

—— (1996). 'Women and politics in Scotland', *Parliamentary Affairs*, 49, 1; repr. in E. Breitenbach and F. Mackay (eds) (2001), *Women and Contemporary Scottish Politics: An Anthology*, Edinburgh, Polygon at Edinburgh, pp. 197–212.

—— (1996). 'Women and Scottish Politics', in J. Lovenduski and P. Norris (eds), *Women and Politics*, Oxford, Oxford University Press.

—— (1998). 'Deepening democracy: women and the Scottish Parliament', *Regional and Federal Studies*, 8, 1, 103–19; repr. in E. Breitenbach and F. Mackay (eds) (2001), *Women and Contemporary Scottish Politics: An Anthology*, Edinburgh, Polygon at Edinburgh, pp. 213–30.

—— (1999). 'Taking their place in the new House: women and the Scottish Parliament', *Scottish Affairs*, 28, 44–50; repr. in E. Breitenbach and F. Mackay (eds) (2001), *Women and Contemporary Scottish Politics: An Anthology*, Edinburgh, Polygon at Edinburgh, pp. 241–7.

——, McCrone, D. and Paterson, L. (1998). *Politics and Society in Scotland* (2nd edn), Basingstoke, Macmillan.

——, Donaghy, T. B., Mackay, F. and Meehan, E. (2002). 'Women and constitutional change in Scotland and Northern Ireland', *Parliamentary Affairs*, 55, 1, 71–84.

Bryant, P. (1998). *The Inclusive Assembly*, Caerphilly, WCVA.

Burrows, N. (2000). *Devolution*, London, Sweet and Maxwell.

Campaign for a Welsh Assembly (CWA) (1988). *Strategy Paper One*, spring, Cardiff, CWA.

Campbell, R. (2004). 'Gender, ideology and issue preference: is there such a thing as a political women's interest in Britain?', *British Journal of Politics and International Relations*, 6, 20–46.

—— and Lovenduski, J. (2005). 'Winning women's votes? The incremental track to equality', *Parliamentary Affairs*, 58, 4, 837–53.

Careers Wales (2002). *A guide for Parents and Guardians: Choices 14+*, Cardiff, Careers Wales.

Carroll, S. J. (ed.) (2003). *Women and American Politics: New Questions, New Directions*, Oxford and New York, Oxford University Press.

Caul, M. (1999). 'Women's representation in parliament: the role of political parties', *Party Politics*, 5, 1, 79–98.

Caul, M. (2001). 'Political parties and the adoption of candidate quotas: a cross-national analysis', *Journal of Politics*, 63, 4, 1214–29.

Chaney, P. (2002). 'Social capital and the participation of marginalized groups in government: a study of the statutory partnership between the third sector and devolved government in Wales', *Public Policy and Administration*, 17, 4, 22–39.

—— (2003a). 'Increased rights and representation: women and the post-devolution equality agenda in Wales', in A. Dobrowolsky and V. Hart (eds), *Women Making Constitutions: New Politics and Comparative Perspectives*, Basingstoke, Palgrave, pp. 173–85.

—— (2003b). *Action Against Discrimination in Pay Systems: A Preliminary Evaluation of the Welsh Assembly Government's Close The Pay Gap Campaign in Wales*, Cardiff, Welsh Assembly Government, the Equal Opportunities Commission Wales, and the Wales TUC.

—— (2004a). 'The post-devolution equality agenda: the case of the Welsh Assembly's statutory duty to promote equality of opportunity', *Policy and Politics*, 32, 1, 37–52.

—— (2004b). 'Women and constitutional change in Wales', *Regional and Federal Studies*, 14, 2, 1–23.

—— (2005). 'Women's political participation in the Welsh Assembly', in J. Aaron and C. Williams (eds), *Postcolonial Wales*, Cardiff, University of Wales Press, pp. 114–33.

—— (2006a). 'Women and constitutional reform: gender parity in the National Assembly for Wales', in M. Sawer, M. Tremblay and L. Trimble (eds), *Representing Women in Parliament: A Comparative Study*, New York and London, Routledge, pp. 188–203.

—— (2006b). 'Public policy', in R. Wyn Jones and R. Scully (eds), *Wales Devolution Monitoring Report: January 2006*, London, University College London, Constitution Unit.

—— (2006c). 'Critical mass, deliberation and the substantive representation of women: evidence from the UK's devolution programme', *Political Studies*, 54, 4, 671–9.

—— (2006d – forthcoming). *Equality and Public Policy: Wales in Comparative Perspective*, Cardiff, University of Wales Press.

—— (2006e – forthcoming). 'A case of institutional decoupling: equality and public policy in post-devolution Wales', *Scottish Affairs*, 56, 22–34.

—— and Fevre, R. (2001a). 'Inclusive governance and "minority" groups: the role of the third sector in Wales', *Voluntas – International Journal of Third Sector Research*, 12, 2, 131–56.

—— —— (2001b). 'Ron Davies and the cult of inclusiveness: devolution and participation in Wales', *Contemporary Wales*, 14, 131–46.

—— —— (2001c). 'Welsh nationalism and the challenge of "inclusive" politics', *Research in Social Movements, Conflict and Change*, 23, 227–54.

—— —— (2002a). *The Equality Policies of the Government of the National Assembly for Wales and their Implementation: July 1999 to January 2002. A Report for: The Equal Opportunities Commission, Disability Rights Commission, Commission for Racial Equality, and Institute of Welsh Affairs*, Cardiff, IWA.

—— —— (2002b). 'Is there a demand for descriptive representation? Evidence from the UK's devolution programme', *Political Studies*, 50, 897–915.

——, Hall, T. and Dicks, B. (2001a). 'Inclusive governance? The case of "Minority" and voluntary sector groups and the National Assembly for Wales', *Contemporary Wales*, 13, 182–202.

——, Fevre, R. and Stephens, N. (2003). 'Setting the agenda? Women and policy-making in post-devolution Wales', paper presented at the seminar Engendering Democracy, Women's Organisations and their Influence on Policy Making, 5 December 2003, Queen's University Belfast.

—— and Mackay, F. (2003). 'Mainstreaming equality – a comparative analysis of contemporary developments in Scotland and Wales', paper presented to the Women and Equality Unit Gender Research Forum, Cabinet Office.

—— and Rees, T. (2004). 'The Northern Ireland Section 75 Equality Duty: an international perspective', in *2004 Review of the Section 75 Equality Duty*, Belfast, Northern Ireland Office.

——, Hall, T. and Pithouse, A. (eds) (2001b). *New Governance – New Democracy? Post Devolution Wales*, Cardiff, University of Wales Press.

——, Scourfield, J. and Thompson, A. (eds) (2004). *Contemporary Wales: Review of the Assembly's First Term*, Cardiff, University of Wales Press/Board of Celtic Studies.

Charles, N. (1994). 'The women's refuge movement and domestic violence', in J. Aaron, T. Rees, S. Betts and M. Vincentelli (eds), *Our Sisters' Land: The Changing Identities of Women in Wales*, Cardiff, University of Wales Press, pp. 34–54.

—— (2004). 'Feminist politics and devolution', *Social Politics*, 11, 2, 297–311.

—— and Davies, C. A. (2000). 'Cultural stereotypes and the gendering of senior management', *Sociological Review*, 48, 4, 544–67.

Childs, S. (2001). 'In their own words: New Labour women and the substantive representation of women', *British Journal of Politics and International Relations*, 3, 2, 173–90.

—— (2002). 'Hitting the target: are labour women MPs "acting for" women?', *Parliamentary Affairs*, 55, 1, 143–53.

—— (2003). 'The Sex Discrimination (Election Candidates) Act 2002 and its implications', *Representation*, 39, 2, 83–93.

—— (2004a). *Women Representing Women: New Labour's Women MPs*, London, Frank Cass.

—— (2004b). 'A feminized style of politics? Women MPs in the House of Commons', *British Journal of Politics and International Relations*, 6, 1, 3–20.

—— and Withey, J. (2004). 'Women representatives acting for women: sex and the signing of Early Day Motions in the 1997 British Parliament', *Political Studies*, 52, 552–64.

—— and Krook, M. L. (2005). 'The substantive representation of women: rethinking the critical mass debate', paper presented to the annual meeting of the American Political Science Association 2005, Washington, DC.

——, Lovenduski, J. and Campbell, R. (2005). *Women at the Top 2005: Changing Numbers, Changing Politics?* London, Hansard Society.

Clements, L. and Thomas, P. (1999). 'Human rights and the Welsh Assembly', *Planet – The Welsh Internationalist*, 136, 7–11.

Cockburn, C. (1989). 'Equal opportunities: the short and long agenda', *Industrial Relations Journal*, 37, 89–114.

—— (1996). 'Strategies for gender democracy: strengthening the representation of trade union women in the European social dialogue', *European Journal of Women's Studies*, 3, 1, 67–82.

Connell, R. W. (1987). *Gender and Power*, Cambridge, Polity Press.

Cosgrove, K. (2001). 'No man has the right', in E. Breitenbach and F. Mackay (eds), *Women and Contemporary Scottish Politics: An Anthology*, Edinburgh, Polygon at Edinburgh, pp. 131–46.

Cowley, P. and Childs, S. (2003).'Too spineless to rebel? New Labour's women MPs', *British Journal of Political Science*, 33, 345–65.

Cowell-Meyers, K. (2001). 'Gender, power, and peace: a preliminary look at women in the Northern Ireland Assembly', *Women and Politics*, 23, 3, 57–90.

—— (2003). *Women Legislators in Northern Ireland: Gender and Politics in the New Legislative Assembly*, Centre for the Advancement of Women in Politics, Occasional Paper 3, Belfast, School of Politics, Queen's University Belfast.

Crwydren, R. (1994). 'Welsh lesbian feminist: a contradiction in terms?', in J. Aaron, T. Rees, S. Betts and M. Vincentelli (eds), *Our Sisters' Land: The Changing Identities of Women in Wales*, Cardiff, University of Wales Press, pp. 42–51.

Cymdeithas yr Iaith Gymraeg (1998). *Agenda ar gyfer y Cynulliad Cenedlaethol Cymru*, Cardiff, Cymdeithas yr Iaith Gymraeg.

—— (2001). 'A paper from Cymdeithas yr Iaith Gymraeg', papers of the Culture Committee, National Assembly for Wales, 18 July 2001, Cardiff, National Assembly for Wales.

Dahlerup, D. (1988). 'From a small to a large minority: women in Scandinavian politics', *Scandinavian Political Studies*, 11, 275–98.

Davies, C. A. (1994). 'Women, nationalism and feminism', in J. Aaron, T. Rees, S. Betts and M. Vincentelli (eds), *Our Sisters' Land: The Changing Identities of Women in Wales*, Cardiff, University of Wales Press, pp. 67–82.

Davies, J. (1993). *The Welsh Language*, Cardiff, University of Wales Press.

Davies, R. (1998a). 'Taking the Assembly forward – Ron Davies announces the next stage', press release, 21 August 1998, W98451-dev, Cardiff, Welsh Office.

—— (1998b). 'Ron Davies raises profile of ethnic and minority groups in the Assembly', press release, 16 September 1998, W98493-dev, Cardiff, Welsh Office.

—— (1999). *Devolution: A Process not an Event*, Gregynog Papers, 2, 2, Cardiff, Institute of Welsh Affairs.

Day, G. (2000). *Making Sense of Wales: A Sociological Perspective*, Cardiff, University of Wales Press.

——, Dunkerley, D. and Thompson, A. (2000). 'Evaluating the "New Politics": Civil Society and the National Assembly for Wales', *Public Policy and Administration*, 15, 2, 25–37.

Deacon, R. (1996). 'Where are the women politicians?', *Planet – The Welsh Internationalist*, October/November, p. 132, pp. 126–8.

Dobrowolsky, A. (2003). 'Shifting states: women's constitutional organizing across time and space', in L. A. Banaszak et al. (eds), *Women's Movements Facing the Reconfigured State*, Cambridge, Cambridge University Press, pp. 141–68.

—— and Hart, V. (2003a). 'Introduction, new politics and constitutional change', in A. Dobrowolsky and V. Hart (eds), *Women Making Constitutions: New Politics and Comparative Perspectives*, Basingstoke, Palgrave, pp. 2–23.

—— —— (eds) (2003b). *Women Making Constitutions: New Politics and Comparative Perspectives*, Basingstoke, Palgrave.

Dodson, D. (2001). 'The impact of women in Congress. Rethinking ideas about difference,' paper presented at the annual meeting of the American Political Science Association, Washington, DC.

Donaghy, T. B. (2003). 'Mainstreaming: Northern Ireland's participative-democratic approach', Centre for the Advancement of Women in Politics, Occasional Paper 2, Belfast, School of Politics, Queen's University Belfast.

—— (2004). 'Applications of mainstreaming in Australia and Northern Ireland', *International Political Science Review*, 25, 4, 393–410.

Dovi, S. (2002). 'Preferable descriptive representatives: will just any woman, black or Latino do?', *American Political Science Review*, 96, 4, 729–43.

Dubé, J. (1988). 'The legible woman: annual conference of the Welsh Union of Writers', *Radical Wales*, 20, 10–11.

Duerst-Lahti, G. and Kelly, R. M. (eds) (1995). *Gender Power, Leadership and Governance*, Ann Arbor, University of Michigan Press.

Edwards, J. (1995). *Local Government Women's Committees*, Aldershot, Avebury.

—— and Chapman, C. (2000). 'Women's political representation in Wales: waving or drowning?', *Contemporary Politics*, 6, 4, 23–33.

—— and McAllister, L. (2002). 'One step forward, two steps back?: Women in the two main political parties in Wales', *Parliamentary Affairs*, 55, 1, 154–66.

—— —— (2003). 'Recent research: women's political representation in the National Assembly for Wales', *Contemporary Politics*, 9, 4, 45–53.

Edwards, S. (1994). 'Include us in', in J. Osmond (ed.), *A Parliament for Wales*, Llandysul, Gomer Press.

Elfyn, M. (1994). 'Writing is a bird in hand', in J. Aaron, T. Rees, S. Betts and M. Vincentelli (eds), *Our Sisters' Land: The Changing Identities of Women in Wales*, Cardiff, University of Wales Press, pp. 89–97.

Elson, D. (1998). 'Integrating gender issues into national budgeting policies and procedures: some policy options', *Journal of International Development*, 10, 7, 929–41.

Equal Opportunities Commission Wales (2003). *EOC Briefing on Gender and Party Breakdown of Regional and Constituency Candidates Assembly Elections 2003*, Cardiff, EOC Wales.

Equal Opportunities Commission Wales/Wales Women's National Coalition (2004). *Who Runs Wales? Pwy Sy'n Rhedeg Cymru?* Cardiff, EOC Wales.

ESTYN (2002a). *The Annual Report of ESTYN (Her Majesty's Chief Inspector of Education and Training in Wales) 2000–2001*, Cardiff, ESTYN.

—— (2002b). *Framework for the Inspection of Schools*, Cardiff, ESTYN.

—— (2004). *Guidance on the Inspection of Secondary Schools*, Cardiff, ESTYN.

European Commission – The European Convention Secretariat (2003). *Draft Constitution, Volume I*, CONV 724/03, Brussels, EC.

Evans, J., Hudson, C. and Smith, P. (1985). 'Women and the miners; it's a whole way of life', *Radical Wales*, 8, 14–15.

Evans, N. and Jones, D. (2000). 'To help forward the great work of humanity: women and the Labour Party in Wales', in D. Tanner, C. Williams and D. Hopkin (eds), *The Labour Party in Wales 1900–2000*, Cardiff, University of Wales Press.

Fawcett Society (no date). *The Need for Positive Action*, London, Fawcett Society.

Fearon, K. (1999). *Women's Work. The Story of the Northern Ireland's Women's Coalition*, Belfast, Blackstaff Press.

Feld, V. (1992). 'What chance for women?', *Planet – The Welsh Internationalist*, 93, 39–43.

—— (2000). 'A new start in Wales: how devolution is making a difference', in A. Coote (ed.), *New Gender Agenda*, London, IPPR.

Ferree, M. M. and Martin, P. Y. (eds) (1995). *Feminist Organizations: Harvest of Women's Movements*, Philadelphia, Temple University Press.

Fischer, F. (2003). *Reframing Public Policy: Discursive Politics and Discursive Practices*, Oxford, Oxford University Press.

Flynn, P. (1999). *Dragons Led by Poodles*, London, Politicos Publishing.

Frederickson, H. G. (2000). 'Public administration and social equity', in W. D. Broadnax, *Diversity and Affirmative Action in Public Services*, Boulder, CO, Westview Press.

Fredman, S. (2000). 'Equality: a new generation?', *Industrial Law Journal*, 30, 145–168.

Gargarella, R. (1998). 'Full representation, deliberation and impartiality', in J. Elster (ed.), *Deliberative Democracy*, Cambridge, Cambridge University Press, pp. 231–56.

Gill, G. (1999). *Winning for Women*, London, Fawcett Society.

Gregory, R. (1989). 'Political rationality or incrementalism? Charles E. Lindblom's enduring contribution to public policymaking', *Policy and Politics*, 17, 2, 139–53.

Grey, S. (2002). 'Does size matter?', in K. Ross (ed.), *Women, Politics and Change*, Oxford, Oxford University Press.

Hain, P. (1999). *A Welsh Third Way?* Tribune pamphlet, London, Tribune Publications.

Hall, P. A. (1986). *Governing the Economy: The Politics of State Intervention in Britain and France*, Cambridge, Polity Press.

Harris, M., Rochester, C. and Halfpenny, P. (2001). 'Voluntary organisations and social policy: twenty years of change', in M. Harris and C. Rochester (eds), *Voluntary Organisations and Social Policy in Britain*, Basingstoke, Palgrave, pp. 67–75.

Hart, E. (2000). 'The official record', Thursday 5 July 2000, Plenary debate on the annual report on equal opportunity arrangements, Cardiff, NAW.

Hart, V. (2003). 'Redesigning the polity: Europe, women and constitutional politics in the UK', in A. Dobrowolsky and V. Hart (eds), *Women Making Constitutions: New Politics and Comparative Perspectives*, Basingstoke, Palgrave, pp. 118–32.

Harvey, C. (2001). 'Human rights and equality', in R. Wilson (ed.), *Agreeing to Disagree? A Guide to the Northern Ireland Assembly*, London, Stationery Office, pp. 76–81.

Hazell, R. (2003). 'The devolution scorecard as the devolved Assemblies head for the polls', in Hazell, R. (ed.), *The State of the Nations 2003: The Third Year of Devolution in the United Kingdom*, Exeter, Imprint Academic, pp. 167–78.

—— (ed.) (2000). *The State and the Nations*, Exeter, Imprint Academic.

Hinds, B. (2003). 'Mainstreaming equality in Northern Ireland', in A. Dobrowolsky and V. Hart (eds), *Women Making Constitutions: New Politics and Comparative Perspectives*, Basingstoke, Palgrave, pp. 185–200.

Howells, A. (1986). 'Honno: the new Welsh women's press challenges the publishing patriarchy', *Radical Wales*, 11, 10.

ICPR (2004). *Changed Voting, Changed Politics: Lessons of Britain's Experience of PR since*

1997. *Final Report of the Independent Commission to Review Britain's Experience of PR Voting Systems*, London, University College London.

Inglehart, R. and Norris, P. (2000). 'Gender gaps in voting behaviour in global perspective', *International Journal of Political Research*, 12, 67–85.

Inter-Agency Network on Women and Gender Equality (IANWGE) (2005). *Summary of the Online Discussions Held in Preparation for the 10 Year Review and Appraisal of the Implementation of the Platform for Action in the 49th Session of the Commission on the Status of Women*, New York, United Nations.

International Parliamentary Union (IPU) (2005), *www.ipu.org*.

Jahan, R. (1995). *The Elusive Agenda: Mainstreaming Women in Development*, Atlantic Highlands, NJ, Zed Books.

Jenkins, D. and Owen, M. E. (1980). *The Welsh Law of Women*, Cardiff, University of Wales Press.

Jewson, H. and Mason, F. (1986). 'The theory and practice of equal opportunities policies: liberal and radical approaches', *Sociological Review*, 34, 2, 56–84.

John, A. (ed.) (1991). *Our Mothers' Land: Chapters in Welsh Women's History*, Cardiff, University of Wales Press.

Jones, B. (1987). 'Slate quarry strike', in L. Dee and K. Keineg (eds), *Women in Wales: A Documentary of our Recent History*, London, Womenwrite.

Jones, J. B. (2000). 'Post-referendum politics', in B. Jones and D. Balsom (eds), *The Road to the National Assembly for Wales*, Cardiff, University of Wales Press.

Jones, K. and Morris, D. (1997). *Gender and the Welsh Language: Research Review*, Cardiff, EOC Wales.

Jones, R. M. (1999). *Hanes Cymru yn y Ugeinfed Ganrif*, Cardiff, University of Wales Press/ Hughes A'i Fab.

Kanter, R. (1977). *Men and Women of the Corporation*, New York, Basic Books.

Karam, A. (ed.) (1997 and 2002). *Women in Parliament: Beyond Numbers*, at *http://www.idea.int/gender/wip*.

Karam, K. (2000). 'Beijing + 5: women's political participation: review of strategies and trends', in anon. *United Nations Development Programme – Women's Political Participation and Good Governance: 21st Century Challenges*, New York, UNDP, ch. 3.

Karvonen, L. and Selle, P. (eds) (1995). *Women in Nordic Politics*, Aldershot, Dartmouth.

Kathlene, L. (1998). 'In a different voice: women and the policy process', in S. Thomas and C. Wilcox (eds), *Women and Elective Office: Past, Present and Future*, London and New York, Routledge, pp. 77–86.

Katzenstein, M. F. (1990). 'Feminism within American institutions: unobtrusive mobilization in the 1980s', *Signs*, 16, 11, 27–52.

—— (1998). *Faithful and Fearless: Moving Feminist Protest inside the Church and the Military*, Princeton, NJ, Princeton University Press.

Knight, J. and Johnson, J. (1997). 'What sort of political equality does deliberative democracy require?', in J. Bohman and W. Rehg (eds), *Deliberative Democracy: Essays on Reason and Politics*, Cambridge, MA, MIT Press, pp. 67–88.

Kriesi, H. (1995). 'The political opportunity structure of new social movements: its impact on their mobilization', in J. C. Jenkins and B. Klandersmans (eds), *The Politics of Social Protest: Comparative Perspectives on States and Social Movements*, Minneapolis, University of Minnesota Press, pp. 152–64.

Lakeman, E. (1982). *Power to Elect: The Case for Proportional Representation*, London, Heinemann.

Leach, R. (2002). *Political Ideology in Britain*, Basingstoke, Palgrave.

Lindblom, C. E. (1960). 'The science of muddling through', *Public Administration Review*, 19, 79–88.

Lister, R (2002). *Citizenship: Feminist Perspectives*, Basingstoke, Palgrave.

Livingstone, S. (2001). *Unequal Opportunities? The Impact of Devolution on the Equality Agenda Devolution in Practice*, Third Seminar Paper of 'Public policy differences within the UK, a joint IPPR/ESRC Devolution Programme project', Queens University Belfast, 3 December.

Lloyd Jones, M. (1994). 'Between two worlds', in J. Aaron, T. Rees, S. Betts and M. Vincentelli (eds), *Our Sisters' Land: The Changing Identities of Women in Wales*, Cardiff, University of Wales Press, pp. 77–83.

Lovenduski, J. (1997). 'Gender politics: a breakthrough for women?', *Parliamentary Affairs*, 50, 4, 708–19.

—— (1999). 'Sexing political behaviour in Britain', in S. Walby (ed.), *New Agendas for Women*, Basingstoke, Macmillan.

—— (2002). *Women's Political Representation: Research Findings and Priorities*, paper presented to the Gender Research Forum, DTI, London.

—— (2005). *Feminizing Politics*, Cambridge, Polity.

—— and Karam, A. (2002). 'Women in parliament: making a difference', in A. Karam (ed.), *Women in Parliament*, Stockholm, *http://www.idea.int*, ch. 5.

—— and Randall, V. (1993). *Contemporary Feminist Politics: Women and Power in Britain*, Oxford, Oxford University Press.

—— and Norris, P. (2003). 'Women and Westminster: the politics of Presence', *Political Studies*, 51, 1, 84–102.

—— —— (eds) (1993). *Gender and Party Politics*, London, Sage.

McAdam, D., McCarthy, J. and Zald, M. (eds) (1998). *Comparative Perspectives on Social Movements*, Cambridge, Cambridge University Press.

McAllister, L. (1995). 'Community in ideology: the political philosophy of Plaid Cymru', unpublished Ph.D. thesis, University of Wales.

—— (1998). 'The Welsh Devolution referendum: definitely, maybe?', *Parliamentary Affairs*, 51, 2, 149–165.

—— (2000). 'Changing the landscape? The wider political lessons from recent elections in Wales', *The Political Quarterly*, 71, 2, 211–22.

—— (2001a). *Plaid Cymru, The Emergence of a Political Party*, Seren, Bridgend.

—— (2001b). 'Gender, nation and party: an uneasy alliance for Welsh nationalism', *Women's History Review*, 10, 1, 51–69.

—— (2001c). 'The National Assembly elections: Plaid Cymru's coming of age', *Contemporary Wales*, 14, 109–114.

—— and Ridley, F. F. (eds) (2000). 'Designing a new democracy: institutions and politics', special issue, *Parliamentary Affairs*, 53, 3.

McCrudden, C. (1996). 'Mainstreaming fairness? A discussion paper on policy appraisal and fair treatment', Committee on the Administration of Justice, Belfast.

—— (2004). 'Mainstreaming equality in Northern Ireland 1998–2004: a review of issues concerning the operation of the Equality Duty in Section 75 of the Northern Ireland Act 1998', in E. McLaughlin and N. Faris (eds), *The Section 75 Equality Duty – An Operational Review*, Belfast, Northern Ireland Office.

Mackay, F. (2001a). *Love and Politics: Women Politicians and the Ethics of Care*, London, Continuum.

—— (2001b). 'The case of zero tolerance: women's politics in action?', in E. Breitenbach and F. Mackay (eds), *Women and Contemporary Scottish Politics*, Edinburgh, Polygon at Edinburgh, pp. 105–29.

—— (2001c). 'Perspectives on social justice: mainstreaming equal opportunities', *Social Justice Annual Report Scotland 2001*, Edinburgh, Scottish Executive.

—— (2003). 'Women and the 2003 elections: keeping up the momentum', *Scottish Affairs*, 44, 74–90.

—— (2004a). 'Women's representation in Wales and Scotland', *Contemporary Wales*, 17, 140–62.

—— (2004b). 'Gender and political representation in the UK: the state of the "discipline"', *The British Journal of Politics and International Relations*, 6, 1, 99–120.

—— (2004c). 'Women and devolution in Scotland', briefing note prepared for the Scottish Parliament Cross-Party Group on Women and the Equal Opportunities Commission Scotland, March.

—— (2006). 'Descriptive and substantive representation in new parliamentary spaces: the case of Scotland', in M. Sawer, M. Tremblay and L. Trimble (eds), *Representing Women in Parliament: A Comparative Study*, Routledge, New York, London, pp. 156–64.

—— and Bilton, K. (2000). *Learning from experience: Lessons in Mainstreaming Equal Opportunities*, Edinburgh, University of Edinburgh/The Governance of Scotland Forum.

——, Myers, F. and Brown, A. (2003). 'Towards a new politics? Women and the constitutional change in Scotland', in A. Dobrowolsky and V. Hart (eds), *Women Making Constitutions: New Politics and Comparative Perspectives*, Basingstoke and New York, Palgrave, pp. 84–99.

——, Meehan, E., Donaghy, T. B. and Brown, A. (2002). 'Women and constitutional change in Scotland, Wales and Northern Ireland', in *Australasian Parliamentary Review*, 17, 35–54.

Macpherson, W. (1999). *The Macpherson Report: The Stephen Lawrence Inquiry*, London. HMSO, 24 February.

McRobbie, A (2000). 'Feminism and the Third Way', *Feminist Review*, 64, 97–112.

Maguire, G. E. (1998). *A History of Women and the Conservative Party, 1874–1997*, Basingstoke, Macmillan.

Mansbridge, J. (1999). 'Should blacks represent blacks and women represent women? A contingent "Yes"', *Journal of Politics*, 61, 628–57.

Masson, U. and Rolph, A. (1997). *Guide to Sources for the Women's Liberation Movement in South Wales, Database and Booklets*, part 1, 'Events', part 2, 'Media', part 3, 'Newsletters', Pontypridd, University of Glamorgan.

Matland, R. E. (2002). 'Enhancing women's political participation: legislative recruitment and electoral systems', in A. Karam (ed.), *Women in Parliament: Beyond Numbers* (updated chapters) at *http://www.idea.int/gender/wip/eng_updates.htm*.

—— and Studlar, D. (1996). 'The contagion of women candidates in single member district and proportional representation electoral systems: Canada and Norway', *Journal of Politics*, 58, 3, 707–33.

Meyer, J. and Rowan, B. (1991). 'Institutionalized organisations: formal structure as myth and ceremony', in W. Powell and P. DiMaggio (eds), *The New Institutionalism in Organisational Analysis*, Chicago, University of Chicago Press, pp. 231–56.

Morgan, K. and Mungham, G. (2000). *Redesigning Democracy*, Seren, Bridgend.

—— and Rees, G. (2001). 'Learning by doing: devolution and the governance of economic development in Wales', in P. Chaney, T. Hall and A. Pithouse (eds), *New Governance – New Democracy? Post Devolution Wales*, Cardiff, University of Wales Press, pp. 126–72.

Morgan, K. O. (1981). *Rebirth of a Nation: Wales 1880–1980*, Oxford and Cardiff, Open University Press and University of Wales Press.

Morgan, Rh. (2002). 'Clear red water', speech to the National Centre for Public Policy, University of Wales Swansea, 11 December.

Murray, C. (ed.) (1994). *Gender and the New South African Legal Order*, Cape Town, Juta.

National Assembly Advisory Group (NAAG) (1998). *Recommendations: National Assembly Advisory Group for Wales*, Cardiff, NAAG.

National Assembly for Wales (NAW) (1999a). *Standing Orders of the National Assembly for Wales*, Cardiff, NAW.

—— (1999b). *The Approach to Equal Opportunities. [A] Paper by the Chair of the Committee on Equality of Opportunity*, Cardiff, NAW.

—— (2000a). *Voluntary Sector Scheme*, Cardiff, NAW.

—— (2000b). *Better Wales*, Cardiff, NAW.

—— (2000c). *Report on Public Appointments*, papers of the Assembly Equality Committee, 25 October, Cardiff, NAW.

—— (2001a). *Equality Training and Raising Awareness Strategy – ETAARS*, Cardiff, NAW.

—— (2001b). *Second Annual Equality Report*, Cardiff, NAW.

—— (2001c). *The National Assembly for Wales Policy for the Appointment of Chairs and Non-Executive Directors to the Boards of Health Authorities and NHS Trusts*, Cardiff, NAW.

—— (2002a). *The National Assembly for Wales, Code of Practice for Ministerial Appointments to Public Bodies*, Cardiff, NAW.

—— (2002b). *Final Report on the Review of Remuneration and Expenses of Chairs and Members of Assembly-Sponsored Public Bodies and National Health Service Wales Bodies*, Papers of the Assembly Equality Committee, 30 January, Cardiff, NAW.

—— (2003). *Progress and Achievements on Public Appointments*, papers of the Assembly Equality Committee, 30 March, Cardiff, NAW.

—— (2004). *Mainstreaming Review*, Cardiff, NAW.

—— (2005). *Report on Welsh Assembly Government Work to Promote Equality 2003–2004*, Cardiff, NAW.

Norris, P. (1996). 'Women politicians: transforming Westminster?', *Parliamentary Affairs*, 49, 1, 89–102.

—— (2004). *Electoral Engineering: Voting Rules and Political Behaviour*, Cambridge, Cambridge University Press.

—— and Lovenduski, J. (2001). *Blair's Babes: Critical Mass Theory, Gender, and Legislative Life*, Faculty Research Working Papers Series, John F. Kennedy School of Government, Harvard University.

Northern Ireland Human Rights Commission (NIHRC) (2004). *Progressing a Bill of Rights for Northern Ireland: An Update*, Belfast, NIHRC.

Northern Ireland Women's Coalition (NIWC) (1998). *A New Voice for New Times: Women's Coalition Manifesto for Assembly Elections*, Belfast, NIWC.

Nott, S. (1999). 'Mainstreaming equal opportunities: succeeding when all else has failed?', in A. Morris and A. O'Donnell (eds), *Feminist Perspectives on Employment Law*, London, Cavendish, pp. 97–115.

—— (1996). *Rhoi'r Bobl yn Gyntaf: Ethol Cynulliad i Gymru/Putting the People First: Electing a Welsh Assembly*, London: Electoral Reform Society.

—— (1997). *Wales in Europe: The Opportunity Presented by a Welsh Assembly Government/ Cymru yn Ewrop: Y Cyfle a Gynigir gan Gynulliad Cymreig*, Cardiff: Institute of Welsh Affairs/Welsh Centre for International Affairs.

O'Cinneide (2003). 'Taking equal opportunities seriously: the extension of positive duties to promote equality', London, Equality and Diversity Forum.

Osmond, J. (1995). *Welsh Europeans*, Bridgend, Seren.

—— (ed.) (1994). *A Parliament for Wales*, Llandysul, Gomer Press.

Parliament for Wales Campaign (PWC) (1994a). *Parliament for Wales Campaign Democracy Conference Programme 5–6 March 1994*, Cardiff, PWC.

—— (1994b). *Empowering the Vision: Response to the Welsh Labour Party's Consultation Paper 'Shaping the Vision: the Powers and Structures of the Welsh Assembly (Agreed by the National Council of the Parliament for Wales Campaign, Rhayader, 1 October 1994)*, Cardiff, PWC.

Paterson, L. and Wyn Jones, R. (1999). 'Does civil society drive constitutional change? The case of Wales and Scotland', in B. Taylor and K. Thompson (eds), *Scotland and Wales: Nations Again?* Cardiff, University of Wales Press, pp. 64–75.

Pearson, R. (1988). 'Double tokenism: the Equal Opportunities Commission in Wales', *Radical Wales*, 17, 18–19.

Pelizzo, R. (2003). 'Party positions or party direction? An analysis of party manifesto data', *West European Politics*, 26, 2, 67–89.

Pettit, A. (1985). 'From Maenclochog to Moscow', *Planet – The Welsh Internationalist*, June, 27–43.

Phillips, A. (1995). *The Politics of Presence*, Oxford, Clarendon Press.

Plaid Cymru (1999). *Plaid Cymru Manifesto for the National Assembly for Wales*, Cardiff, Plaid Cymru.

—— (2003). *Plaid Cymru Manifesto for the National Assembly for Wales*, Cardiff, Plaid Cymru.

Pollack, M. A. and Hafner-Burton, E. (2000). 'Mainstreaming gender in the European Union', *Journal of European Public Policy*, 7, 3, 432–56.

Porter, N. (2001). 'Baroness attacks Welsh men', *Welsh Mirror*, 29 June.

Putnam, R. (1976). *The Comparative Study of Political Elites*, Englewood Cliffs, Prentice Hall.

Rawlings, R. (1998). 'The new model Wales', *Journal of Law and Society*, 25, 4, 461–509.

—— (2003). *Delineating Wales: Constitutional, Legal and Administrative Aspects of National Devolution*, Cardiff, University of Wales Press.

Rees, G. (1985). 'A new politics?', in *Planet – The Welsh Internationalist*, October/ November.

—— (2004). 'Democratic devolution and education policy in Wales: the emergence of a national system', *Contemporary Wales*, 17, 28–43.

Rees, T. (1994). 'Women and paid work in Wales', in J. Aaron, T. Rees, S. Betts and M. Vincentelli (eds), *Our Sisters' Land: The Changing Identities of Women in Wales*, Cardiff, University of Wales Press.

—— (1999a). *Women and Work: 25 Years of Gender Equality in Wales*, Cardiff, University of Wales Press/Board of Celtic Studies.

—— (1999b). 'Women in Wales', in D. Dunkerley and A. Thompson (eds), *Wales Today*, Cardiff, University of Wales Press.

—— (1999c). 'Mainstreaming equality', in S. Watson and L. Doyal (eds), *Engendering Social Policy*, Buckingham, Open University Press, pp. 56–67.

—— (2002a). 'The politics of mainstreaming gender equality', in E. Breitenbach, A. Brown, F. Mackay and J. Webb (eds), *The Changing Politics of Gender Equality in Britain*, Basingstoke, Palgrave, pp. 94–9.

—— (2002b). *What is Gender Mainstreaming?*, a paper presented to the Equal Opportunities Commission Conference on Gender Mainstreaming, Hilton Hotel, Cardiff, 7 February.

Reeves, R. (1988). 'A Welsh patchwork', in A. Sebestyen (ed.), *'68, '78, '88: From Women's Liberation to Feminism*, Bridport, Prism Press.

Reingold, B. (2000). *Representing Women: Sex, Gender, and Legislative Behavior in Arizona and California*, Chapel Hill, University of North Carolina Press.

Renc-Roe, J. (2003). *The Representation of Women in the Political Decision-Making Process in Poland: Existing Problems and Advocated Solutions*, paper prepared for the ECPR Joint Session: Changing Constitutions, Building Institutions and (Re)defining Gender Relations, University of Edinburgh, 28 March–2 April.

Rhodes, R. A. W. (1997). *Understanding Governance*, Buckingham, Open University Press.

Richard Commission (2004). *Report of the Richard Commission on the Powers and Electoral Arrangements of the National Assembly for Wales*, Cardiff, Richard Commission.

Richardson, N. (2003). 'A new politics', in J. Osmond and J. B. Jones (eds), *Birth of Welsh Democracy, The First Term of the National Assembly for Wales*, Cardiff, IWA.

Rolph, A. (2003). 'A movement of its own: the women's liberation movement in south Wales', in G. H. Koloski, A. Neilson and E. Robertson (eds), *The Feminist Seventies*, University of York, Raw Nerve Books, pp. 127–38.

Roulston, C. (1999). 'Inclusive others: the Northern Ireland Women's Coalition in the peace process', *Scottish Affairs*, 26, 1–13.

Rowlands, T. (2004). 'Whitehall's last stand: the establishment of the Welsh Office, 1964', *Contemporary Wales*, 16, 1, 39–52.

Royles, E. (2004). 'The National Assembly for Wales: democratising the policy process?', *Contemporary Wales*, 16, 101–21.

—— (2007a). *The Impact of Devolution on Civil Society in Post-devolution Wales*, Cardiff, University of Wales Press.

—— (2007b). 'Devolution to Wales – democratising economic governance? Civil society and the structural funds in Wales', *Regional and Federal Studies*.

Rubenson, D. (2000). *Participation and Politics: Social Capital, Civic Voluntarism, and Institutional Context*, paper presented to the ECPR joint sessions of workshops, University of Copenhagen, 14–19 April 2000.

Rubery, J., Figueiredo, H., Smith, M., Grimshaw, D. and Fagan, C. (2004). 'The ups and downs of European gender equality policy', *Industrial Relations Journal*, 35, 6, 603–28.

Rule, W. and Zimmerman, M. (eds) (1994). *Electoral Systems in Comparative Perspective: Their Impact on Women and Minorities*, Westport, CT, Greenwood Press.

Russell, M. (2000). *Women's Representation in UK Politics: What Can Be Done Within the Law?* London, Constitution Unit, UCL.

—— (2003). 'Women in elected office in the UK 1992–2002: struggles, achievements and possible sea-change', in A. Dobrowolsky and V. Hart (eds), *Women Making Constitutions*, Basingstoke, Palgrave, pp. 68–83.

——, Mackay, F. and McAllister, L. (2002), 'Women's representation in the Scottish Parliament and National Assembly for Wales: party dynamics for achieving critical mass', *Journal of Legislative Studies*, 8, 2, 49–76.

Ryan, M. (1990). 'Women in the new Europe/women and self-government', in *Plaid Cymru Summer School 1990: Self-Government in the Nineties*, Cardiff, Plaid Cymru, pp. 13–14.

Sawer, M. (2000). 'Parliamentary representation of women: from discourses of justice to strategies of accountability', *International Political Science Review*, 75, 56–71.

—— (2002). 'The representation of women in Australia: meaning and make believe', *Parliamentary Affairs*, 55, 1, 5–18.

Scottish Constitutional Convention (SCC) (1992). *Recommendations: Shaping the Scottish Parliament*, Edinburgh, SEC.

—— (1995). *Scotland's Parliament, Scotland's Right*, Edinburgh, Cosla.

Scottish Labour Party (SLP) (2003). *A Scotland We can All be Proud to Call Home*, 2003 Scottish Parliament election manifesto, Edinburgh, SLP.

Scottish Liberal Democratic Party (SLDP) (1999). *Scottish Parliament Manifesto 1999: Raising the Standard for Our Schools, Our Hospitals, Our Jobs – For Scotland's Future*, Edinburgh, SLDP.

Scottish National Party (SNP) (1999). *Enterprise, Compassion, Democracy: The SNP Manifesto for the 1999 Scottish Parliament Elections*, Edinburgh, SNP.

Simon, H. A. (1947). *Administrative Behaviour*, London, Macmillan.

—— (1957). *Models of Man*, London, John Wiley.

Sinn Féin (1999). *Sinn Féin 6 County Assembly Election Manifesto 1999: For Real Change – Building a New Ireland*, Belfast, Sinn Féin.

Skard, T. and Haavio-Mannila, E. (eds) (1986). *Unfinished Democracy: Women in Nordic Politics*, Oxford, Pergamon.

Skeije, H. (1991). 'The rhetoric of difference', *Politics and Society*, 19, 2, 25–45.

Snow, D. and Benford, R. D. (1992). 'Master frames and cycles of protest', in A. Morris and C. McClurg (eds), *Frontiers in Social Movement Theory*, New Haven, CT, Yale University Press, pp. 133–55.

Stonewall Cymru (2004). *Annual Review 2003–04*, Cardiff, Stonewall Cymru.

Studlar, D. T. and McAllister, I. (2002). 'Does critical mass exist? A comparative analysis of women's legislative representation since 1950', *European Journal of Political Research*, 41, 233–53.

Sudbury, J. (1998). *'Other Kinds of Dreams': Black Women's Organisations and the Politics of Transformation*, London, Routledge.

Swers, M. L. (2002). *The Difference Women Make*, Chicago, University of Chicago Press.

Tarrow, S. (1994). *Power in Movement: Social Movements, Collective Action and Politics*, Cambridge, Cambridge University Press.

Taylor, M. (2001). 'Partnership: insiders and outsiders', in M. Harris and C. Rochester (eds), *Voluntary Organisations and Social Policy*, Basingstoke, Palgrave.

—— and Bassi, A. (1998). 'Unpacking the state: the implications for the third sector of changing relationships between national and local government', *Voluntas – International Journal of Third Sector Research*, 9, 113–36.

Taylor-Robinson, M. M. and Heath, R. M. (2003). 'Do women legislators have different policy priorities than their male colleagues? A critical case test', *Women and Politics*, 24, 4, 77–101.

Thomas, S. (1994). *How Women Legislate*, Oxford, Oxford University Press.

—— (1996). *How Women Legislate*, New York, Oxford University Press.

—— and Wilcox, C. (eds) (1998). *Women and Elective Office: Past, Present and Future*, Oxford, Oxford University Press.

Thomson, K. (2003). *Wales Life and Times Studies, 2001 and 2003: Technical Report*, London, National Centre for Social Research.

Tomos, A. (1994). 'A Welsh lady', in J. Aaron, T. Rees, S. Betts and M. Vincentelli (eds), *Our Sisters' Land: The Changing Identities of Women in Wales*, Cardiff: University of Wales Press, pp. 78–89.

—— (2001). *Cnonyn Aflonydd*, Caernarfon, Gwasg Gwalch.

Tremblay, M. and Andrew, C. (eds) (1998). *Women and Political Representation in Canada*, Ottawa, University of Ottawa Press.

—— and Trimble, L. (eds) (2003). *Women and Electoral Politics in Canada*, Toronto and Oxford, Oxford University Press.

Trimble, L. and Arscott, J. (2003). *Still Counting: Women in Politics Across Canada*, Peterborough, Ontario, Broadview Press.

True, J. (2003). 'Mainstreaming gender in global public policy', *International Feminist Journal of Politics*, 5, 3, 368–96.

United Nations (1995). *Beijing Declaration and Platform for Action, Fourth World Conference on Women, 15 September 1995*, A/CONF.177/20 (1995) and A/CONF.177/20/Add.1 (1995), NY, UN.

—— (1999). *Commission on the Status of Women, Forty-second Session, Synthesized Report on National Action Plans and Strategies for Implementation of the Beijing Platform for Action, Report of the Secretary-General*, NY, UN.

—— (1999). *Commission on the Status of Women, Follow-up to the Fourth World Conference on Women: Review of Mainstreaming in Organizations of the United Nations System Follow-up to and Implementation of the Beijing Declaration and Platform for Action, Report of the Secretary-General*, NY, UN.

Voluntary Sector Partnership Council (VSPC) (2000). *Minutes of the VSPC*, 15 December 2000, item 1.8, 'Capacity building', Cardiff, VSPC.

—— (2001a). *Black Voluntary Sector Network Wales*, Cardiff, VSPC.

—— (2001b). *Volunteering Issues*, discussion paper March, papers of the VSPC, Cardiff, VSPC.

—— (2001c). *VSPC Voluntary Sector Scheme Implementation Plan*, July, papers of the VSPC, Cardiff, VSPC.

Wales Assembly of Women (1994). *Action for Equality, Development and Peace: A Report for the Fourth United Nations World Conference on the Status of Women, Beijing 1995*, Cydweli, WAW.

Wales Council for Voluntary Action (WCVA) (1999). *Our Design for Life: The Voluntary Sector and the National Assembly*, Cardiff, WCVA.

—— (2003). *Annual Report 2002–2003*, Cardiff, WCVA.

—— (2004). *Annual Report 2003–2004*, Cardiff, WCVA.

—— (2005). *Analysis of All-Wales Database of Voluntary Organizations*, http://www.WCVA.org.uk.

Wales Labour Party (WLP) (1994). *Shaping the Vision: A Consultation Paper on the Powers and Structure of the Welsh Assembly*, Cardiff, WLP.

—— (1996). *Preparing for a New Wales*, Cardiff, WLP.

Wales Trades Unions Congress Cymru (WTUC) (2004). *Response to the Welsh Assembly Government's Consultation – Tackling Domestic Abuse: The All Wales National Strategy,* Cardiff, WTUC.

Wales Women's National Coalition (WWNC) (2001). *Annual Report,* Cardiff, WWNC

—— (2003). *Canu ein Clodydd / Blowing Our Own Trumpets,* Cardiff, WWNC.

Wängnerud, L. (2000). 'Representing women', in P. Esaiasson, and K. Heidar (eds), *Beyond Westminster and Congress: The Nordic Experience,* Columbus, OH, Ohio State University Press, 140–54.

Weale, S. (2003). 'At last! The new Welsh Assembly is the first legislative body in the world made up of equal numbers of men and women', *Guardian,* 9 May, posted at *Guardian Unlimited, http://www.guardian.co.uk.*

Webb, P. (2000). *The Modern British Party System,* London, Sage.

Welsh Assembly Government (WAG) (2001a). *First Annual Report on the Voluntary Sector Scheme,* Cardiff, WAG.

—— (2001b). *A Paving Document: A Comprehensive Education and Lifelong Learning Programme to 2010 in Wales, The Learning Country,* Cardiff, WAG.

—— (2002). *Reaching Higher – Higher Education and the Learning Country: A Strategy for the Higher Education Sector in Wales,* Cardiff, WAG.

—— (2004a). *National Assembly for Wales Code of Practice for Ministerial Appointments to Public Bodies,* Cardiff, WAG.

—— (2004b). *The Strategy for Older People in Wales,* Cardiff, WAG.

—— (2005). *A Budget for the Future of Wales: The Assembly Government's Spending Plans 2005–06 to 2007–08,* Cardiff, WAG.

Welsh Conservative Party (WCP) (1999). *Fair Play For All: Your Voice in the Assembly,* Cardiff, WCP

—— (2003). *A Fairer Wales: The Welsh Conservative Party Manifesto 2003,* Cardiff, WCP.

Welsh Labour Party (WLP) (1999). *Working Hard for Wales: Labour's Manifesto for the National Assembly,* Cardiff, WLP.

—— (2002). *Welsh Policy Forum: Reports to Conference 2002,* Cardiff, WLP.

—— (2003a). *Working Together for Wales: Welsh Labour's Manifesto 2003,* Cardiff, WLP.

—— (2003b). *Working Together for Equalities,* Cardiff, WLP.

White, E. (1984). 'Peace and protest', *Radical Wales,* 9–10.

Welsh Office (1997). *Llais Dros Gymru / A Voice For Wales,* Cm 3718, London, Stationery Office.

Welsh Liberal Democrats (WLD) (1999). *Guarantee Delivery: Liberal Democrat Manifesto for the National Assembly for Wales,* Cardiff, WLD.

Williams, C. (2005). 'Problematizing Wales: an exploration in historiography and post-coloniality', in J. Aaron and C. Williams (eds) (2005), *Postcolonial Wales,* Cardiff, University of Wales Press, pp. 3–23.

—— and Chaney, P. (2001). 'Inclusive governance for excluded groups: ethnic minorities', in P. Chaney, T. Hall and A. Pithouse (eds), *New Governance: New Democracy,* Cardiff, University of Wales Press, pp. 78–102.

Wilson, F. L. (1990). 'Neo-corporatism and the rise of new social movements', in R. J. Dalton and M. Kuechler (eds), *Challenging the Political Order: New Social and Political Movements in Western Democracies,* Cambridge, Polity Press, pp. 177–96.

Woman's Claim of Right Group (1989). *A Woman's Claim of Right in Scotland,* Edinburgh, Polygon.

Wyn Jones, R. (1996). 'Deffra Gymru!', *Barn*, 401, 4–5.

—— (1997). 'O'r chwyldro felfed i'r chwyldro go-iawn', *Barn*, 413, 7.

Young I. M. (2000). *Inclusion and Democracy*, Oxford, Oxford University Press.

Young, L. (2000). *Feminists and Party Politics*, Vancouver, University of British Columbia Press.

Index

Note: page references followed by 't.' indicate material in tables; page references followed by 'n.' indicate material in notes.